The Bible Speaks to You

The Bible Speaks to You

BY ROBERT McAFEE BROWN

The Westminster Press
PHILADELPHIA

PRINTED IN THE UNITED STATES OF AMERICA
9 8 7 6 5 4 3 2

Library of Congress Cataloging in Publication Data

Brown, Robert McAfee, 1920–
  The Bible speaks to you.

  Includes indexes.
  1. Bible—Criticism, interpretation, etc. 2. Theology,
Doctrinal—Popular works. I. Title.
BS538.B74 1985   220.6   84-19578
ISBN 0-664-24597-8

Contents

A New Preface After Thirty Years

It is a scary thing to reread something one wrote thirty years ago. Will it sound terribly dated? Will it be just plain wrong? Will it instill the wish that it had gone out of print years ago, rather than rising up once more to haunt its author?

I avoid such interior dislocation by the simple, if cowardly, device of seldom rereading my books once they have been published, unless I'm *really* convinced they are good—an experience that happens with sufficient infrequency to keep me reasonably humble.

But in the case of *The Bible Speaks to You,* a confrontation was inevitable. Taking account of the gratifying fact that the book has continued to attract readers for thirty years, the publisher asked the author, Are there any small changes you would like to make?

Yes, there was one "small" change the author would like to make immediately: getting rid of all that embarrassing sexist language and replacing it with inclusive language. For while sexist language had not even loomed as an issue in the early fifties, it had become a powerful blemish in a text for the middle eighties. So the task was begun with a blue pencil. But when the changes per page began to mount into the twenties, it was clear that although beginning the enterprise seemed morally necessary, completing it was going to be financially disastrous, since subsequent production costs for resetting would raise the price of the book to a figure that could be contemplated by none but the fiscally élite.

Out of this practical bind, a guiding principle reluctantly emerged: Let the text stand; let the book be read for what it is—a product of the early 1950s, with whatever strengths and weaknesses such a product embodies. For in the process of resetting almost the entire text, many other substantive changes would also cry out to be introduced, which would, in effect, make it a new book. And if a new book is called for, let it be brand new, rather than a patchwork. There is, after all, that New Testament image about not sewing new cloth on old garments.

Would I do the book differently today? Of course. I have lived thirty years in the interval, thirty very tumultuous years, and have gone through some theological and human revolutions of my own, mostly (I want to stress) based on trying to keep in touch with the biblical materials, and if any reader wants an inkling of new directions, a book entitled *Unexpected News: Reading the Bible with Third World Eyes* (Westminster Press, 1984) speaks to the concern. (*Unexpected News,* incidentally, was my original and enthusiastic nomination for the title of what became *The Bible Speaks to You.* The motion died, back then, for want of a second. Over the long haul, persistence sometimes pays off.)

While I am willing, on the whole, to stand by the text of so long ago, there are a few emphases in it (in addition to the omnipresent sexist language) that now make me uneasy, and I list them briefly here, so that new readers can do their own further wrestling with the biblical material.

1. In comments about the early church, about Judaism and Christianity, and about the relationship of law and gospel, there are occasional statements that might be bent, if one chose to do so, toward a position I explicitly disavow: namely, that the appearance of Christianity superseded and made unnecessary the ongoing existence of Judaism. Contrary to such an implication, I believe it is particularly important for Christians to affirm the continuing existence of Judaism as part of the divine plan for humanity, and I find strong biblical support for this in Romans 9–11.

2. The treatment of war seems to me, in retrospect, not nearly urgent enough. A great deal has happened in human history since the early fifties, especially in our knowledge of the threat to human survival posed by the presence of nuclear weapons, and I now believe that Christians (and others) are called upon to say a clear "no" to any use of nuclear weapons by anyone. There seems to me no possibility of squaring the use, deployment, or manufacture of such weapons with God's will for the human family.

3. Although the book tries to guard against facile resolutions of the juxtaposition of God and evil in the world, I would make

this tension even stronger now. Like many of my generation, I could not, for many years, really deal with the moral and theological implications of the Holocaust, the systematic destruction by the Nazis, of six million Jews. I have recently had to begin to do so and am convinced that we will as long as there are human questioners with the "why" of that event, and not come up with "answers." There is no overall divine pattern into which such an event can be made to fit. If there were, it would create an even deeper moral dilemma than the one with which we now have to struggle.

4. My ongoing reading of the Bible has forced me to acknowledge that its challenge to our established white, middle-class social structures and systems is much more radical (i.e., deep-rooted) than I had suspected when I wrote *The Bible Speaks to You*. Specific issues, such as work, politics, war, and democracy, need more thorough systemic challenge than they receive here. Pervasive racism (to which, in retrospect, I discover the book makes very little reference) and classism (a category of social analysis I had scarcely heard of in the early fifties) deserve fuller attention in the light of the biblical message. Some of the consequences of this new perspective are developed in *Unexpected News*.

I am grateful to the many people who have written to me over the years concerning one point or another in the text of this book. Their ongoing response sustains me in feeling that a new edition, even without extensive change, will meet an ongoing need.

ROBERT MCAFEE BROWN

Pacific School of Religion
June 1984

Preface

"A book about the Bible" is likely to be a snare and a delusion.

People may get the idea that if you read "a book about the Bible" you don't need to read the Bible itself. Actually, this is about as sensible as saying that you'd just as soon read about the President of the United States (or the National League batting champion) as meet him at first hand and watch him in action. Books about the Bible give you the Bible at second hand. And their sole purpose must be to push you toward the Bible, to make you pick it up and read it, and to give you enough information and hints so that when you do read it you won't give up the first time you begin to flounder in a sea of "begats."

As we will see in the following pages, the Bible isn't "just another book" with a lot of interesting information about God. It is a book in which people find God "coming alive," making his way into their hearts and demanding that they do something about him. He's not a "safe" or a "tame" God, securely lodged behind the bars of a distant heaven; he has the most annoying manner of showing up when we least want him; of confronting us in the strangest ways. And he usually turns out to be very different from the sort of God we would have invented for ourselves. We have to be prepared for surprises and unexpected news.

If you are prepared for surprises, you will find this unexpected news popping up all over the place, and while you will go back to other books more learned than this one for further information (commentaries and such), you will ultimately

9

*have to return to the Bible itself and let it speak to you, as it
has spoken to so many people before you. And if you do that,
it may be that for you too God will cease being just an "idea"
and become a reality. For you will have found him at the point
at which he has been seeking you all along.*

ACKNOWLEDGMENTS

All sorts of people helped to write this book. At the risk of
leaving many people out, I must mention a few. The book could
never have gotten started without the willingness of Dr. Charles J.
Turck, president of Macalester College, to lighten my teaching
load there for one semester so that I might have more time to work
on it. Not all college presidents would have been so understanding.
Furthermore, I have taken many ideas from other books, and although I don't imagine anyone can ever avoid that, a few of the
ideas I have used are so clearly dependent upon other people's
creations that they must be acknowledged. The "man from Mars"
incident in Chapter 6 is adapted from Chad Walsh's *Campus
Gods on Trial* (The Macmillan Company), and the story of the
Early Church in San Francisco in Chapter 15 is adapted from Dix,
The Shape of the Liturgy (The Dacre Press). The analogies of
the victrola record and the windowpane in Chapter 3 come originally from the writings of Emil Brunner. There are many other
"borrowings," but the above are the most brazen. Let it also be
recorded that I have received untold help from the editors of the
Presbyterian Board of Christian Education and The Westminster
Press. If there are still dull phrases and ambiguous sentences in
the pages that follow, it is not their fault; their batting average
on the first two drafts was phenomenally high.

It has been true for me (in terms of a metaphor I have seen
variously ascribed to Coleridge, Newton, Herbert, and Perrault)
that if I have been able to see any vision of the spiritual horizon, it
is because I have been carried on the shoulders of giants. But it
is *also* true that if the vision is blurred and indistinct, it is because
I have been forced to view the landscape with my own eyes rather
than theirs.

ROBERT McAFEE BROWN

The Bible Speaks to You

Getting Our Bearings

(What Is the Bible?)

STUDENT *(with mounting vehemence)*: But why should I bother with a book that was written over a thousand years ago! I'm interested in what's going on right now. What difference does it make to me how people solved their problems in 700 B.C.? I've got problems of my own to solve right now. Why should I bother to read the Bible?

SUNDAY SCHOOL TEACHER *(who was obviously not prepared for this sort of thing)*: Well . . .

That's a fair question. It's also a tough one. No theoretical answer will do. And if there is an answer it must come out of the life and situation of people today. Here's one answer (and it happens to be a true one) which may give us some help. We will call it

RESURRECTION IN MID-PACIFIC

The Navy transport had 1,500 Marines on board who were being brought back to the United States from Japan for discharge. On the second day out a small group of them came to the chaplain and, to his intense surprise, asked him to lead them in a Bible study class each morning. Swallowing his amazement, the chaplain jumped at the chance.

Toward the end of the trip the group read the eleventh chapter of John, which describes the raising of Lazarus from the dead. The chaplain suggested that the incident *dramatized* what Jesus said on that occasion: "I am the resurrection, and the life: he that believeth in me, though he were dead, yet shall he live: and whosoever liveth and believeth in me shall never die." More important even than the reanimation of a corpse in A.D. 30 was the question of whether or not that statement of Jesus was true in (what was then) A.D. 1946.

He told them the story of Raskolnikov, a man in Dostoevsky's *Crime and Punishment* who had killed his very self in the act of murdering another, but had in truth been brought back to life as these words of Jesus were read to him.

There was a little discussion. A couple of questions were raised. But on the whole there was nothing to indicate to the chaplain that he had made his point particularly well.

When the discussion was over, a Marine corporal followed the chaplain back to his cabin. After a few false starts, he got down to the point. "Chaplain," he said, "I felt as though everything we read this morning was pointed right at me. I've been living in hell for the last six months, and for the first time I feel as though I'd gotten free."

As he talked, the story came out. He had just finished high school when he was called into the service. He had spent a long time in the occupation forces in Japan. He had gotten bored. Finally he had gone off one night with some friends and gotten into trouble. Serious trouble. Fortunately (so he thought) no one else knew about it. But *he* knew about it. And he was sure God knew about it. He felt guilty, terribly guilty. And each day the ship got nearer to San Francisco, his feeling increased that he had ruined his life and that he would never be able to face his family back home.

But somehow that wasn't the end, after all. He kept repeating one idea, over and over again: "Up until today, Chaplain, I've been a dead man. I have felt utterly condemned by myself, by my family (if they knew), and by God. *I've been dead,* but now, after reading about Jesus and Lazarus, I know that I am alive again. The forgiveness of God can reach out even to me. The resurrection Jesus was talking about is a real thing, after all, right now."

When the corporal left the cabin, it was clear that he still had a lot of problems to iron out, and that things wouldn't automatically be easy in this "new life," but as the chaplain watched him go, he knew that on that day, on that ship, in the middle of the Pacific Ocean, the miracle of resurrection had taken place. It was quite evident that Jesus' words *were* true: "He that believeth in me, though he were dead, yet shall he live."

What Happened?

Now let's face it. On the surface nothing would seem more completely irrelevant to a Marine, tortured in soul, sitting on a coil of rope in a troop transport, than the story of a first century raising from the dead. But, for some strange reason, the story was not irrelevant. How did it happen that after reading it a Marine could speak of having been dead and now being alive? The thing that happened was that the living truth of the story became living truth *for him*. It was not ancient history; it was *his* story, an account of *his* situation. The message of new life reached across the pages, grasped him, and transformed him. The Bible was not merely describing something that had happened in the first century. It was describing something that was happening in the twentieth century.

Even supposing, as is quite possible, that the chaplain missed the "point" of the Lazarus story (and I am very much aware of this possibility since I was the chaplain), nevertheless, the power of the Biblical message "broke through" to that Marine, with its message of healing and new life.

This is not an isolated instance. This sort of thing has happened to people ever since the Bible was written. It is a fact that when people expose themselves to the message of the Bible, things begin to happen.

> People act in daring ways.
> Lives are transformed.
> Weaklings become courageous.
> A dead Church comes alive again.

Take, almost at random, three names from the history of the Church: Saint Augustine, the architect of Western Christian thought; Martin Luther, the first of the great Protestant Reformers; and John Wesley, the founder of what we now call Methodism. Each of these men came to his mature Christian faith the hard way. No easy transition from "the religion of boyhood" or anything like that, for them. It was a rough, tough battle. And with each man it was contact with the living message of the Bible that finally tipped the scales.

This same thing is happening today. Not only to distraught Marines, but to men and women everywhere. In fact, the most significant thing in the last twenty-five years of our Protestant Church life has been what we can call "the rediscovery of the Bible." People are finding out that the Bible is *not* out of date, but that it is astonishingly contemporary, and that as they turn to the Bible it casts increasingly fresh light on their own situations in 1946, or 1955, or 1964.

What Is the Bible?

If this is true, there is real point to asking once more: "Just what is the Bible anyway? Why does it continue to make this kind of impact? Why do people keep being transformed by it?" Let's try to find out.

If you were handed a Bible for the first time in your life, and given a couple of hours to jot down some impressions, you might end up with a list like this:

a VERY *long book*
two main divisions (O.T. and N.T.—what do these
    terms mean?)
actually not one book, but many books (66 on actual count)
some books very long, others less than a page
all sorts and kinds:
  history
    short stories
      a play
        a love poem
          philosophy
            law codes
              informal letters
                some which baffle me completely
seems to be mainly about the Jewish people and later on one
  of them in particular (Jesus)

If you did a little digging into the history of the book itself, you would come up with a few further facts:

> *book a long time being written—about 1,000 years*
> *first part written in Hebrew, second part in Greek,*
>   *couple of dashes of Aramaic (what's that?)*
> *parts of it since translated into* OVER 1,000
>   LANGUAGES!!
> *latest translation (into English) called "biggest*
>   *publishing venture in history"*

Of course, such information doesn't begin to answer the question, What is the Bible? But if you kept at it, you'd finally come up with something like the next few paragraphs.

It wouldn't be enough to say that the Bible is the record of *man's search for God,* a report on the slow, agonizing, upward quest from primitive origins to a highly developed monotheism (belief in one God). True, there are many examples of the development of the concept of God as it becomes purified and ennobled in the course of Jewish history. But as a means of understanding the Bible, this isn't enough. It is much closer to the truth to say that *the Bible is the record of God's search for man.* Throughout the Bible people seem bent on trying to escape from God. And in spite of this, God continues to seek after those same people, refusing to give up, continuing the pursuit in spite of countless rebuffs and evasions.

It has all the excitement and thrill of a detective story, in which the detective relentlessly chases the criminal through chapter after chapter. The same kind of relentless pursuit dominates the interpretation that the Jewish people put on their historical past, in the Old Testament. The search culminates in the New Testament, where the claim is made that God has so desired fellowship with man that finally he has not just sent emissaries or ambassadors or prophets or representatives—in Jesus Christ he has come himself! It is the most

astounding word that has ever been spoken. It is the most
stupendous claim that has ever been made. If anything is
"unexpected news," this is.

But there is more to it even than that. The Bible not only
tells how God sought his people in the past; *it is also a means
by which he seeks us out today.* It is not just part of the dead
past: it is also part of the living present. We cannot read it
without a sense of being involved. For the experiences of the
Biblical characters are basically our experiences. They ask
questions:

> If a man die, shall he live again? (Job 14: 14)
> What do you think of the Christ? (Matt. 22: 42)
> Who are you, Lord? (Acts 9: 5)
> What shall I do, Lord? (Acts 22: 10)
> Why does the way of the wicked prosper? (Jer. 12: 1)
> Why are you cast down, O my soul? (Ps. 42: 5)

And we ask the same questions, even though we use different
words:

> What happens to me when I die?
> Is this Jesus really more than a great man?
> Who is God?
> What difference does believing in God make?
> What's the point of "being good"?
> Why does life sometimes seem so horribly futile?

To the extent that we really ask such questions (and it takes
courage to ask them honestly) we find ourselves involved in
the asking and answering which goes on in the Bible. To be
sure, we shall not find answers given on a silver platter, but
answers were not given to the Biblical characters on a silver
platter either. The answers they got had to be hammered home
to them in the "blood, toil, tears, and sweat" of a tragic history. They were not spun out in a philosopher's study, or even
in a Sunday school classroom. They emerged from the rough
and tumble of life, and it is in the rough and tumble of life
that we discover how right the Bible's answers are.

But it is not only in questions and answers that we find God seeking us in the Bible. Not only are God's demands and promises brought home to us, but *God himself* "comes alive," and speaks to us, as we take the Bible seriously. It is for this reason that Christians speak of the Bible as "the Word of God." This does not mean that God's "words" are recorded in the Bible as though someone had had a celestial tape recorder and then transcribed the message on paper. For, as we shall see, God "speaks" to people, not so much through statements as through his creative activity right where people are. The supreme revelation of his "Word," his creative power, is the "event" of Jesus Christ, in his life, death, and resurrection—the "Word made flesh," as the Fourth Gospel says.

The Bible, then, tells us of these times when God has acted upon the lives of men, and as we read it, the possibility is opened up that God can speak through those acts and events directly to us. "The Bible is a special delivery letter with your name and address on it," is one way of putting it. So it is more than a record; it is a call, an invitation, an urgent message to us.

Using the Bible

Now if this is true, then there is a high priority question to be asked: How can I use the Bible so that it will speak to me in this way? Let us look at some of the ways in which Christians have tried to answer this question.

1. One method which people have used since very early times, particularly with difficult passages, has been to interpret the Bible *allegorically*. An allegory is a story that has hidden meanings which do not appear on the surface. If I write, for example, "The raccoon had a splinter in its paw until it got to the riverbank," this may be my allegorical way of saying that the Christian (raccoon) is involved in sin (splinter) until he has been baptized (riverbank), and I may be seriously trying to write about Christian faith in the form of an allegory about animals.

Many of the Early Church Fathers interpreted portions of the Bible in this fashion. Take Jesus' parable of the Good Samaritan, a story illustrating what it means to be a good neighbor (look it up in Luke 10: 25-37 if you've forgotten how it goes). Augustine made an allegory out of the story, giving every detail a hidden significance. "A certain man" was Adam. Jerusalem was the heavenly city. The robbers were the devil and his angels. The Samaritan was Jesus himself. The inn was the Church. The innkeeper was the apostle Paul. And so on. The story of the Good Samaritan was transformed from a tale about true neighborliness into an allegory of the whole Christian drama of salvation.

Since religious language must always make use of imagery, the method of allegorical interpretation can sometimes serve a useful function. The danger is that one who is not a scholar and expert can "twist" a story to mean whatever he wants it to mean, and not only may the real point of the story be lost, but utterly false meanings may be "read in."

2. In sharp contrast to the allegorical method is the view that the Bible is to be interpreted *literally*, often with the further claim that since every word is directly inspired, all parts are therefore of equal profit and value. This is a much newer way of interpreting the Bible than the allegorical way. Luther, for example, the first Protestant Reformer, made sharp distinctions between various parts of the Bible, calling James an "epistle of straw," and stating that he saw little religious value in the book of Revelation. Whether his judgments were correct is not so important, for the moment, as the fact that he felt free to make them. But later Reformers, having continued with Luther to repudiate the absolute authority of the pope, turned more and more to a belief in the absolute authority of the Scriptures, interpreted in such a way that to be a Christian meant believing the words of the Bible, the statements contained within the covers of the book, as literally true in all particulars. In what way did this raise a problem?

For one thing, it is true that religious language must resort to symbolism, imagery, and poetic description on certain occasions, and such use of language loses its religious significance if taken literally. When Jesus told us to be as little children, for example, he didn't mean that we were supposed to wear diapers.

There is an ethical difficulty in the position "literalists" sometimes adopt, that all the parts of the Bible are equally true and inspired. There is—or ought to be—a clear difference between the attitude of Ps. 137 toward the enemy, "Happy shall he be who takes your little ones and dashes them against the rock!" (v. 9) and Jesus' attitude toward his enemies, "Father, forgive them; for they know not what they do" (Luke 23: 34). Such statements are clearly not on the same level of spiritual significance. To put every part of the Bible on the same level of importance as every other part is to find oneself in the difficulty which faced the man who opened his Bible at random to get advice on a difficult problem, and had the misfortune to light on the words, "And Judas went and hanged himself." Not content with this cold comfort, he tried again, this time opening to the words, "Go and do likewise."

The Bible is not a static collection of proof-text answers to questions, to be used in such fashion as this, and such a realization exposes the main difficulty of approaching the Bible as a series of statements each one of which is literally true and of equal worth. The question is whether or not the God of the Bible actually chooses this way of revealing himself. Although we will be pursuing this problem in the next chapter, we must repeat again what has already been said, that in the Bible we find God revealing himself not so much in statements as in events, and persons, and acts. In other words, a personal God strives to enter into personal relationship with his children. We cannot enter into personal relationship with an impersonal book, but we *can* enter into personal relationship with a person, with Jesus Christ. And it is thus the person about whom the book is written, rather than the book itself, who is the subject and object of our faith. Protestants firmly believe in "the authority of the Bible," but this is because it is the Bible which has brought them face to face with Jesus Christ. God confronts them in a living person, not merely in information about that person.

It is somewhat like a letter from a friend. You don't value the letter so much for its phrases and style as because it brings the friend closer and helps you to know him better. The constant presence of the letter may be nice, but it is a pretty poor substitute for the constant presence of the friend. (Anybody who has been in love will understand this.) Luther made the point well—if we may change our image rather abruptly—when he said, "The Bible is the cradle in which Christ lies."

3. Another way of using the Bible has been to interpret it *critically*, that is, from the point of view of a literary study of the text. For a long time scholars have studied early Biblical manuscripts, trying to determine when the books of the Bible were written, by whom they were written, to whom, the situation out of which they came, and so forth. Since people sometimes deride this way of interpreting the Bible, it must be stressed that Christians today owe an immense debt to these scholars. Because of their efforts, we now have the tools for a better understanding of the Bible than has ever been possible before. To know when a book was written, by whom, for whom, what the author's intention was—all this is clear gain.

The main difficulty with this approach, therefore, is not that it is wrong or irreverent, but that by itself it is incomplete. It is interesting to learn, for example, that there are *two* Creation stories in Genesis, and it is fascinating to compare their similarities and differences. But this is valuable only as a tool to help us toward more fundamental problems: What is the *meaning* of the stories of the Creation? What do they tell us about God's concern for us? What are the implications of the notion that God has made the earth, and particularly that he has made us? The critical approach by itself does not give us answers to these questions.

4. The above ways, then, are not fully adequate ways of understanding and using the Bible. Is there a more significant way? The way that will be suggested here (and will be presupposed throughout the rest of this book) is that we read the Bible as actors who are involved in the Biblical drama of God's search for men.

We are part of this drama. We cannot separate ourselves from it. We cannot understand the Bible as an ancient manuscript chiefly of interest to antiquarians or museum keepers. We must understand it as a living book addressed to us, in which we identify ourselves with those who stand under God's judgment and those who receive God's forgiveness. The fatal error is to read the Bible as a spectator rather than as a participant, to make the faulty assumption that we can sit in a box seat watching the drama, when actually we are on the stage taking part in the drama.

This means that when Amos thunders out to the people of Bethel that they are guilty of wrongdoing, we hear him speaking to us as well. He not only tells us what was wrong in Bethel—he is telling us what is wrong in Minneapolis or Houston or Grovers Corners or wherever we may be living today.

It means that when Jesus says to the disciples, "Who do men say that I am?" that is a question that is being directed at us as well. Who do *we* say that he is? We are being asked to decide, just as the disciples were being asked to decide.

It means that whether Jesus says, "Come to me, all who labor and are heavy-laden," or whether he says, "You also outwardly appear righteous to men, but within you are full of hypocrisy and iniquity," he is talking to us as well as to his first century audience.

We become actors or participants, then, not only by knowing something of the historical situation in which a word is spoken or an event takes place, but chiefly by seeing that word or that event in relation to our own situation, so that the word becomes a word addressed to us, the event an event charged with meaning for us. We take part in the demands and the promises made by God, and in the hopes and fears of his people as they walk across the pages of this book. Their story is now our story. As they are "his people," so are we.

Here's one example of how it works. Shortly after Holland was overrun by the Nazis in World War II, a group of Dutch Christians were put in jail by the Gestapo. Months later, when one of them was to be released, he offered to take a message to the families of the others. What should they say? One of them finally produced a letter, which in rough translation went as follows:

> *Please try to understand that what has happened to us has actually worked out for the advancement of the gospel, since the prison guards and all the rest here are coming to know Christ. In fact, we hear that many of you on the outside have gained courage because of our imprisonment and are speaking the truth more boldly than ever before.*
>
> *We hope that we shall not need to be ashamed because of our witness but that we may be bold enough so that Christ's influence will be spread by us, whether we live or whether we die.*

Now those sentences should have a familiar ring. For what the writer of the letter had done was to take portions of a letter which Paul had written while he too was in prison, 1,900 years before (Phil. 1: 12-20), and make them his own. The Dutch Christians, in sending this letter, were testifying that the experience of Paul was their experience, the message of Paul was their message, the God of Paul was their God.

They were participants in the Biblical drama.

Mostly Facts and Figures

(Where Did the Bible Come From?)

We have, then, a complete Bible—printed, bound, ready to be read. But ask anyone *how* it came to be in its present form, and you're in for trouble. Instead of answers, you're liable to create a chaos of questions. Something like this:

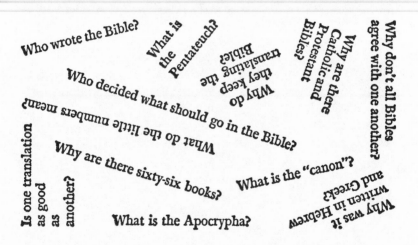

We must try to bring some order out of this chaos. Only as we know something of how this book came to be what it is can we fully appreciate it.

Two Points to Start With

Right off the bat we need to remember two things.

Point number one. The Bible is not a book that "fell out of heaven" complete from start to finish. To believe such a thing may be good Mohammedan doctrine, for Moslems believe that the Koran made its appearance in finished form; it may be good Mormon doctrine, for Mormons believe that the Book of Mormon was given as a finished product to Joseph Smith. But it is not good Christian doctrine, for Christians are aware that the Bible did not suddenly appear all finished and done, but that it was "a long time in the making"—over 900 years! Close this book and think for two minutes about the fact that Jesus was able to read what we call the Old Testament, and that when he was reading it, almost two thousand years ago, not a single one of the New Testament books had yet been written.

Point number two. The Bible was not written in English. Our Bible is a translation. Jesus did not speak English. Moses did not talk with a Boston accent. Luke had never read Shakespeare. And unless you learn Hebrew and Greek, with a dash of Aramaic thrown in (something few readers of this book are likely to attempt in the near future), you will never read the Bible in the language in which the authors wrote it. Our English Bible is simply an attempt to give an accurate translation of materials which were originally written in other languages.

How It All Started

Suppose, for the sake of argument, that something wonderful has happened to you.

You have gotten 100 per cent in an algebra test you were *sure* you were going to flunk.

Or, you have gotten a good job for the summer.

Or, you have fallen in love.

What do you do?

You have to share the news with someone else. This doesn't mean necessarily that you are being boastful. You just have to let your joy "spill over" to someone else.

Now suppose, for the sake of argument, that something even more wonderful has happened.

> You have had a lot of puzzling perplexities about the meaning of your life, and an experience has clarified them.

> Or, you have fitfully tried to pray and one day found out that you were not praying to a Blank, but were in communion with the living God.

> Or, you have experienced a bitter tragedy and discovered that you were not alone but that God was there with you.

What do you do?

Although at first you may be very shy about it, sooner or later you find that once again you have to share the news with someone else. That life makes sense, that God is real, that you are not alone—these are things of such monumental importance that you simply cannot keep quiet about them once you know their truth.

Now suppose, once more for the sake of argument, that this loving God whom you now know makes it plain to you that he wants to use you to make him and his will more real to those about you.

What do you do this time?

Even though you may at first be timid and afraid, you finally must speak. You must share the news with all who will listen. You find yourself in the same situation as the prophet Amos: "The Lord God has spoken," he said, "who can but prophesy?" (Amos 3: 8).

If you can imaginatively put yourself in these situations, then perhaps you can begin to understand why and how the Bible came to be written. If people have good news, they share it. If they have bad news, they share that too. And if they are conscious that God is real, and if they see life in terms of his demands, and his promises, then they have to share that viewpoint, and all that it implies, with others.

It is this sort of thing that we find taking place in the Bible. Some of the Biblical writers find that God has forced them to speak out in his name. These men we usually call "prophets." And the things they say are so important that they are written down for others to read. Or a great event takes place in Jewish history (a victory over the enemy, let us say) and a song is composed for the occasion. The song interprets the event as a vindication of the power and glory of God, so it becomes an important part of the people's understanding of how God relates himself to their lives. Or a tragic event takes place (a nation forced into exile, let us say) and someone has the God-given insight to see that this is the way God's love has to express itself toward those who rebel against him. The message is saved and the people begin to see that all history must be viewed as the theater where God is the chief actor. Or the songs which are written for their public worship of God come to be a means by which God's presence is realized even when they are not in the Temple—so the songs are preserved and written down, along with the other sacred writings.

The point is that all these writings are a response to God's activity and concern with his people—and over the centuries a sizable body of literature is built up. This literature takes on significance precisely because it *has* developed in this gradual way, for it makes plain that God deals with people right where they are, right in the struggles and agonies of their real flesh-and-blood history.

Getting It Down—with an Alphabetical Twist

Our Old Testament is the end product of this gradual process. And our appreciation of its contents can be heightened by a recognition of how this process of "getting it down" into its present form was done. It is, of course, possible to read these books profitably without extensive knowledge of their origins, but to know how the accounts were woven together is often a help when we run across two or three different accounts of the same event. (You needn't remember every detail of what follows, but it will help if you can keep the general picture in mind.) Let us see how the first six books of the Old Testament (called the "Hexateuch," from the Greek meaning "six scrolls") came into their present form.

Here's how it happened. Perhaps as long ago as 900 B.C. (nearly 3,000 years ago!) an early writer compiled a series of stories about the tribes in southern Palestine, and sometime later additions were made to this account so that the Northern tribes would not be left out of the story. In these accounts, the Hebrew word used for God was one which we would write as "Yahweh," and which in Hebrew would be YHWH (or, as it is sometimes written, JHVH). For this reason the document is called the "J" document, and where JHVH occurs in the early part of our Old Testament we can be pretty sure that the passages in question are from "J."

Later on (perhaps between 750-700 B.C.) another writer wrote a similar account of the history, this time with chief emphasis on the Northern tribes. Since he did not believe that the "name" of JHVH was known until the time of Moses, he used another Hebrew word for God, Elohim. His document is therefore known as the "E" document. Later on the accounts were woven together, to form what you should be able to guess is called "JE."

Now the Northern tribes, who had by this time become a kingdom, met a disastrous military defeat in 722 B.C., and in the chaos following this experience a group of people came to feel that the disaster was due to the faulty worship of God. Consequently they wrote another history, with special emphasis on how worship should be conducted. About a hundred years after the defeat, in 621 B.C., this document was discovered

in the Temple. It led to sweeping reforms. Much of this document seems to be contained in what we call "Deuteronomy,"
so it is called, naturally enough, "D." So important did it become that it was woven into the other historical accounts, to
form "JED."

There was a final step. The Southern Kingdom likewise
went down to military defeat, and the people were taken into
exile. Once again they wrote their history, this time with special
emphasis on the importance of Jerusalem as a center of worship and of the priests as the directors of the religious life of
the people. Because of its "priestly" emphasis this document
is known as "P." The four documents were woven together to
form "JEDP," and it is out of this composite that the books
of Genesis through Joshua come. In the opening chapters of
Genesis, for example, the account of the Creation in Gen. 1:
1 to 2: 4 is from the "P" strand, while the account in ch. 2: 4f.
is from "J."

These different writers sometimes stress different elements
in their nations' history, but they are united in their belief
that their nations' history can be understood only in terms of
God's sovereignty over that history. History as the workshop
of God—that is their theme. God speaks to them through these
historical events, and they come to discern his will as they read
the events in the light of that belief.

The Process Jells at Jamnia

While all this was going on, other books were being written,
so that by about 200 B.C. most of the Old Testament material
had been gathered together. In addition to the Hexateuch
there were other historical narratives, the writings of the
prophets, a hymnbook, a short story, a book of sad wailings,
regulations ranging from where to worship to the accepted
way to slaughter animals, and so forth. The variety was covered under three headings. The first heading was known as
the *Law*, and covered the first five books of the Old Testament.

The *Prophets* comprised the second grouping, and included not only the major and minor prophets, but also many of the historical books, such as Joshua, Judges, etc. The remaining books were known simply as the *Writings*.

This collection, which came to 39 books in all, became more and more generally accepted, and a council of Jewish rabbis, meeting at Jamnia, Palestine, about A.D. 90 or 100 decided that no more books should be admitted to the group of sacred writings.

The First Translation

Remember that, except for a few scattered verses in Aramaic, these books were all written in Hebrew. Now the Hebrew alphabet had no vowels and no punctuation. What is more, all the letters were run together. If you wrote that way in English, you would get something like this:

MTHLRDYRGDWHBRGHTYTFTHLNDFGYP

TTFTHHSFBNDGYSHLLHVNTHRGDSBFRM

If you can guess where the vowels go, and what they are, and how to divide the words thus found, you can finally figure out that this sentence reads:

I AM THE LORD YOUR GOD, WHO BROUGHT YOU OUT OF THE LAND OF EGYPT, OUT OF THE HOUSE OF BOND-AGE. YOU SHALL HAVE NO OTHER GODS BEFORE ME.
(Ex. 20: 2, 3)

And even though omitting the vowels saves space, it is obviously quite a stunt to read this kind of writing; to deal with this problem "vowel points" began to be used on later manuscripts, little marks placed under or over the consonants to indicate what vowels should be inserted where.

As time went on, more and more Jews learned Greek, and fewer and fewer could read Hebrew accurately. Therefore, beginning about 270 B.C. and extending up into the Christian

Era, Jewish scholars made translations of the Old Testament from Hebrew into Greek. These documents were the ones used by the early Christians, and are known as the Septuagint (from *septuaginta*=seventy) because according to a tradition seventy (-two) scholars produced the translation in seventy (-two) days.

About a dozen books in the Septuagint were not included among the approved Jewish Scriptures by the Council of Jamnia. These books are called the Apocrypha (meaning "hidden" or "obscure"). Our Old Testament does not include them, since it is based upon the Hebrew documents. They are included in Roman Catholic Bibles, since the official Roman Catholic translation made extensive use of the Septuagint.

A "New" Testament

It took about 700 years to get the Old Testament written down. The New Testament, by contrast, was completed in about 100 years. Its books were not written in Hebrew but in Greek. They were not written in the stately classical Greek of Plato, but in an ordinary, market-place dialect, known as *koine*. At that, the Gospels represent a kind of "translation," for Jesus and his disciples spoke, not Greek, but Aramaic, and their spoken Aramaic had to be translated into written Greek. You can find a few Aramaic expressions in the Gospels, such as Jesus' cry from the cross, "Eloi, Eloi, lama sabachthani" (Mark 15: 34), and his words to a girl, "Talitha cumi" (ch. 5: 41).

Many people fail to realize that the earliest New Testament writings are not the Gospels, but Paul's letters. The first of these, I Thessalonians, may be as early as A.D. 50. Paul had no idea that he was writing "sacred Scripture"; his letters were "occasional pieces," jotted down to help churches to deal with specific problems. They were almost always circulated among the early Christian churches, and a collection of them gradually developed. They form a substantial part of our New Testament.

The rest of the New Testament writings (except for the Gospels, which will be discussed in Chapter 9) fall into two main classifications. Some of them were written during times of persecution, such as the letter to the Hebrews, the letter called First Peter, and (while you might not guess it from a quick glance) Revelation. In these writings we get a clear witness to the bravery of the early Christians as they stood firm against a hostile pagan world.

Other letters combat a heresy which was common around the end of the first century. (A "heresy" is not a belief that is totally false; it is a belief that overemphasizes part of the truth, and can thus pretend to be the truth itself.) The stock heresy in this period was the notion that while Jesus was God incarnate, he was not fully man, but only *seemed* to have a human body. Hence the belief was called "Docetism," from the Greek word meaning "to seem." It goes without saying that if this belief had won the day it would have destroyed Christian faith, since the whole point of Christian faith was precisely the claim that Docetism denied, namely, that in Jesus God fully indwelt a human life, and that this was a true human life, not a fake. This situation helps us to appreciate more fully the emphasis of the Fourth Gospel, on "the Word made *flesh*," and similar statements in the three letters of John. Second Peter and portions of the "Pastoral Epistles" (I and II Timothy and Titus) combat this and other false positions.

This does not mean that the New Testament books are merely negative, but only that we can understand their positive message more adequately if we also know what they were seeking to deny.

The Development of a "Canon"

Marcion, an early heretic, came to the false conclusion that the Old Testament and the New Testament were about two different gods. He decided to draw up a list of sacred writings that would meet with his approval. He began by excluding the entire Old Testament, and in his New Testament included only the Gospel of Luke and ten of Paul's letters that he felt were "safe."

Because of such antics, and because of the prevalence of other heresies, the Early Church gradually began to develop a standard list of authorized writings. They included the Old Testament, of course, seeing in it the preparation for the mighty acts of God fulfilled in the New Testament in Jesus Christ, and they gradually reached agreement about which, out of the many new Christian writings, should be approved. By A.D. 200 there was pretty general agreement about the Gospels, The Acts, and Paul's letters. Other writings were "on the border" for some time, but by A.D. 367 a list had been approved which contained the 27 books that comprise our present New Testament. These writings came to be known as the "canon," coming from a Greek word meaning "norm," or "standard," since they were the norm or standard for Christian faith, and still are.

Testament = Covenant = Agreement

It is time we cleared up one minor mystery.

The word "testament" has been smuggled into this discussion a number of times, without making clear just what it means. As a matter of fact, just what it means is by no means easy to say, since it is a poor translation of a Hebrew word. The better English word would be "covenant," an extremely important Biblical word (as we shall see in Chapter 15) which means the agreement or relationship established between God and man. The "Old Covenant" (what we call the Old Testament) is an account of the agreement between God and his people. The "New Covenant" (what we call the New Testament) is the account of the new relationship established between God and man in the person of Jesus Christ. Since the

New Covenant completes rather than wipes out the Old Covenant, both Covenants or Testaments are included within our present Bible.

Jerome Produces the Vulgate

By the third century A.D. you could get a Greek Bible (the Septuagint) or one in Greek and Hebrew.

But perhaps you didn't read Greek, let alone Hebrew. The only language in which you knew your way around was Latin. And since most educated people were in the same situation, the pope commissioned a scholar named Jerome to translate the Bible into Latin. This translation, done between A.D. 385 and 405, is called the Vulgate (from the Latin *vulgatus* meaning "usual" or "common") because it was in the common or "vulgar" tongue of the people. It became the official translation of the Roman Catholic Church.

There is one interesting effect that this translation had on later Church history which illustrates the problem of translating the Bible. The Greek word used in Matt. 4: 17 is *metanoite,* which we would translate in English as "repent, turn about, begin again, get a fresh start." ("Repent, and believe in the gospel.") The Latin which Jerome used was *poenitentiam agite,* which can be translated "repent" but which can also be translated "do penance," and it was in this latter sense that Jesus' command was understood in medieval Christendom. Jesus' words thus became, "Do penance and believe in the gospel," and they are so translated to this day in the Douay (Roman Catholic) New Testament. Around this notion the sacrament of penance developed, and the belief that we must do certain things in order to secure God's forgiveness. When Protestant scholars went back to the original Greek, instead of stopping at the Latin, they found that there was no clear basis for the sacrament of penance in this verse, and it was abolished from Protestant practice.

Luther Brings the Bible to the People

By the end of the Middle Ages, only priests and highly educated people (not necessarily synonymous) could read and understand Latin. Now new translations were needed in the languages ordinary people spoke, particularly since the Protestant Reformation had restored the Bible to the central place in the life of the Christian.

When a group of Martin Luther's friends spirited him off into hiding, at a time when his life was in danger, they probably had no idea that their concern for his safety would result in one of the most influential of all Biblical translations. Luther, hidden in the Wartburg Castle, used his time of enforced leisure to translate the New Testament into German (1522), just as later on he did the Old Testament (1534).

The German people had not had the full Bible in their own tongue before this time, and Luther did his translation in such a way that the Bible became a living book that they could understand. Instead of making a wooden literal translation, he tried to get the flavor of the events, so that people could imagine them taking place in their own locality. There were robbers on the road between Jerusalem and Jericho—it must have been just as dangerous as going through the Black Forest at night! When Luther translated Ps. 46 ("God is our refuge and strength") he conveyed this idea by conjuring up the picture of a strong medieval castle with thick walls, a wide moat, safe and strong and protecting, and gave the psalm the subtitle, "A mighty *fortress* is our God." The Germans knew what that meant! To make sure that they could understand the sacrificial requirements in Leviticus correctly, Luther checked the material with his butcher.

First Glimpses of an English Bible

But how did the Bible get into English?

Legend says that back in the seventh century a stable hand

at Whitby named Caedmon had sung portions of the Creation story and the life of Jesus in English, and we know that in the eighth century a great churchman known as "the Venerable Bede" translated the Fourth Gospel into English.

The first complete English translation, however, came from the pen of John Wycliffe (or Wiclif or Wyclif or Wickliffe or Wycklife—they weren't particular about spelling in those days). Together with some scholars, he finished the New Testament in 1380 and the rest of the Bible by 1382, using Jerome's Vulgate as his text. All the copies, of course, had to be written out in longhand, and Wycliffe sent out groups of people called Lollards to read these Bibles and expound them to the people in the market places. On the basis of what he found in the Bible, Wycliffe opposed many elements in medieval Christianity, and was a forerunner of Protestantism. As a result, his writings were condemned and his books burned. Since Wycliffe had inconsiderately died before they could burn him too, the authorities dug up his bones and burned them. Such was the price one had to pay to make the Bible available to the people.

Smuggling for the Glory of God

The next translator, William Tyndale, was less fortunate, for Tyndale was still alive when the authorities clamped down on him, and he was strangled and burned for his pains. But Tyndale had two advantages in making his translation that Wycliffe did not have. Johann Gutenberg had invented movable type, so that Tyndale's translation was able to be printed in large quantities. And the Dutch scholar Erasmus had produced a scholarly edition of the Greek New Testament, so that Tyndale was able to base his translation on the original tongue, rather than being dependent on the Latin.

When things got too hot for Tyndale in England, he went to Germany and had his English Bible printed there. The Bibles were then smuggled into England in great bales of cotton. One angry bishop bought a lot of the Tyndale New Testaments and burned them publicly. Tyndale took the profits made from the bishop's purchases and printed a new edition!

A Rash of New Translations

Although Tyndale met a martyr's death, the impact of his work was felt, and it gradually became safer to produce an English Bible in England. In 1535, just ten years after Tyndale's New Testament appeared, the first complete printed Bible appeared in English, the work of Miles Coverdale, who used much of Tyndale's translation, but completed the Old Testament, which Tyndale had only partially done. Most of the portions of the Bible used in the present Episcopal *Book of Common Prayer* are based on Coverdale's version.

New translations appeared thick and fast in the ensuing years. The Great Bible (1539) had royal approval, and got its name because of its size. Copies of it were chained in the churches. Later a group of Puritans fled to Geneva, Switzerland, to be free from persecution during the reign of "Bloody Mary" (so called because of her persecution of Protestants), and while they were there, they produced the Geneva Bible (1560), which was the first Bible to contain numbered verses. This Bible was very unpopular among the English bishops because the translators put Calvinistic interpretations in the margins. The bishops countered with the Bishops' Bible (1568), but it was never popular except among the bishops.

The most famous of the English translations was the Authorized Version, usually called the King James Version (1611). Forty-seven scholars were appointed by King James I of England to do a new translation based on the original languages of Scripture and making use of all the available English translations thus far made. And although many translations have been made into English since then, no one of them has seriously challenged the popularity of the King James Version, until recently.

The Need for a New Translation

Why bother with new translations, if we still have the King James Version, with its incomparably beautiful English prose? Here are just a few reasons:

1. The usage of *English* words has changed tremendously since 1611. In 1611, the word "prevent" meant "precede." In 1611, Phil. 4: 14 was translated, "Notwithstanding, ye have well done, that ye did communicate with my affliction." That may have been clear in 1611, but it is not very clear today. It simply means, "Yet it was kind of you to share my trouble."
2. A more basic reason for a new translation is that the sources available to the translators in 1611 were pitifully meager compared to those now on hand. The King James translators had a couple of dozen imperfect Greek manuscripts, none earlier than the tenth century, and their New Testament text had over 5,000 copyists' errors.
3. Recent archaeological discoveries have clarified our understanding of certain parts of the Biblical texts. Today there are thousands of manuscripts which have been dug up in Palestine and Egypt, and by comparing these, the translators can understand the original meaning of disputed passages much better. In 1948, for example, in a cave near the Dead Sea, a group of manuscripts were discovered, some of which were written between the second and first centuries B.C. This is incomparably old for a manuscript—a thousand years older than other existing manuscripts—and the scroll that contains The Book of Isaiah has clarified passages that up until now have always been obscure.

The Newest Translation

For these and other reasons a new, up-to-date, and reliable English translation of the Bible has recently been completed—the product of fourteen years of intensive work by outstanding scholars. The New Testament appeared in 1946, and the Old Testament in 1952. If you have ever been puzzled, for example, over those perplexing verses at the beginning of Ps. 8 in the King James Version, "Out of the mouth of babes and sucklings hast thou ordained strength because of thine enemies," you will find the difficulty resolved in the Revised Standard Version:

> Thou whose glory above the heavens is chanted
>   by the mouths of babes and infants,
> Thou hast found a bulwark because of thy foes,
>   to still the enemy and the avenger.

Here are other examples of similar clarification:

K.J.V.: Take no thought for your life. (Matt. 6: 25)
R.S.V.: Do not be anxious about your life.

K.J.V.: Be not high-minded. (Rom. 11: 20)
R.S.V.: Do not become proud.

K.J.V.: My brethren, have not the faith of our Lord Jesus Christ, the Lord of glory, with respect of persons. (James 2: 1)
R.S.V.: My brethren, show no partiality as you hold the faith of our Lord Jesus Christ, the Lord of glory.

Translating Will Continue

The "R.S.V." will probably become the standard translation in our lifetimes, though the King James Version can continue to be used with it, with immense enrichment. But new translations will be made, and will continue to be made, as long as people read the Bible. For word usages will change, and new manuscripts will be discovered which will cast further light on the intent of the original writers. Thus it is never right to "freeze" the translation process and assume that, say, the King James Version bound in black leather and printed on thin paper is the only "real" Bible. Until the end of time men will be engaged in one of the most significant of all pursuits— the attempt to render the Word of God in the words best suited to make that God come alive in the hearts and minds of men.

On Asking the Right Question

(How Does God Make Himself Known?)

Q. What is the chemical formula for salt?
A. You can get salt out of a saltshaker on a sticky day if you put a few grains of rice in the shaker beforehand.

Q. How can the subway system show a profit?
A. The best way to get from Grand Central to Broadway and 110th Street is to take a shuttle to Times Square and a northbound express with two red lights.

Question and Answer have somehow failed to make connections. One reason the answers are pointless is because they are answers to unasked questions. They might be very good answers if the questions were "How do you get salt out of a saltshaker on a sticky day?" or "How can I get from Grand Central to Broadway and 110th Street by subway?"

And part of our job, as we approach the Bible, is to learn to ask the right kinds of questions, the questions to which the Biblical answers are real answers. It is pointless to ask of the Biblical writers:

Q. How can we prove the existence of God?

For the Biblical writers that kind of question would be quite beside the point. They were not talking about an idea of a "something somewhere" that might or might not exist. They were talking about the living Reality who had confronted them, changed their lives, entered into relationship with them. To try to "prove his existence" would be as though you and Joe discussed the question, "Does Fred really exist?"—right under Fred's nose, with Fred perhaps contributing to the discussion from time to time. You are entitled to take Fred's existence for granted since you already know him. And that is what the Biblical writers do with God. He is the first and last fact of their lives. They don't waste their time trying to "prove" him; they try to see how he makes himself known, and what he demands of them.

So if we want to understand the Biblical answers we must ask the right question:

Q. How does God make himself known?

Then perhaps we can get somewhere.

How the Bible Answers the Question

Once upon a time a group of non-Jewish slaves tried to find out about the God of the Jewish nation. But it seemed hopeless. "Truly," they cried, "thou art a God who hidest thyself" (Isa. 45: 15). God is a hidden God! For many people this has been the end of the matter. And yet there is a further meaning to the cry. For while the slaves realize that God does indeed hide himself, they now know where he is to be found. He is to be found in Israel. If you want to know where this hidden God is revealed, they are saying, look at the events of the life and history of the Jewish nation, for it is there that God has made himself known. To the Israelites they say: "Only in thee is God—and not elsewhere, no Godhead at all! Truly with thee God hideth Himself. Israel's God is a Savior" (Isa. 45: 14, 15, translated by G. A. Smith).

To say this is to say, in effect, "If you want to know how God makes himself known, then look at the events of the history of the Jewish people, and you will find him at work there, you will find him making himself known there, showing those people who he is, what he is like, what he demands of them, what he promises them." And so the Bible gives us the history of that nation Israel, and finally (in the New Testament) the story of the one in whom God is most fully made known.

Now this is extremely surprising. It is even shocking. For this Jewish nation was not a "great" nation as nations go. It was a tiny nation, always being overrun by the great nations, getting into trouble, carried off into captivity, having its cities, villages, and peoples uprooted and destroyed time and time again. On the stage of world history it was the doormat on which the great empires scuffed their boots—hardly a fit place to expect to find God at work! If we had been planning things we would certainly have chosen a different way to do it. But we were not planning things, and so we must listen to the Biblical claim that this is the way God planned it, and see why he did it his way rather than ours. What, then, is the Biblical answer to the question, "How does God make himself known?"

God Reveals Himself

The first thing to be said is not so obvious as it might appear. The Bible makes it plain that God reveals *himself*. He does not simply reveal information *about* himself. Put another way, what we find in the Bible is not an accumulation of data about God, but rather a living God in living relationship with living people. These people have not lifted themselves by their own bootstraps into the presence of God. They testify that God has taken the initiative and sought them out. Their job is to respond, but the initiative lies with him. He reveals to them not just ideas or information, but himself. As a matter of fact, this is the only way in which it could possibly be done so that a *relationship* between God and man could result.

Look at it this way. A new high school student moves in next door. "On your own hook" you can discover a good deal about him: he is fifteen, has brown hair, goes to the same school you do, rides a bicycle expertly, has a dandy first baseman's glove, and gets perfumed letters, in tinted envelopes, written in delicate female script, about twice a week. All these facts you can discover by a little patient sleuthing.

And yet, do you really know him?

Of course not.

And how can you come to know him?

Only, in the last analysis, *if he chooses to make himself known to you,* if he is willing to take the initiative of entering into a relationship with you so that in that relationship he reveals himself to you. If this happens, you will not simply know things *about* him, you will know *him.* You and he will have met in living encounter.

This is something like the claim which the Bible makes about God. It says that God is known in the same kind of living encounter by which we come to know a living person. Unless he reveals *himself* he remains forever hidden from us. We cannot truly know him if all we have is information about him. We can't enter into relationship with information about God; we can enter into relationship only with God himself. So the Bible is not a textbook of doctrinal statements (though doctrinal statements can be derived from it)—the Bible is an account of an encounter between God and his people.

God Reveals Himself in Historical Events

Where do we find this God at work? Here the Bible is quite clear. God reveals himself right where people are—in the midst of their hopes and hates, their loves and fears, their businesses and battles, which is to say, in historical events, and particularly in the historical events of the Jewish nation. As people for whom God is real look at the past, the present, and the future, they find their belief in him corroborated, clarified, and sometimes corrected. He *does things*—history is his workshop. He gives evidence right where people are of who he is and what he wills to do. And though this always remains in part a mystery, nevertheless the place where some meaning enters in upon the mystery, the place where true relationship replaces mere information, is always in the midst of people's actual "human situation."

This claim that God is at work right where people are is a tremendously significant claim. It means that to know God and be known of him you do not need to go off into a mystic trance, or cut yourself off from men, or go into permanent seclusion. God is right where you are, in your situation—not somewhere else. Look at three examples of God's meeting people in their own historical situations:

EXAMPLE ONE: When the Children of Israel finally escaped from Pharaoh's pursuing armies, and got across the Red Sea, they did not congratulate themselves on their expert tactical maneuvering. On the contrary, they gave thanks to God who had delivered them from the enemy. And that interpretation of the event colored the whole of their later history. God had delivered them in their hour of peril; he was at work right where they were, with them in time of crisis.

EXAMPLE TWO: Centuries later these same Israelites were thoroughly trounced by the Babylonians and taken into captivity. And yet even in the whole tragic event of their defeat and exile they could see God revealing himself, showing them the consequences of failure to do his will. They discovered him at work, not by turning their backs on history, but right in the midst of history.

EXAMPLE THREE: When God finally revealed himself in a human life, this too occurred right where people were. The accounts of Jesus' birth remind us of this. The chance to see the Christ-child was not offered to the shepherds while they were making a pilgrimage or even while they were in church, but while they were doing their proper job, which was taking care of sheep. The same news came to the Wise Men right where they were, engaged in their proper work, which was scanning the heavens. Christ himself is part of our history. He was born "in the days of Herod the king." He suffered "under Pontius Pilate." His life was datable.

The encounters between God and man take place right where people are, within the arena of human history.

Note to the careful reader: But here we have a puzzler. Many people say, "God reveals himself in *nature,* and that is where I find him." And it is true that the natural world, as God's creation, gives us some indications of the character of the creator. "The heavens declare the glory of God; and the firmament showeth his handiwork" (Ps. 19: 1). But neither the psalmist nor the other Biblical writers ever argue from nature to God, as though you could figure out from nature who the God of Biblical faith is. To argue from the world of nature that there "must" be a God, or that nature "proves" God's existence, is a dubious undertaking. For if nature produces lovely sunsets, it also produces cancer and tornadoes and tigers clawing at one another. God cannot be "explained" by nature. It is the other way around. Because they already believe in God for other reasons, the Biblical writers can see evidence of God in his created order. But the true arena of the encounter between God and man is not just the world of nature, but the world of human events, where people suffer, struggle, hate, love, live, and die.

God Reveals Himself Through Persons

How do we know about the activity of God in the world of human events? We cannot just look at a complicated group of "events" and infer God from them, any more than we can look at nature and infer God from it. What we find in the Bible, in the face of this problem, is not merely a recital of history, but an *interpretation* of history.

The claim that God is at work in Jewish history, for example, is an interpretation put upon that history by men who look at it from a special point of view. The inner meaning of the Red Sea episode is a meaning that is communicated to us by persons whose belief in God causes them to understand that event in a very special way.

We find that to some people God seems to grant special insight. Through them his will and purpose come closer to the rest of us than would otherwise be the case. These men are called "prophets." We often think of a prophet as one who foretells the future, as though he had a divinely guaranteed crystal ball. While it is true that the Old Testament prophets often talked about the future and what it would bring, their main significance was as spokesmen of God, *forth*tellers of God's will quite as much as *fore*tellers of the future. And they spoke with authority. They did not say timidly,

"It seems to me a reasonable possibility that under certain circumstances we might just possibly interpret the will of God to be thus-and-so."

No, when they had something to say, they thundered forth,

"THUS SAITH THE LORD!"

and then proclaimed the will of God for that particular situation. The prophets told the people what God was going to do, and what he was at that moment doing; they pointed out that God was active, that he participated, that he did not sit back and leave things to run themselves. And in thus witnessing to an acting God, they were, and have been, a means by which that God has been revealed to the rest of us.

We shall be looking at the insights of these prophets in some detail as we go through this book. For the moment, simply notice the kind of God with whom the prophets acquaint us. He is a God of strict justice, who demands that we take justice seriously in our human dealings (Amos); he is a God also of great compassion and mercy, unwilling to forsake his people even though they deserve to be forsaken (Hosea); he is holy, high, and lifted up, someone "other" than us (Isaiah). Much of our own awareness of God is the result of the arresting claims of the prophets.

God Reveals Himself Supremely Through One Person —Jesus Christ

The entire Old Testament has a forward look about it. Some of the prophets talk about an Anointed One ("Messiah" is the word in Hebrew) who will come from God to show the people who God is, and what he demands of them. In other words, among all the things that were to happen in Jewish history, one thing was going to happen that would have more meaning than anything else; among all the persons of Jewish history there was going to be one person who would be more meaningful than anyone else, and through the events of the life of this person, the revelation of God would be made more fully than it had been made before. The Old Testament waits for "the fullness of time" when these things shall come to pass. At one stage, the people cry to God in a vivid image, "Oh that thou wouldest rend the heavens, that thou wouldest come down" (Isa. 64: 1).

The New Testament claim is that the cry has been answered. God has come to men, since men could not get to God. He has come in the only way they could possibly understand, as a person like themselves. This, so Christian faith claims, is the supreme revelation of God to man: God makes himself known most fully in the events clustered around one Jesus, who is called the Christ. ("Christ" is the Greek equivalent of the Hebrew "Messiah." The words can be used interchangeably.) While the Old Testament talks in general terms about the Word of God, or creative power of God, the New Testament says in very specific terms as it looks at Jesus Christ, "The Word was made flesh, and dwelt among us" (John 1: 14).

The implications of this momentous claim, the most staggering ever made, will occupy much of our attention throughout this book. What we must see clearly at this point is that when the Bible speaks of God it does not just talk *about* God; it shows us God at work on the human scene, in a human life. How, then, does God make himself known to us? Finally and conclusively, God makes himself known by coming to us himself in Jesus Christ, who enters into fellowship with us, taking upon himself the limitations of our human lot, even suffering and dying as the ultimate expression of God's love for us and

of his desire to enter into fuller fellowship with us. And we
have to decide what to do about him.

God Reveals Himself
Through the Life of a Community

Those who decide that the claims made about him are true
comprise what is called the Christian Church. And in the life
of the Church God continues to be active, to work, to reveal
himself. Before we explore that notion we must remind ourselves that the Church did not just suddenly spring into existence "from scratch" about A.D. 30. The early Christians,
as a matter of fact, often referred to themselves as the "new
Israel," suggesting that they stood in a continuity with the old
Israel. And the old Israel, as we have seen, was a nation called
out, set apart, through whom God revealed himself. The
Israelites came to see that they must be "a light to the nations"
(Isa. 42: 6), that is, that they in their turn must make known
to the rest of the world the God with whom they stood in such
intimate relationship.

Now this is precisely the task which the New Testament
claims fell upon the Christian Church. The early Christians
tried to spread the "good news" of what God had done in
Christ to all men across the face of the earth. The "new Israel"
took upon itself the job that the old Israel did not do because
the old Israel did not accept Jesus as the promised Messiah. So
from the Christian standpoint, the task of the Jewish nation
is picked up and becomes the task of the Christian Church.
And the claim is that through the history of that ongoing community, as recorded in both the Old and the New Testaments,
the activity of the everliving God is still revealed. A quick
look at the book of The Acts, for example, one of the most exciting documents in all literature, will show you how in the
life of the Christian community the power and presence of the
living God continued to be manifested in new ways. Since God
is living and not dead, his activity does not cease at any point

in time, but continues through the channel of his appointing—the fellowship of believers known as the Church.

God Reveals Himself Through a Book

How do we know all these things? They are recorded on the printed pages of our Bibles. Thus the Bible itself is a means by which God reveals himself to us, since it is by reading the Bible that we find him confronting us.

But we must be careful here. There is a difference between God and statements about God. The statements in the Bible have come out of the historical events which the Bible describes, and these statements have been gathered together, written down, pieced together, and translated, by men. We believe that these men were moved by the power and spirit of God in a singular way, but this did not make them cease to be men. We will therefore hear the word of men within the Bible as well as the word of God.

Perhaps a couple of illustrations can make this clear. Imagine that you have bought a victrola record. On the label you see the slogan "His Master's Voice." Listening to the record, you can hear the voice of a great master—a Caruso, a Flagstad, or even a Bing Crosby. And yet, it is not *just* the master's voice. There are also other noises—scratches which are the result of the fact that the record has been made by human beings. This does not mean that we fail to hear the master, but simply that we must be careful to distinguish between the noises that are the master's voice and those which are the surface noises of the record. So with the Bible, we are always faced with the responsibility of distinguishing between the sounds that are the Master's voice, and those that are the result of the human situation in which men wrote down the words we now have.

Or imagine that you are standing in front of a solid brick wall. Only if there is a window in the wall can you see through it. Even then, if you look *at* the windowpane, you cannot focus on the view beyond. So you must look *through* the windowpane and focus your attention on what lies beyond. Similarly, the Christian does not so much look *at* the Bible as *through* the Bible to the encounters between God and man which are described on the printed page, and which we could not see at all if we did not have the printed page. If we just look *at* the Bible, its statements and propositions, the image beyond may be blurred; we have not come to know God as fully as we should. But if we look *through* the Bible, it serves as a kind of window by means of which God and Christ are brought into true focus. Thus the Bible is the means by which God can make his impact upon us today.

The Tally

This is what it adds up to, then:

God reveals himself.

God reveals himself in historical events.

God reveals himself through persons.

God reveals himself supremely through one person—Jesus Christ.

God reveals himself through the life of a community.

God reveals himself through a book.

And our next job is to try to find out more about the God who reveals himself in these amazing ways.

God, Genesis, and Geology

(Where Did Everything Come From?)

To say that most people want to know God, is nonsense.

To say that most of us want to get away from God and have him let us alone, is a lot closer to the truth. At least, that's what the Bible says, and it is a rather surprising idea.

How to Escape from God
—in Four Easy Lessons

We have an account of one Biblical writer's attempt to escape from God, and what happened. This account is in Ps. 139. It is a good place to begin a study of the God of the Bible, because it will keep us from becoming "sentimental" about him.

God has come too close to this writer, who is terrified by the thought that the Lord of heaven and earth is very near. If you have a friend who can "see right through you" when you are bluffing, and who knows you almost too well, you can get a dim notion of how the writer felt, for he had discovered that God knew him all too well: "There is not a word in my tongue, but, lo, O Lord, thou knowest it altogether" (v. 4). A rather unpleasant situation!

And so, since God's nearness makes him squirm, he decides to put a lot of distance between himself and God. This is what people invariably do when the living God gets too close. (It is only the "tame" gods that we manufacture ourselves in whose

50

presence we can remain comfortable.) For the living God makes demands. So the psalmist imagines four ways of escape:

1. He will "ascend up into heaven," seeking refuge, apparently, in a world that is so well-ordered that God will become unnecessary, a veritable "heaven" of his own imagination.
   But it doesn't work. God is there.
2. So he decides to make his bed in Sheol, "the pit," the one place he can be sure God won't be.
   But, worse luck, God is there, right where he has no business being!
3. The writer is panicky now, so he decides to run away, to the ends of the earth, "the uttermost parts of the sea." God won't be able to keep pace with him. He'll outwit God yet!
   No luck. God is there ahead of him.
4. Finally, he decides to take cover under "darkness."
   Once more, God finds him.

No exit. No escape.

The Moral: You Can't Escape from God

This is intolerable! No matter where the psalmist goes, God is there first. What the writer had said at first is true at last: "Thou hast beset me behind and before, and laid thine hand upon me." He is trapped. He cannot get away. This relentlessly pursuing God goes after him no matter where he attempts to flee.

And then, apparently, the psalmist realized that he was engaged in a losing battle. He couldn't get away from God. God was determined to have control over his life. Perhaps, strange thought, this was what life was all about. Perhaps he was made to surrender, to acknowledge this God, to turn about and meet him, rather than fleeing him. And so a new note enters into the psalm (v. 13). The writer turns from fear to praise. And now God's thoughts, instead of being fearful, are "precious" (v. 17). Now instead of fleeing from God for fear he will have to be remade, he turns to God in perfect trust and confidence and asks to be remade:

Search me, O God, and know my heart!
Try me and know my thoughts!
And see if there be any wicked way in me,
    and lead me in the way everlasting!

(Ps. 139: 23, 24)

A note to the careful reader: Verses 19-22 of this psalm, as
you will have seen in your Bible, are angry and bitter. The
writer hates God's enemies "with perfect hatred" and cries for
their destruction. This is a good reminder to us of the humanity of the writer of the psalm. He reacts very much as we
would react. (Think of the worst enemy of God you know and
see if it is not rather easy to say these verses about him.) These
verses can therefore remind us that even in a moment of high
spiritual insight we may corrupt that insight. This makes vs.
23, 24 even more important.

A Danger, a Difficulty, a Directive, and a Diagnosis

This experience of the psalmist warns us against speaking
too glibly about the God of the Bible. Let us therefore keep
in mind a few further things.

First, *a danger.* There is something extremely arrogant in
our presumption that we can understand or (even worse) write
about God. For we always run the danger of reducing God to
an "object," into a "something" about which we can write de-
scriptions or make diagrams. Also, we need to remember that
we haven't got "the whole story on God," that even when we
have said all that we can say we have still barely scratched the
surface. No one has a full and unimpeded vision of the pure
divine majesty, and the story of Moses being allowed to see
only God's "back" is a very early attempt to drive home this
point. (See Ex. 33: 17-23.) So let us never think that we can
reduce God to a series of statements or to four chapters in a
book.

Second, *a difficulty.* We find it difficult to think of God except in terms that come from our own human experience. As

a result we describe God in terms that seem to make him like us—larger, perhaps, and older and more experienced, possibly with a long beard, sitting on a throne. This kind of limitation of God to grade-school notions must certainly be avoided. And yet, on the other side of the argument, we may notice that categories drawn from our own experience are the only categories in which we are able to think, and if we do not claim too much for them, some of the human categories we use may be a lot closer to the mark than impersonal ones. When we say that God is "personal," for example, we do not mean that he is "a person" like us, with arms, legs, and fingernails, but that, whatever else we may say about him, he is *at least* one with whom we can enter into personal relationship and fellowship. He may be much more (and certainly is), but since we enter into relationship with persons and not with stones, we use human rather than geological categories to talk about our relationship with God.

Every attempt to "put God into words" will involve a measure of distortion, since we are trying to describe in terms of our own experience someone who is vaster than all our experience. We must recognize the inadequacy of our human symbols at the same time that we continue to use them—since we have no others. It is like the artist trying to depict three dimensions on his flat two-dimensional canvas. Let us say that his picture has railroad tracks which disappear at the horizon. Actually, the tracks are parallel right to the horizon. But on the canvas they are not parallel. They converge toward each other and finally join. When we see the painting in an art gallery, the painter succeeds in telling us the truth (the tracks are parallel) by painting something else (his tracks are not parallel). Language about God is much the same. For we too, like the artist, are trying to put into the dimension of our own experience something which is vaster than our own experience can fully understand.

Third, *a directive*. We must remember that the Biblical

understanding of God always retains a sense of mystery. The Latin phrase, *mysterium tremendum,* should ring a bell for anyone who tries to talk or write or think about God. There will always be an element of awe, of wonder, of something akin to fear and yet not quite the same as fear. Cold, descriptive words do not capture what this means, but an excerpt from *The Wind in the Willows* makes the point superbly. You may recall the time when Rat and Mole were looking for Portly, a baby otter who had gotten lost. They were transfixed by the unearthly music of the "piper at the gates of dawn," the animal's god Pan. They made their way toward the source of the music.

Then suddenly the Mole felt a great Awe fall upon him, an awe that turned his muscles to water, bowed his head, and rooted his feet to the ground. It was no panic terror—indeed he felt wonderfully at peace and happy—but it was an awe that smote and held him and, without seeing, he knew it could only mean that some august Presence was very, very near.

Finally the Mole dared to look up, and found himself in the presence of "the Friend and Helper," with whom, safe and content, was the baby otter.

"Rat!" he found breath to whisper, shaking. "Are you afraid?"
"Afraid?" murmured the Rat, his eyes shining with unutterable love. "Afraid! Of *Him?* O, never never! And yet—and yet—O Mole, I am afraid."

In this "pagan" experience, Kenneth Grahame has unforgettably captured an authentic Biblical note, a note which is expressed in such passages as Isa. 6: 1-8; chs. 40; 45; Ex., ch. 3; Job 42: 1-6; and countless others.

Fourth, *a diagnosis.* We must face the disturbing fact that there are differing conceptions of God in the Bible, particularly in the Old Testament. At times he seems like a bloody tyrant, exulting in the death of men and women. At other times he embodies mercy and forgiveness. At times he is only one god among many, and at other times the only God.

What can we say to this? We have simply to remember that the Old Testament comes out of the life and experience of hundreds of years of Jewish history, in which the sensitivity of the people is deepened, and through the course of which God makes himself more fully known to them as they are able to bear it and respond to him. God reveals himself to people where they are, and not somewhere else. He comes to their clouded vision, in the midst of their imperfect cultures, in their sin and idolatry, and they respond to his demands *as they understand them,* then and there. Their response is not perfect, for they are men and not God. Consequently, they bequeath to us insights that are not of uniform worth and significance. The Christian, who has seen this process of revelation come to its culmination in Christ, can use him as the "measuring stick" by which to judge all events within the Biblical revelation. We would not want to emulate many of the bloodthirsty things which the Israelites did in response to what they felt was the will of God for them. But we have this at least to learn from them—that just as they were trying to be obedient to God's will as it came to them in their time, so we have a similar obligation to be obedient to God's will as it comes to us in our time.

Likewise, when we come across references to "other gods" in the earlier Biblical writings, we must place this belief in the context of the later firmly established Jewish belief that there is one God and only one, and that all men are to give allegiance to him. "Hear, O Israel: The Lord our God is one Lord" (Deut. 6: 4) is the basic affirmation of mature Old Testament belief, and all else must be judged in the light of it.

In what follows, then, let us remember the danger, the difficulty, the directive, and the diagnosis. The story of the "evolution" of ideas about God is an interesting story, but it is not our concern here. We shall try to see the living God entering into the lives of the people of the Bible, so that we may be prepared for him to enter into our lives also.

God the Creator

In the long, tortuous history through which the Jewish nation came to know the Lord, monotheism (belief in one God) finally became absolutely fundamental. And once the Jews had realized that there is one God and one God alone, a very important consequence of this belief became apparent to them: the one God, the ruler of all things, is also the creator of all things. The relationship of these ideas is strikingly illustrated in a passage from Isaiah, written during the Babylonian Exile:

> For thus says the Lord,
> who created the heavens
>   (he is God!),
> who formed the earth and made it
>   (he established it;
> he did not create it a chaos,
>   he formed it to be inhabited!):
> "I am the LORD, and there is no other."
>   (Isa. 45: 18)

This note recurs again and again in the later chapters of Isaiah. These chapters, together with Gen., chs. 1; 2 (which in their present form also come from the Exilic period), are our main sources for the Biblical understanding of God as creator.

The Genesis Stories—with Supplements

One fact about the Bible which "every schoolboy knows" is that the opening chapters of Genesis tell about the creation of the world. Actually, as not every schoolboy knows, there are two accounts of the Creation, one in Gen., chs. 1: 1 to 2: 4a, and the other in Gen. 2: 4b-25. Before you continue this book, take five minutes to read them over, and another five minutes to think about them.

What is the real religious significance of these stories? When we attempt to answer such a question we discover that the accounts are much more profound than they appear to be on the surface. Here are some starters:

1. *The stories are first of all stories about God.* They breathe throughout the atmosphere of his majesty and power and holiness. The term "holy" in the Bible suggests the idea of "otherness"; that is, that God is *other* than, *more* than, the created order. To use a very long word, God is "transcendent"; that is, he is not to be confined within the world, but is above, beyond, outside, greater than, that which he has created. This understanding of God is implied throughout the Genesis stories, and it is made very explicit in the Isaiah writings, which were written at about the same time. The prophet of the Exile makes his point with incomparable beauty:

> Who has measured the waters in the hollow of his hand
>   and marked off the heavens with a span,
> enclosed the dust of the earth in a measure
>   and weighed the mountains in scales
>   and the hills in a balance? . . .
> Behold, the nations are like a drop from a bucket,
>   and are accounted as the dust on the scales;
>   behold, he takes up the isles like fine dust.
> Lebanon would not suffice for fuel,
>   nor are its beasts enough for a burnt offering.
> All the nations are as nothing before him,
>   they are accounted by him as less than nothing and
>   emptiness. . . .
> Have you not known? Have you not heard?
>   Has it not been told you from the beginning?
>   Have you not understood from the foundations of the earth?
> It is he who sits above the circle of the earth,
>   and its inhabitants are like grasshoppers;
> Who stretches out the heavens like a curtain,
>   and spreads them like a tent to dwell in;
> who brings princes to nought,
>   and makes the rulers of the earth as nothing.
>
> (Isa. 40: 12, 15-17, 21-23)

This is the God of creation—a God of majesty, power, transcendence, before whom we must stand in awe.

This means that one who thinks Biblically can never practice "nature worship," or believe that nature is God. Such a belief (called "pan-theism," that is, everything is God) is a pagan belief, which is repudiated by the Biblical emphasis that God creates nature, and is above and beyond nature. One of the psalms makes this distinction well.

> Of old thou didst lay the foundation of the earth,
>   and the heavens are the work of thy hands.
> They will perish, but thou dost endure;
>   they will all wear out like a garment.
> Thou changest them like raiment, and they pass away;
>   but thou art the same, and thy years have no end.
>   (Ps. 102: 25-27)

2. A second thing we learn from the Creation stories is that *all that is, is dependent upon God.* I am not "the master of my fate" or "the captain of my soul." God is. We have not placed ourselves here. God has. "It is he that made us, and we are his" (Ps. 100: 3). Life is not something we have earned or deserved, but something that has been given to us. It is a gift. We did not ask for it, or earn it. We simply received it. The girl you are in love with, the parents who look after you—these are the gifts of the creator God. Everything derives its meaning and significance from God. He is not only the creator of the universe, but its sustainer.

Take a brief "time out" over that last word. To believe in creation in the Biblical sense is to believe that *at every moment in time,* the created order is dependent upon God for its continuation. Without him it would cease to be. It is not enough just to think of God as creating the world "once upon a time," and then sitting back and saying: "There now! I'll let it run itself." The Bible stresses the fact that creation is God's ceaseless activity. "My Father is working still, and I am working" (John 5: 17) was the way Jesus summed it up.

3. The Creation stories emphasize very explicitly that *creation is good,* since it is God's handiwork. This theme is stressed particularly in the first Genesis story. On four occasions the identical wording about creation is used: "And God saw that it was good." (Compare Gen. 1: 12, 18, 21, 24.) God also saw that "the light was good" (v. 4) and toward the conclusion we find the summary statement, "And God saw everything that he had made, and behold, it was very good" (v. 31). (The natural reaction, "Then what about all the evil in the world?" we shall try to deal with in Chapters 11 and 12.)

God's world, then, is good. This means that we are to have a positive attitude toward it. We are not to "reject" the world, or throw up our hands in dismay at the thought of doing anything significant in it. Nobody who takes the goodness of creation seriously can say, "The world is so evil that I must escape it," or, "People are so bad that I hate them all," or, "There's no more point to living." Biblical religion is one of "world-affirmation" rather than "world-denial" precisely because of its belief in the goodness of creation. (We will see this more clearly in the chapters later on Biblical ethics.)

4. Finally, the Creation stories remind us that since God created the world, there is meaning and purpose behind it. The world in which we live didn't "just happen." It is not simply the product of chance or fate. Rather, the universe is the result of God's purposeful activity. We are not "trapped" in an unfriendly and hostile universe. Rather, God has a plan and a direction for it. It follows that our main task is to try to discover that plan and make our lives fall into line with it, so that we are working with the creator God rather than against him. We are to help, rather than to hinder, the bringing about of those things which God had in mind when he created the world.

"But What About Genesis and Geology?"

It would be pleasant to leave the matter there. This could be a short chapter. We could feel that everything had worked out rather nicely. Unfortunately, we can't leave the matter there. For these opening portions of Genesis have been the subject of so much controversy that we cannot ignore the fact.

The difficulty arose about a hundred years ago when scientists began to point out that the world had taken millions, perhaps billions, of years to evolve into its present form. The stanch believers in the Bible said that this was blasphemy. Didn't the Bible say that God created the world in "six days"? Nobody was going to tell them that

$$6 \text{ days} = 1,000,000,000 \text{ years (or so)}.$$

Who was right—the "religionists" or the scientists? To ask the question this way (as we usually do) is to miss the point. Let us rather ask first of all what these Creation stories are trying to say and what they are not trying to say. As we have seen, they are stories praising God, a God so great that he has created the universe. They are dealing with the religious question, "Why?" Why the world? Because God in his greatness and love has brought it into being. Now in making this profoundly important religious point, the authors say something of "how" God did all this, and it is here, and here only, that science raises some questions. For science investigates answers to the question, "How?" The authors of the Creation stories quite naturally based their stories on the scientific information available to them about 500 B.C. The fact that our scientific knowledge has changed considerably since then does not undercut or disprove the *religious* insights of the authors. There is no real "conflict" in believing in the scientific accuracy of modern evolution and at the same time believing in the religious accuracy of the Genesis stories.

Two Ways of Thinking

Let us make sure we understand that when we are dealing with religious questions and scientific questions, we are dealing with two different ways of describing reality, and that the two should not be confused. Genesis is not a scientific account of the Creation, and should not be so interpreted. It deals with "Why?" and its answer is "God." Modern science looks at the world and asks, "How?" and its answer is that the world slowly evolved—an answer that in no sense undermines belief in God.

Here are four statements:

$2+2=4$.

I love you.

Babe Ruth hit 619 home runs in his major league career.

I love you too.

It should be clear that statements one and three are of a different order from statements two and four. One and three are factually verifiable: "you can look them up." Statements two and four cannot be "proved" in the same way; but they can be much "truer" for the meaningful living of life than any number of so-called "factual" statements.

Look at the point in one other way, since it is important. In Shakespeare's play *As You Like It,* we are told that there are "... tongues in trees, books in the running brooks, sermons in stones." The speaker is saying that there are lessons to be learned from the woods. The metaphors help to underline the truth of his statement. But the statement is obviously not "true" as an actual literal set of facts. Just let some factually minded proofreader get ahold of Shakespeare's play, and he would soon set Shakespeare straight! He would revise it as follows:

trunks/ ~~tongues~~ in trees, (books) in the running brooks, /*trans.* sermons in (stones)

which we would decode to read "trunks in trees, stones in the running brooks, sermons in books." These statements would be factually true but quite unimportant. Shakespeare's statement is a valuable description of the woods, while the proofreader's statement is pointless, even though scientifically accurate.

Return now to the Creation stories. The point of the Creation stories is not illumined by a squabble over the number of hours in each "day" (and let it be remembered that the Bible says that "one day is with the Lord as a thousand years," so that there is really no conflict from that point of view). The important thing is that *God created*. (Read that sentence out loud twice, emphasizing first one, and then the other, italicized word.) Whether it was done in 24 hours, or 24,000 years, or 24,000,000,000 years, is quite beside the point. In other words, we can accept all that science has to tell us within its legitimate field of inquiry (which is answering the question "How?") and not be disturbed when we turn to religious inquiry (which deals with the question "Why?"). Our only quarrel will be with the people who claim that science has *all* the answers, that it can answer the question "Why?" as well as the question "How?" The scientist has a perfect right to tell us how old the world is, and how it has come to be what it is, by analyzing rock structures, tree rings, and so forth. But if he tries to tell us *why* the world has come into being at all, he is immediately in an area where he has to go beyond the strict scientific evidence.

The Genesis stories, then, are the product of religious devotion meditating on the significance of the Creation, and pointing out its inescapable religious truth and relevance to us.

Two Sides of the Same Coin —and a Summing Up

(What Do Words Like "Judge," "Redeemer," and "Trinity" Mean?)

Books have to have chapters. But don't let this new one fool you. We are simply picking up right where we left off on the last page of the last chapter. We are still talking about the same God. In this chapter we shall examine the assertion that he is Judge and that he is Redeemer. (There is a final section to the chapter also, but you will have to wait and see what that is.)

God as Righteous Judge

The Bible tells us that this creator God is also a righteous God, who expects his children to live righteously, and who holds them accountable when they do wrong. In other words, he is a judge. We can trace a kind of three-beat rhythm in the Biblical recognition of this fact—the recurrent rhythm of *demand, disaster, renewal*.

1. *God makes demands.* He expects his children to live up to these demands. You are expected to do justice, for example, rather than injustice. You are expected to love God rather than idols or false gods. You are expected to love your neighbor as yourself, rather than to "do him dirt." And so on. There is no evading these demands. No one, not even you, can

63

wriggle out from under them, nor can they be avoided.

2. *When these demands are not heeded, disaster follows.*
This disaster is interpreted as God's judgment upon human
sin. The Book of Amos is a good place to see this principle
at work. Amos looks at the nations surrounding Israel one by
one—Damascus, Gaza, Tyre, Edom, Ammon, Moab, and
Judah—and says that each one will be punished for having
defied God's will. And then comes the pay-off, the pay-off to
end all pay-offs. For the very same thing will happen to the
"people of God" themselves—they too will be judged by God
for their wrongdoing. No escape for them, just because they
are the "chosen people." In fact, precisely *because* they are the
chosen people, their punishment will be stiffer—they should
have known better. All men are judged. No exceptions.

3. *What is needed to change the situation is for man to re-*
pent. The situation is not completely black. The prophets do
not simply talk of gloom, but they talk of gloom in order to
"wake men up," so that they will change before it is too late.
As Amos puts it:

> Seek good, and not evil,
> that you may live;
> and so the Lord, the God of hosts, will be with you,
> as you have said.
> Hate evil, and love good,
> and establish justice in the gate;
> it may be that the Lord, the God of hosts,
> will be gracious to the remnant of Joseph.
>
> (Amos 5: 14, 15)

To talk of God as judge, then, is to insist that history has
moral meaning, that when people do wrong, they do not "get
away with it" indefinitely. There comes a time when they are
held accountable. Human life is in the hands and destiny of
the righteous God, and if people defy him, they must expect
to suffer the consequences. They will be judged by him and
found wanting. The only way out is for men to change drastically.

To Be Continued . . .

Now this is a grim picture. And it leaves us with a real problem: How can this talk of judgment be squared with the many Biblical assertions about God's love and mercy?

We need to remember that when we have spoken of God as judge, the description is still "to be continued" as the next section of this chapter will show. But before turning to the other affirmation about God we need to remember that we cannot eliminate the Biblical emphasis on God as judge. The danger is that we will sentimentalize God's love to such a degree that justice and judgment are no longer present. But love itself may have to include an element of stern judgment. Sentimental indulgent love may not be real love at all. The parents who say: "We can't understand why Johnny went wrong. We always gave him everything he wanted," may be less loving than the parents who sometimes said "No" to him and helped him to realize that he was living in a world where Johnny could not call all the signals.

Human wrongdoing and sin are an offense to God. They degrade his world and they represent a repudiation of his Lordship. He cannot simply "wink" at sin or refuse to take it seriously. It is wrong and must be punished. Otherwise there is no moral meaning to the universe and all we can say is that "anything goes." We are thus in the curious position of realizing that judgment can be the "negative side of love," love as it must express itself toward wrongdoing. Love must not let wrongdoing "get away with it." Thus justice and love are two sides of the same coin.

This means that God's judgment has a purpose behind it, which is redemptive. He does not punish simply to "be mean," but to try to change the wrongdoers. If they will not respond to persuasion, perhaps they will respond to sternness. Judgment is a kind of "shock treatment" which God employs to bring erring nations and peoples to their senses. The Biblical writers are able to appreciate that judgment is a way of making God's love reach them. The author of Ps. 76 points out that "God arose to establish judgment to save all the oppressed of the earth" (Ps. 76: 9). There we have it in a nutshell—"judgment to save." Judgment for the purpose of salvation is an indispensable part of the Biblical notion of God as judge. With this in mind, we can turn to the "other side of the coin."

God as Redeemer

Granted, the word "redeemer" sounds old-fashioned. But it is an important Biblical word, and we can't get along without it. To "redeem," in common usage, is to buy back something we once owned. Thus we speak of redeeming a pledge (from a pawnbroker) or redeeming a promise (which we had broken but which we still want to make good).

In this sense, God seeks to "redeem" men, that is, to buy them back, or, more properly in his case, to win them back, or even to woo them back, to fellowship with him. The situation is as though men, who belong to God, had run away from him and gotten lost—but that even though it was their fault, he had sought them out and reclaimed them for his own. The word "redemption" is thus a hopeful word. It says that God has not forsaken us, even if we have forsaken him, but that he seeks us constantly.

The clearest Biblical expression of this redemptive activity of God is the whole story of the coming of Christ into the world as God's outgoing, redemptive love made concrete and personal. Since Chapters 7 to 10 will develop this theme, we will look for the moment at other Biblical insights into God's redemptive activity.

There is no need to be theoretical about this. We can look at a specific person, the prophet Hosea. Hosea knew that God was a God of justice and that he punished wrongdoing. But he also knew that that was not the end of the story. The realization of God's redemptive love came to him through a tragic personal experience. Hosea discovered that his wife Gomer was not faithful to him, but was an adulteress. The relationship between Hosea and Gomer was thus spoiled. Then Hosea realized that the same thing was true of the relationship between God and Israel. Israel too had proved faithless. She was likewise an adulteress, giving herself to other gods. Just as Gomer had broken her promise to be faithful to Hosea, so Israel had broken her promise to be faithful to God.

So Hosea had to put Gomer out of his house. But he made an astonishing discovery. He discovered that even though Gomer had been unfaithful to him—he still loved her! Although she did not "deserve" his love, that love was still there. Could he dare to believe this also of God—that although Israel had been unfaithful to him he still loved her?

Hosea dared to believe it. His restoration of Gomer to his own household dramatized what he felt certain God would do for his people. They would first be put out of "God's house" and sent into exile. But there would be a return! God's love for his people was such that he could not and would not give them up. Even when they were faithless, he would encompass them with "bands of love."

And I will betroth you to me for ever; I will betroth you to me in righteousness and in justice, in steadfast love, and in mercy. I will betroth you to me in faithfulness; and you shall know the Lord.

(Hos. 2: 19, 20)

A redeeming God, then, is *a seeking God, willing to restore fellowship because of his deep love.*

There are three parables of Jesus, each of which underscores a part of the italicized statement:

One: In the parable of the Lost Sheep (Luke 15: 3-7) we are reminded that God is a seeking God. The shepherd does not wait at the sheepfold for the straggler to return. He goes out into the night to find the one sheep that has gotten lost.

Two: In the parable of the Lost Boy (Luke 15: 11-24) we are reminded that God is a forgiving God. When the boy finally comes to his senses and returns home, expecting the worst, he finds his father waiting, ready to forgive him.

Three: In the parable of the Workers in the Vineyard (Matt. 20: 1-16) we are reminded that God's redeeming love is a gift, not something that can be earned. A number of men work from dawn to dusk for a denarius. But at various times during the day other men are employed, some at nine, some at noon, some at three, and some just before quitting time. And the master who has hired them gives each one the same wage—even those who worked only a few minutes! The parable is not a lesson in labor relations but a description of the Kingdom of God and of the fact that God's love toward each man is not expressed in terms of what each man earns, but is rather a sheer gift. God loves because it is characteristic of him to love, not because men have deserved it.

Echoes in the Psalter

Such a God is one with whom men can enter into personal relationship, through worship. This point has significance. If you want to know what people really believe about God, then do not look simply to their history, or their great leaders. Look also at their devotional life—the moments when they lift their hearts in praise, abase themselves in penitence, rejoice with thanksgiving, or entreat with heartfelt need. These moments we find recorded in the Jewish hymnbook, the Psalter. In it we find hints about the kind of relationship with the redeemer God that can be real for men. Here are a few snippets to tease you into examining the Psalter for yourself:

> Be mindful of thy mercy, O Lord,
>   and of thy steadfast love,
>   for they have been from of old.
> Remember not the sins of my youth,
>   or my transgressions;
>   according to thy steadfast love, remember me,
>   for thy goodness' sake, O Lord!
>
>   (Ps. 25: 6, 7)

> The Lord is merciful and gracious,
>   slow to anger and abounding in steadfast love.
> He will not always chide,
>   nor will he keep his anger for ever.
> He does not deal with us according to our sins,
>   nor requite us according to our iniquities. . . .
> As a father pities his children,
>   so the Lord pities those who fear him.
>
> (Ps. 103: 8-10, 13)

> Have mercy on me, O God, according to
>   thy steadfast love;
>   according to thy abundant mercy blot out
>   my transgressions. . . .
> Create in me a clean heart, O God,
>   and put a new and right spirit within me.
> Cast me not away from thy presence,
>   and take not thy holy Spirit from me.
> Restore to me the joy of thy salvation,
>   and uphold me with a willing spirit.
>
> (Ps. 51: 1, 10-12)

The Impact of God on the New Testament Folk

Now let us jump across many centuries, to about A.D. 55 or 60. We find Paul ending a letter to the Corinthians with the words, "The grace of the Lord Jesus Christ and the love of God and the fellowship of the Holy Spirit be with you all" (II Cor. 13: 14). This is curious talk! Is Paul referring to one God, or three? Are God, Christ, the Holy Spirit, all the same, or are they different?

We are treading upon formidable ground here, ground that goes by the name of the doctrine of the Trinity. There is no formal "doctrine of the Trinity" as such in the New Testament. But it is out of the experience of New Testament Christians that the doctrine of the Trinity was later formulated. Let this fact be underlined: *The doctrine of the Trinity is not an attempt by theologians to make things tough for the average Christian by introducing a celestial mathematics which says 3 = 1. The doctrine of the Trinity is an attempt to describe, as systematically as possible, the content of the Christian experience of God.*

FATHER . . .

Take one of these early Christians like Peter. He has grown up in a Jewish home. He knows the God of his fathers, the God and Lord of history to whom his Jewish people stand in special relationship. Through the worship of the synagogue, through studying the law, and through the experiences of his own life, this God has been a reality for Peter, one with whom he has had personal relationship. He knows with countless other Jews that God pities those who fear him, "as a father pities his children" (Ps. 103: 13). Perhaps Peter has even called this God "Father."

. . . SON . . .

But then one day Peter meets a man who is more than a man. This man confronts Peter as he mends nets, or fishes all night without luck. Peter makes himself the follower of this man Jesus and lives in close relationship with him. He finds that human categories won't explain him. So when Jesus asks Peter, "Who do you say that I am?" Peter replies, "You are the Christ, the Son of the living God" (Matt. 16: 16). When Jesus confronts Peter, Peter cannot escape the conclusion that *God* is confronting him. This man is God—and yet he is still man.

. . . AND HOLY SPIRIT

But the time comes when Jesus is no more physically present with the disciples. In spite of this fact, they do not feel that God has left them, for he has sent "the Holy Spirit." This is not another God, this is the same God, making himself known to them as a constant abiding presence and the source of their power. Peter has known God as Father, he has known God as Son, now he knows God as Spirit, and his life becomes a constant surrender to that power which is not his own, but rather God active and at work in him. God isn't to be talked about in the past tense—he is active and at work right now in the present, with the promise that he will continue to be so in the future.

Thus the New Testament writers talk about God in these three ways. They are not constructing an intellectual puzzle; they are simply describing how the living God works upon their lives.

About This "Holy Spirit"

In our own day we generally have our greatest difficulty when we try to talk meaningfully about the Holy Spirit. If God the Father is little more than "a benevolent oblong blur," the Holy Spirit is just a blur. We are not alone in this difficulty. The same thing bothered certain early Christians.

SCENE: Ephesus. The home of some disciples. Enter Paul.
PAUL (*anxious to get better acquainted*): Did you receive the Holy Spirit when you believed?
DISCIPLES (*wondering what on earth Paul is talking about*): No, we have never even heard that there is a Holy Spirit.
(Acts 19: 2)

And for us the situation is made even more confusing by the frequent ecclesiastical use of the old-fashioned word "ghost": for "Holy Spirit" read "Holy Ghost" in most hymnals, prayer books, and sermons. We think of "ghosts" in terms of the old Scottish collect:

From goblins and ghosties and long-legged beasties,
And things that go BUMP in the dark,
Good Lord, deliver us.

"Since we don't believe in ghosts of that sort any more, why should we believe in a Holy Ghost?" is a not unnatural rejoinder. As a matter of fact, the old Anglo-Saxon word from which this comes, *gast*, originally meant "breath," or "spirit," or "soul," which (as we shall see) is not far from the original Biblical meaning. How can we overcome these confusions?

Let us remember that the Holy Spirit is, in simplest definition, *God in action*. To be possessed by the Spirit is not simply to be "feeling inspirational" or to be imbued with "team spirit," but to be possessed by God. He was central to the experience of the early Christians, and he has been central for authentic Christian experience ever since. His reality is perhaps most clearly felt in community experience. Paul, you remember, talked about the "*koinonia* [community, fellowship] of the Holy Spirit" (II Cor. 13: 14). The Church, then, is the sphere where His power is most fully operative. It is significant that almost everything that the early Christians do in the book of The Acts is attributed to the power of the Holy Spirit. "It has seemed good to the Holy Spirit and to us . . ." (Acts 15: 28) is mature Christian conviction.

As we look at the notion of "spirit" in the Bible, certainly the dominant impression we gain is of "spirit" as a source of *power*. The Hebrew word used in the Old Testament, *ruach*, is developed from the notion of "wind," and comes to mean a manifestation of God's activity and presence. ("Take not thy holy *ruach* from me," Ps. 51: 11.) The new Testament word *pneuma* stands likewise for the dynamic activity of God at work in the lives of men. As Jesus put it, "You shall receive power when the Holy Spirit has come upon you" (Acts 1: 8). The word-images that the early Christians use for the Holy Spirit also reflect this fact. He is not gentle and passive. On the contrary, "The place in which they were gathered together was *shaken;* and they were all filled with the Holy Spirit" (Acts 4: 31). In the account of the descent of the Holy Spirit at Pentecost, the apostles hear "a sound from heaven like the rush of a mighty wind." When they try to picture the Holy Spirit in a visual image, he appears as "tongues of fire." (Cf. Acts 2: 1-4.)

The Heart of the Matter

The transforming, pulsating, vibrant power of God expressing himself in human life—God in action—is something of what we mean when we talk about the Holy Spirit. Such matters can never be fully expressed in cold type. Music should be the best descriptive medium. Unfortunately, most hymns about the Holy Spirit are so vapid and unexciting that it is difficult to imagine people becoming empowered by the Holy Spirit if he is no more dynamic than they suggest. Make it a point, therefore, to get hold of a recording of Bach's *B Minor Mass,* and listen to the chorus about the Holy Spirit, "Cum Sancto Spiritu." If you do, you will come closer to an understanding of the Holy Spirit than you will by reading a dozen books. Bach does not present an anemic "still, small voice of calm." On the contrary, the music is vibrant, pulsating and alive, dynamic, rushing from start to finish, vitality personified. It is a thrilling experience to hear it, and even more thrilling to sing it. And it can give you at least a little inkling of what would be most thrilling of all—to be possessed by the One about whom you were singing.

A Claim and Some Challenges

(What About Predestination and Miracles?)

When Pascal, the famous French scientist, died, a small document was discovered on his person which contained the statement, "God of Abraham, God of Isaac, God of Jacob, not of the philosophers and scholars." Pascal wasn't interested in some vague idea of God as "the undifferentiated unity" or the "all-cohesive source of reality." He was concerned about the God of history, the God who is not aloof and unconcerned about men, but who acts, who *does things,* on the historical scene. This is right in line with the Bible's understanding of God, where we learn that God sent . . . .

God spoke . . . .

God called . . . .

God delivered . . . .

God worked . . . .

History is God's workshop, the place where he is active.

The Claim: God Is Sovereign

Now this is a tremendously far-reaching conception. The fact that God becomes known in the events of Jewish *history* and that he finally reveals himself in the *historical* event of Jesus Christ, "in the days of Herod the king" (Matt. 2: 1), indicates how seriously God as the Lord of history is taken by Biblical faith.

74

Instead of looking at this claim in terms of generalities, let us do a little honest-to-goodness grappling with a specific passage, one from The Book of Isaiah. The background of the passage is this: Assyria has arisen as a menacing world power, and is now ready to pounce on Judah, where Isaiah lives and is prophesying. Problem: How can God's activity in history be discerned in the devouring of Judah (the people of God) by Assyria (a pagan monster nation)? Isaiah answers that Assyria, the pagan nation, is an instrument of God's purposes! God speaks:

> Ah, Assyria, the rod of my anger,
>   the staff of my fury!
> Against a godless nation [that is, the Jews who had forsaken God]
>   I send him,
>   and against the people of my wrath I command him,
> to take spoil and seize plunder,
>   and to tread them down like the mire of the streets.

But Assyria, a proud, boastful nation, is not aware that it is being used:

> But he [the Assyrian nation] does not so intend,
>   and his mind does not so think;
> but it is in his mind to destroy,
>   and to cut off nations not a few;
> for he says: . . .
> "Shall I not do to Jerusalem and her idols
>   as I have done to Samaria and her images?"

Assyria *will* conquer Jerusalem as it has already conquered Samaria. But Assyria's king will be proud and think that he has accomplished this by his own power:

When the Lord has finished all his work on Mount Zion and on Jerusalem he will punish the arrogant boasting of the king of Assyria and his haughty pride. For the king says:

> "By the strength of my hand I have done it,
>   and by my wisdom, for I have understanding;

I have removed the boundaries of the people,
    and have plundered their treasures;
    like a bull I have brought down those who sat on
        thrones. . . ."

This attitude will be the undoing of Assyria, for this is an attempt to repudiate God's Lordship over history. Isaiah goes on tauntingly:

Shall the ax vaunt itself over him who hews with it,
    or the rod magnify itself against him who wields it?
As if a rod should wield him who lifts it,
    or as if a staff should lift him who is not wood!

The result will be disaster for the idolatrous Assyrians who worship only themselves:

Therefore the Lord, the Lord of hosts,
    will send wasting sickness among his [the Assyrians'] stout
        warriors,
and under his glory a burning will be kindled,
    like the burning of fire.
                    (Isa. 10: 5-8, 11-13, 15, 16)

To get the full force of this remarkable passage read it again:

1. For "Assyria," substitute "an enemy nation."
2. For the "godless nation" (Judah), substitute your own nation.
3. For "Jerusalem," substitute the capital of your own nation.
4. For "Samaria," substitute the latest country to come under the domination of the enemy nation you listed in No. 1.

Then you will be able to see the sledge-hammer impact this passage has.

We can now detect some disturbing implications. Is the Bible really suggesting that *God* raises up Hitlers and Stalins? Are they the way his will gets accomplished in the world? We must look carefully at what this passage really tells us about God as the Lord of history.

1. The passage affirms that *history is in God's hands*. Assyria seems to be the boss, but Assyria is not. God is. This is not easy

to understand. We cannot say that it is God's will that Hitler should murder six millions of Jews and that thousands of innocent people should be slaughtered in World War II. However, we must say that in a world of which God is in final control, a large-scale neglect of his laws can lead only to large-scale disaster. If God is righteous, then wrongdoing cannot go unnoticed. Let's bring it right down to home: America, France, Britain, and others have been, by and large, "godless nations," just as Judah had been. We have served God with our lips and denied him with our lives. A modern Isaiah or Jeremiah or Amos would have a good deal to say to us. To exploit the underprivileged, to be rich while others starve, to be idle while men break their backs at slave labor—these things bear heavy interest, which sooner or later has to be paid. Such statements are hard to say and hear, but they are true to prophetic insight. In such situations, when men in their freedom defy God, forces like Nazism and Communism develop. And what the Bible underlines is that *even* such forces are brought under God's sovereignty. He is not defeated by a Hitler or a Stalin. On the contrary, God is able to make such use of them that in the long run *his* purposes rather than theirs are effected. He uses the wrath of man to praise him. (See Ps. 77.)

2. To say that history is in God's hands is to say that *it has a moral meaning*. If Judah becomes a "godless nation," then Judah must be expected to pay the price, which is defeat by Assyria. When a crisis comes, and Assyria is ready to pounce, this is not just a freak of history—it has moral significance. It can be interpreted as a warning. Isaiah tells Judah that repudiation of God has consequences, grim historical consequences, in the face of which man must repent. To see history in this way is to see its moral significance. Today, for example, the passage can remind America that it is the richest nation on earth, and that if its wealth is used just for itself, the judgment of God is sure to follow.

3. *Even the nation that is the "instrument" of God's pur-*

poses stands under God's judgment. God uses Assyria without Assyria's being aware of it, and since Assyria does not acknowledge God, Assyria stands under judgment just as Judah does. To say, "By the strength of *my* hand I have done it," as the Assyrian king does, is to court disaster by refusing to acknowledge God's sovereignty. This is a grim warning to nations that imagine that they have enough power to do as they please. When a nation becomes popular or powerful, it is particularly easy for it to claim the credit, and say, "By the strength of my hand I have done it." Assyria was guilty of this. Judah was guilty of this. America can easily become guilty of this. The same point is made in Deuteronomy. There the Jewish people are warned not to forget God when power and prosperity come to them.

Beware lest you say in your heart, "My power and the might of my hand have gotten me this wealth." You shall remember the Lord your God. . . . And if you forget the Lord your God and go after other gods and serve them and worship them, I solemnly warn you this day that you shall surely perish. Like the nations that the Lord makes to perish before you, so shall you perish, because you would not obey the voice of the Lord your God (Deut. 8: 17-20).

The Challenges

The claim, then, is that God is sovereign. He is in control. This is a fundamental Biblical insight which no amount of text-juggling can dislodge. But this gets us into deep water at a number of points, and we must look at two of the challenges that face us when we take the claim seriously. (A third challenge, the relationship of evil to God's sovereignty, is faced in Chapters 11 and 12.)

PROBLEM ONE: GOD'S SOVEREIGNTY AND "PREDESTINATION"

The problem arises this way. If God is sovereign, the "ruler of all things," then we seem to be saying that *everything* that happens is ordained by God. And this appears to destroy our freedom. If you choose to serve God, that is because he determined that you would choose him. If you choose to reject God, that (so many Christians have held) is also because God determined that you would reject him—and suffer the consequences. Either way, he has "predestined" your action. What can we say about such an alarming conclusion?

We must not confuse Biblical belief in the sovereignty of God with fatalism. It is not the Biblical contention, for example, that you are powerless to choose a ham sandwich for supper since it has been previously determined that you will eat peanut butter. Such a view would mean that you were simply a puppet, a pawn of fate, and that no effort, nor moral striving or choosing, on your part could make the slightest difference. That would not be Biblical faith, but pagan fatalism.

Two Inescapable Affirmations

Biblical faith proceeds in a different way, with two apparently dissimilar affirmations:

The *first* real fact about life is God, and the first fact about God is that he *is God*—sovereign, all-powerful. That conclusion cannot be avoided without distorting the Biblical message. This means that everything is seen, ultimately, as "under God." This is his world, not ours. We are placed here by him, not by ourselves. We are to do his will, not our own. He is not a little tin god who is only one of many objects in a hostile universe; he is the first and the last, surrounding all that is.

But Biblical faith makes another claim. This is the claim that we are morally responsible agents, and that we cannot escape responsibility for what we do. We have been given the gift of freedom. Even when we abuse that freedom and make wrong choices, we cannot shove the blame off on God. We cannot say, "I'm not responsible, it's God's fault." On the contrary, the Bible everywhere affirms that we must shoulder the blame, and that we cannot slide out from under it.

Now on the face of it, these two ideas don't "jell." God is all-powerful. I am responsible. If the first is true, the second is false. If the second is true, the first is false. So it would seem. Logically, they certainly disagree. However, we must notice that life does not always conform to strict logic. Very often, the most real things in life fly in the face of logic:

"Do you honestly think Anne is beautiful?"

"Well, no, she's not exactly beautiful."

"Is she a brain?"

"No, I can't honestly say she's a brain."

"Is she a witty conversationalist?"

"Well, no. . . ."

"Good grief. Does she have money?"

"No, not a cent."

"Is there *anything* particularly wonderful about her?"

"Well, I can't exactly describe it."

"And yet you love her?"

"You bet I do!"

The conclusion doesn't follow logically—and yet it is a true conclusion! He *does* love her. They're being married next month. There are areas of life where logic is not the final court of appeal.

We can follow up this clue in looking at the problem of predestination. For it may be that two things logically irreconcilable may be reconciled in religious experience. Paul is a help here. "Work out your own salvation with fear and trembling," he says, emphasizing *our responsibility,* and then in the same breath goes on, "for God is at work in you, both to will and to work for his good pleasure," emphasizing *God's sovereignty* (Phil. 2: 12, 13). In one sentence he combines two apparently irreconcilable attitudes. The point is that while logic may not be able to understand this joining together of God's sovereignty and man's responsibility, religious experience can and does. Put it to any religiously sensitive person:

Q. Did you become good through your own efforts?

A. Of course not. It was due to the grace of God. I can't take the credit.

And then ask:

Q. Well, then, what about the lie you told last week? I suppose that was God's fault?

A. Of course not. That was my fault. I can't blame God for that.

Authentic religious experience of God seems to demand both answers. As Paul says again and again, "It was I, yet it was not I, it was the grace of God." To give a different answer to either question would be hypocrisy.

The Significance of "Election"

The question of predestination is also raised when we take seriously the Old Testament claim that God has "chosen" the Jewish people as his special concern. (See further the section on "the covenant" in Chapter 15.) And when we realize that God chose them, not because they deserved it, but simply because he loved them, it all sounds highhanded and arbitrary. Why should God "choose" one nation instead of another? And what about those who are not chosen?

An important part of the answer is the reminder that the Jews were "chosen" not for special privileges but rather to bear special responsibilities. They did not have an easier time because they were God's chosen people. They had a tougher time. The pagans could in a sense be excused for their wrongdoing, but the Jews had no excuse—they knew better! So we must rule out any notion of "favoritism" in the sense that election made things easier for the elected.

Furthermore we must see the election of the Jews in terms of its ultimate purpose, which was that through them God's love and concern could be expressed to *all* people: "I will give you as a light to the nations, that my salvation may reach to the end of the earth" (Isa. 49: 6). And it is a matter of sober fact that it *was* through the events of Jewish history that the nations did come to see God at work, and were prepared for his final manifestation in Jesus Christ.

Notice further that in doing all this God does not override the gift of freedom which he has given us. The Jewish people can accept God or reject God. They usually reject him, just as we do. But this does not defeat God. He makes use of the very facts of their sin and rejection, working them into his plan, using them as a way of showing more clearly who he is and what he demands. It is almost as though a composer of a piece of orchestral music were to stand behind us as we played, and as we made mistakes, he were to alter the succeeding measures of the score to make use of those mistakes and weave them into the pattern of the piece. He would control the ultimate direction and outcome of the music, but he would do so in relation to the way we fulfilled his directions or failed to fulfill them. He would be master of the situation, and we would still be free.

The Biblical belief in election is a *positive* belief. It does not say, "God deliberately rejects most people and chooses only a few." It affirms that God does choose, and that those so chosen are the ones through whom he reaches out toward all men. It is not our job to puzzle about the fate of those "not chosen," and gloat over the fact (as Christians sometimes have) that "we made the team" and somebody else didn't. As a matter of fact, nobody but God knows who is "on the team." The "bad pagan" may actually be a lot closer to the Kingdom of God than you.

"Why Bother?"

A further question which is raised when God's sovereignty is taken seriously, goes like this: "If God is really in control, why bother? He'll see that we do the things he wants us to do. Relax!"

Here is another area where what seems like a logical conclusion just doesn't follow. It is a matter of simple historical fact that people who have been convinced of the sovereignty of God have been extremely "active." If he has chosen them to do his will, then they must strive mightily to do just that! At the time of the Protestant Reformation, for example, the Calvinists were the people who took predestination most seriously. But there were no more active and responsible individuals in that entire period than the Calvinists. Why? Because they were convinced that God had chosen them to do his work, and that therefore nothing, absolutely nothing, could defeat them. Who could stand against the Lord's elect? Consequently they had a vigor that was marvelous (and sometimes terrifying) to behold. A seventeenth century writer put it clearly: "I had rather meet coming against me a whole regiment with drawn swords than one lone Calvinist convinced that he is doing the will of God."

PROBLEM TWO: GOD'S SOVEREIGNTY AND MIRACLES

Let us now look at our second main challenge. The Bible speaks a great deal about the "mighty deeds" which the Lord of history performs. And there is probably no greater stumbling block for the modern reader than these miracles. (Here we will deal only with the Old Testament miracles. Chapter 9 discusses Jesus' miracles.) It seems impossible to a twentieth century reader that axheads should float, or that sticks should change to snakes, or that city walls should crumble because a trumpet was blown. What about it?

Faith vs. Faith—Not Faith vs. Nonfaith

There is a false way of getting at the problem that must be shattered. This is the view that says that to believe in miracles takes a monumental act of faith, while not to believe in miracles is simply common sense, because miracles cannot happen. Notice carefully that the claim, "Miracles cannot happen," is just as dogmatic a statement, just as much an act of faith, as the claim, "Miracles can happen." Each statement implies a whole view of the universe to which the speaker has committed himself. The choice, then, is not a choice between faith or nonfaith. It is a choice between rival faiths. One person is saying, "I believe in a universe in which God can work in ways that I may not totally understand." The other person is saying, "I believe in a universe in which nothing can happen that I don't understand."

You can decide which view makes more sense to you.

What Is a Miracle?

We must make clear what we mean by "miracle." A popular definition of miracle is that it is something that is "contrary to nature." There are certain rules or laws at work in the universe. Every now and then something happens that is contrary to those laws, and this is a miracle.

But miracle can also be interpreted as something that is "contrary to what we know of nature." This definition, though more modest, may be more valuable. For it recognizes the limitations of our outlook, and suggests that there may be a more complete outlook than the one we possess. And it is precisely this that Biblical faith insists upon—that God's outlook is the ultimate one and that we can never claim to share it. He may do things that seem strange to us but are not strange to him. It would even be true to say that from God's outlook there are no miracles—God is simply working in ways that are "natural" to him, even if they appear "supernatural" to us. We have no right to limit God only to activities that we can understand.

Let's put it this way. Suppose you are a man from Mars. As your flying saucer circles above an American city, you see traffic and traffic lights. After a while you decide that there is a law which goes, "Cars move when the light is green, and stop when the light is red." But then a strange thing happens. All the cars pull over to the side of the street and a couple of cars race through six or seven red lights without stopping. Then the other cars start up again.

This leaves you highly perplexed. For this is contrary to the law. But actually it is not contrary to the law; it is only contrary to what you (a man from Mars, remember) know of the law. For the thing you do not know, sitting in a flying saucer, is that there is a provision in the law to take care of emergencies. When an ambulance and police car appear with sirens going, the other cars are required by law to pull over to the side of the street, and give them the right of way, red lights or no. The ambulance and the police cars are not breaking the law; they are illustrating part of the law that you didn't happen to know about. Your theory was all right as far as it went, but it didn't go far enough.

What More Is a Miracle?

However, it would not be enough just to leave the matter there. In the Bible, miracle is not simply "what we don't know." There is the more positive assertion that miracle is a recognition of God's power, that we are in no position to tell God what he can or cannot do. He determines that! The Biblical writers were quite aware that God's "mighty acts" went beyond any human possibility of explanation. They are a way of asserting God's sovereignty over all that he has created. He is not "bound" by creation in the way we are. If God is truly the living Lord of all creation, then we must allow that he can express himself as *he* chooses, and not as we dictate. To believe in miracle is to believe that God can do *new things*. And it is from this sort of perspective that we must approach the fact of miracle in the Bible. We must make room for the possibility that God can do things that seem new and even strange from our point of view, although they may not be new or strange from his point of view.

The Fundamental Miracle

This is not the same thing as saying that all the recorded miracles are of equal *religious* importance. The most important matter is not the question of the floating axhead or the sun standing still at Joshua's command. The most important matter is whether or not we are grasped by the fundamental miracle of Biblical faith. And if we are, we are entitled to and obligated to look at other reported miracles in relationship to the fundamental miracle.

What is the fundamental miracle? Surely, it is the fact—the miraculous, inexplicable fact—that God loves stumbling, sinful people like us. As this theme is developed throughout the Bible—in God's choosing of Israel, his continued forgiveness, particularly his sending of his Son, his gift of the Holy Spirit, his concern with us to this very day—we come to see how miraculous it all is, how totally unexpected, how far beyond anything we have a right to expect, how contrary to what we know of the way life usually goes. That God loves sinful men and enters into fellowship with them is the heart of the Biblical assertion. It is the fundamental miracle. Particularly as we see it focused in Jesus Christ, we see that it is *the* really important matter. After we understand that, we can go on to ask about this or that miracle not only concerning the trustworthiness of our report of it, but, more important, how and to what extent it helps to illumine and further clarify our understanding of the fundamental miracle of Jesus Christ.

So let us turn to examine more fully the fundamental miracle.

The Unexpected Character of the Good News

(What Makes Jesus So Important?)

Be It Hereby Enacted:
*that every three years all people shall forget whatever they have learned about Jesus, and begin the study all over again * * ***

In some ways, a law like that wouldn't be a bad idea. It would at least force us to go back and read the Gospels and Epistles again "for the first time," and come face to face with the Person who is portrayed there. Seeing him free from the distortions and limitations with which our minds inevitably clothe him, we would be amazed—we might even be shocked—at what we saw.

87

Who Is Right?

You notice the limitation when you read books *about* Jesus. Almost everyone gives you something less than the "whole" Jesus. You often learn more about the person who writes the "life of Jesus" than you do about Jesus himself.

> A man with socialist leanings writes a book about Jesus and Jesus emerges as the great champion of the underprivileged.

> An advertising executive writes a life of Jesus and Jesus emerges as one who is particularly clever in his use of advertising principles.

> A humanist writes a book about Jesus and Jesus emerges as a great teacher, humanitarian, and friend.

Which picture is right? Is he "gentle Jesus, meek and mild," and at the same time a fiery denouncer who can use very harsh language and condemn the Pharisees? Is he a vague mystic concerned only with "spiritual things" and at the same time a person who can urge us to pray for such crassly material things as our daily bread?

The Point of the New Testament Claim

The reason for such puzzling contradictions springs from the fact that the New Testament makes two apparently contradictory claims about Jesus. To some people, the claims cancel each other out. To others they appear absurd. But to the vast procession of Christians down through the ages, it has seemed necessary to insist upon *both* affirmations. They can be stated in a number of ways:

> Jesus is both God and man.

He is both human and divine.

He shows us who God is and he shows us what we ought to be.

Or, to put the same thing in Biblical terminology, "in him the whole fulness of deity dwells bodily" (Col. 2: 9), and yet he is one who "in every respect has been tempted as we are" (Heb. 4: 15).

Well-meaning Christians come to grief when they attempt to make one of these affirmations without the other. There are plenty of people, for example, who are willing to admit that Jesus was a very, very, very good man, or even a very, very, very, *very* good man—but they balk at the notion that he is divine.

On the other hand there are Christians who assert emphatically that because Jesus was divine, he knew everything, and there was nothing he could not do. They are annoyed if you point out to them that Jesus got tired, hungry, discouraged, and lonely like any other normal human being, even though these facts are repeatedly stressed in the Gospels.

Both groups of people miss the point of the New Testament. Take the opening verses of the Fourth Gospel, for example. The author has been talking about the "Word" of God, which in the Old Testament was a way of describing the power and creativity of God: "By the word of the Lord the heavens were made" (Ps. 33: 6). God's "Word" is his creative power, by means of which he enters into relationship with men, addresses them, tells them and shows them who he is. And what does the Fourth Gospel say? It says, "The Word *became flesh* and dwelt among us" (John 1: 14). "Became flesh" means, quite simply, "became a man" like us. Here is the showing forth of God's creativity and power, in a flesh-and-blood human life. God is not just pretending to be a human being. He has become one of us, in a man who was called Jesus Bar-Joseph, son of a Nazareth carpenter. When Jesus gets hungry, it is real hunger, and not just a pretense. When nails are driven into his hands, they hurt, and real blood flows from the wounds. And the thing which the New Testament dares to assert is that in the life and the teaching, the death and the resurrection, of this man God himself was present in a unique way, so that if you want to see most clearly who God is and what he has done, you look at this same Jesus Bar-Joseph.

An Astounding Claim

Now this is an astounding claim. We need to remember that. We ought to be somewhat surprised every time we read it or hear it made. This is not something to be believed lightly. It takes, as we say, "some believing." And almost as astonishing as the claim itself is the fact that people have believed it without realizing that it is astonishing. Such a claim, if it is true, is obviously the most important thing that has ever happened in the course of human history. That God, the creator of the ends of the earth, beyond and before all time and space, should have lived a life like one of us is headline news. That men should have resented God's doing this, that they should have spat upon Jesus and put him to death in a fiendishly cruel way, is a shocking tale. But we can get more concerned over the death of a pet turtle than we do over the fact that Jesus Christ was executed on a hill outside Jerusalem on the charge that he was dangerous to the public safety. The story has become so commonplace that it no longer arouses us. It no longer shocks us. It no longer repels us. It no longer even excites us.

And yet—the events of Jesus' life and death did make an impact on the people of his time. These things did rouse people. They shocked people. They repelled people. They even excited people.

What Men Were Looking For

Why were people so violent in their reactions to Jesus? Try to imagine what they were looking for. They were Jews.

That means they had been outcast and downtrodden for hundreds of years. Whenever they seemed to be getting somewhere, a large empire would swoop down from the north or swoop up from the south and take them captive. And so they were looking for a vindicator, a deliverer to whom they could give the title "Messiah" (meaning "the Anointed One"), a Messiah whom God would send to deliver them and set them free, and through whom the reign of God would be established on earth. What would this Messiah be like? A first century "Gallup poll" would have gone something like this:

FIRST MAN (*very matter-of-factly*): Me? I'm looking for a descendant of David, to come and rule the way King David did. Those were the days! We had land, food, prestige, and a great king. Someday God will send another David who will rule over us. Then we'll have peace and justice, and the enemy will be destroyed. I only hope he comes soon.

SECOND MAN (*with a snarl*): I don't know just how we'll recognize the Messiah, but I can tell you this. He'll be a great warrior. He'll push those blasted Romans back into the sea, and we'll have our own land once again, without a bunch of foreigners ruling us, taking all our money in taxes and keeping us poor. I'll join up with his army first thing, and we'll hatch a revolution that will smash the Romans to bits.

THIRD MAN (*rather wild-eyed*): No, it won't be as easy as that. We're in too deep for any mere man to deliver us. Our only hope lies in a heavenly creature, sent down from the clouds of heaven, with legions of angels. The sort of thing The Book of Daniel talks about. He'll smite the oppressive Romans and deliver us from them, and then set up his heavenly Kingdom right here in Palestine. That's the only thing that can save us.

These were typical of the dreams and aspirations of a captive people, living under the hard rule of an "army of occupation," powerless to resist, too bitter to come to terms, too proud to accept their fate lying down. They felt sure that even in their humiliation God had not forgotten them, and that he would send his Anointed One, even though they were not all agreed as to just what the Anointed One would be like.

What Men Found

Did these people find in Jesus the Messiah they were looking for?

Not by a long shot.

Perhaps some of them did at first. They may have felt at the very beginning that Jesus would turn into this kind of Messiah. Judas, perhaps, was one of those who became progressively disillusioned because Jesus would not be Judas' kind of Messiah. And one disciple, Simon the Zealot (not Simon Peter), seems to have been a member of a fanatical band who were trying to start open revolt against Rome, and who had joined up with Jesus, hoping that he would lead in the fight.

But Jesus had his own conception of what the Messiah should be like, and it turned out to be very different from everybody else's conception. He was not willing to be a tool for the nationalist ambitions of the first century Israelites. God had something more profound to reveal to men through the Messiah than that. What we find, therefore, is that the Messiah whom Jesus claims to be is not the Messiah who was expected by the people. Jesus put his understanding of Messiahship in terms that were shocking and unthinkable to people of his day, shocking and unthinkable even to the most intimate of his followers.

It all came out into the open shortly before the end of his life. After a brief ministry around the Sea of Galilee, Jesus and his intimate followers went north for a while, probably to take stock of the situation. Things weren't going too well. A crisis was at hand. And Jesus, after asking his disciples what opinions they had heard about him, put the question point blank to them, "Who do *you* say that I am?" (Mark 8: 29). Peter was the one who answered, "You are the Christ." He meant by this, "You are the Messiah, the Anointed One sent from God."

But it soon turned out that what Peter meant by this term was something totally different from what Jesus meant. Jesus combined two notions which had heretofore not been combined in Jewish thought. The first was the notion of the "Son of Man," which probably meant, not what it appears to mean—a simple human being—but rather the heavenly creature pictured in the Daniel passage referred to above. The second was the notion of the "Suffering Servant," the one who suffers on behalf of others, who takes upon himself the consequences of the sins of those who are persecuting him (see especially Isa. 52: 13 to 53: 12). Jesus combined these two notions in the electrifying statement, "The Son of man must suffer . . ." (Mark 8: 31).

Now this was sheer nonsense to Peter. The Son of Man suffer? Preposterous! The Son of Man might come on the clouds of heaven, or he might be a great warrior king, or he might be a nationalistic leader, but suffer and die? Never! That would be precisely what he would not do. How could he accomplish the great things God was going to do through the Messiah in that fashion? And Peter's bewilderment and amazement were underlined by the rest of the people who came into contact with Jesus. If he went to his death, if he did not accomplish all that the people had dreamed of for centuries, then he was obviously not the Messiah after all. He must be a crank, an impostor, someone who should be put out of the way.

What Men Did

So the people reasoned. And so they acted. The very manner in which they did away with Jesus seemed to be an ironic confirmation that they were right. For there was a verse in the Jewish law, "Cursed be every one who hangs on a tree" (quoted in Gal. 3: 13), suggesting that a man who is put to death by crucifixion ("tree"=wood=cross) is one who stands under the curse of God. What could be more obvious than that Jesus' crucifixion meant that he had been rejected by God, and that he was not the promised Messiah after all? Messiahs don't "hang on a tree"; they conquer, they rule in glory.

Now that, whether we like it or not, is the way most first century people reasoned when confronted with the preposterous claim that Jesus was the Messiah for whom they had been waiting. We have to face very squarely the fact that this is so. Jesus did not win all the multitudes to him by a pleasant personality. He won a few people, yes (though most of them deserted him in the pinch and left him to go to his death without them). But many other people rejected him vigorously and absolutely. They flatly denied his claim, called it a blasphemy, and did their best to get him executed once and for all.

They succeeded.

Or at least, they thought they did. The fact that his death was not the end of the story is a fact we shall presently have to examine. But before we do so, we must realize that his life was a "failure" in the sense in which we ordinarily use that word. What kind of Messiah would be put to death in the first century equivalent of an electric chair, as a common, ordinary criminal, after successful prosecution by both the religious and the civil authorities? A strange Messiah indeed, hardly worth a second glance!

The Tiny Minority Who Disagreed

And yet, there were those who *did* take a second glance. They were the ones who flew in the face of the facts, talked about victory when only tragedy was apparent, spoke in cheerful voices when they should have been sad, smiled when they should have been weeping. Why were they different from the other 99½ per cent? Take a look at them.

Look at these followers of Jesus immediately after their leader has been captured, convicted in a "framed" trial, and put to death. They are *bewildered* by the quick reversal of fortunes which they and their leader have suffered. Jesus, who had been with them at supper just a night or two ago, now lies cold and dead in a tomb. They are *disillusioned*. Jesus had talked of such wonderful things. He had done such wonderful things. But that was all over now. He had only been spinning out a dream. When the real pinch came he was powerless, and the dream had dissolved like a puff of smoke. You can see them getting ready to sneak out of Jerusalem and go back to their fishing nets, saying to one another, "I'll never get taken in like *that* again." They are *frightened*. They are meeting behind locked doors. Why? The reason is very simple. They were afraid. They had been seen with Jesus. Jesus had been killed. Who would be next? The Romans had plenty of crosses. Let the Committee on Un-Roman Activities look their way, and they too would be going through a "framed" trial, and death by torture.

That is what the disciples were like immediately after the death of their leader. An unpromising group of men, bewildered, disillusioned, and frightened. Nobody would expect them to amount to anything.

But they did amount to something. They very soon began to amount to a great deal. And to complete the story we must look at another picture of the same group of men. This time the canvas can't be confined to a little room with a barricaded door. It has to be wide enough so that eventually it will include the whole Roman Empire. Take another look.

Instead of being bewildered, they are immensely sure of themselves. They have been galvanized into action, and are going far and wide proclaiming what they call "good news," in temples and market places, to fish peddlers and Roman officers. Instead of being disillusioned, they are full of confidence, and have an almost naïve joy in sharing a tremendous experience which has transformed them. Rather than walking about with leaden feet, they are filled with a mysterious power which they call holy. Instead of being frightened, they are full of an infectious courage, and are going all over the place literally shouting about the same sorts of things for which their leader had so recently been killed. The more they are told to keep quiet, on pain of death, the more gladly do they speak. In fact, they made such a dent on the people around them, that very soon their enemies (not their friends, but their enemies) were calling them "men who have turned the world upside down" (Acts 17: 6).

Why They Disagreed with the Majority

What brought about this amazing transformation? Quite inescapably, it was their unshakable conviction that Jesus had not been held by the grave in which he had been put after he was quite dead, but that God had raised him from the dead and that he was with them, beside them, among them, as a living and active presence. The "risen Christ" was no theory to them, but a fact, a fact of their own experience. They knew he was alive because he and they were once again in intimate fellowship. And as we look at the record of the things they did, the sermons they preached, the letters they wrote, the stories of Jesus which they compiled, a startling fact emerges. The basis of the whole enterprise was not (as we are often led to believe) the ethical teachings of Jesus, but rather the "good news" of the resurrection.

It was indeed "good news" on every level of life. It vindicated the claims of Jesus, and the faith the disciples had had in him. It showed that even out of a catastrophe like the crucifixion God could make something supremely good. It showed that death need no longer be feared, since God is more powerful than death, the Lord of life *and* death. It showed that God could take human sin (even the terrible sin of those who put Jesus to death) and triumph over that. It demonstrated, in short, that through death could come resurrection, that out of tragedy could come triumph, that even when men did their very worst, God could do his very best. This good news "upset" everything that people had believed before about God and his manner of working.

What Is the Evidence?

A quick look at the evidence should make clear how central this message was. The earliest specific written references to the resurrection are in Paul's letters. In his first letter to the Corinthians, for example, he says that this resurrection faith is "the gospel," the good news. He "received" it when he became a Christian. It is "of first importance . . . , that Christ died for our sins . . . , that he was buried, that he was raised on the third day" (I Cor. 15: 3, 4). But this is not just something Paul has been told. He lists those to whom the risen Christ has appeared, and then says, "He appeared also to me" (v. 8). The experience has been real for Paul himself. This resurrection faith *is* the Christian faith: "so we preach and so you believed" (v. 11). Put even more strongly, "if Christ has not been raised, then our preaching is in vain and your faith is in vain" (v. 14).

This kind of testimony stands out on almost every page of the New Testament. Christ is risen from the dead! Sing it! Shout it! Let everyone know! Because it changes everything.

We naturally have questions. We want to know as much as we can about such an event. Paul doesn't give us any details. For specifics we have to turn to the concluding chapters in each of the four Gospels (Mark, ch. 16; Matt., ch. 28; Luke, ch. 24; John, chs. 20; 21), although it is important to remember that the resurrection is presupposed throughout each book. What do we find?

The accounts give overwhelming testimony to the central fact of the resurrection, with differences about some of the details. Any honest person must recognize both these things. On the important matters there is agreement: Christ was not held by the tomb, he was raised from the dead, he appeared to his followers, they became sure of his living presence, and their lives were transformed by him. When you pin down the details you find, naturally enough, less than full agreement. Four writers, long before newspapers, telephones, printed journals, have different recollections and stress different things. They are not sure, for example, just who was at the tomb when the women got there to anoint the body. They are unable to agree as to precisely the kind of body the risen Lord had, so that in some stories he can eat boiled fish with them and in others he can appear and disappear at will.

These facts are pointed out since they often perplex readers of the stories. Why are there even minor disagreements? Let us imagine an unexpected event taking place today.

Two cars collide on the main street of your town in front of the high school.

You see the crash from the grocery store window.

Your cousin sees it from a parked car a block away on the other side of the street.

Members of the tenth-grade class see it from the playground.

An eleventh-grader sees it from a second-story window of the high school.

A policeman sees it from the corner.

A lot of passers-by see the cars just after the collision.

If all these witnesses were haled into court a few months later, any lawyer worth his salt would be suspicious if their stories tallied exactly on every last detail. People simply don't notice things that minutely, or remember them that well. The lawyer would suspect them of getting together to "put one over on him" by concocting a uniform tale.

Now imagine that thirty or fifty years later the witnesses are asked for information about the accident. What would they recall? They would be able to give clear and convincing evidence that there *had* been an accident. No disagreement there. But on the secondary details, the color of the cars, the speeds at which they were going, and so on, there would be understandable differences.

Now there is a considerable difference between an auto accident and a resurrection from the dead. And there is an element of mystery in the unparalleled character of the resurrection event which can be lost whenever we try to make too neat an analogy to explain it. A resurrection from the dead can never be fully "explained." But over and beyond that, our example can be at least dimly suggestive. When we look again at the resurrection accounts in the Gospels, we can see that the very differences of detail are a tribute to the fact that no one is "putting one over" on us. Four accounts (written by different men in different places in different years) which dovetailed neatly with each other would arouse our suspicions. The very differences underline the integrity of the central claim on which they all agreed—that the cross was not the end, but that God raised Jesus from the dead.

Had the cross been the end, let us remember, the disciples would have dispersed, cynical and disillusioned, and Christianity would never have gotten started. The thing that did get it "started" was the disciples' conviction that God had raised Jesus from the dead, that he was in fellowship with them, and that this world-shaking news had to be proclaimed at whatever cost, since it completely transformed the meaning of life. Since that day, the fundamental note of Christian faith has been not sorrow but joy, not defeat but triumph. And the badge of the Christian has been not a long face but a radiant one.

The Choice Open to Us

What are we to make of this amazing story? We can, it seems, do one of two things with it. We can accept the testimony of Jesus' contemporaries, and let the startling fact work the same transformation in our lives that it did in theirs. Or, we can refuse to accept it, insisting that "dead people stay dead." We can say that the Biblical claim is so world-shaking that it couldn't possibly be true, that it is a bit of pious fiction, or a shabby invention by a group of deluded men who couldn't face the awful reality that their leader had been destroyed.

Both those options treat the Christian claim with something like the respect it ought to have. Both understand that this is a stupendous claim, not to be treated lightly or accepted glibly. Both understand that this claim is either the most significant truth of all time or the most barefaced nonsense ever perpetrated on the human race.

The thing which we are *not* entitled to do with this story is to try to eliminate it from the Christian account, to suggest that the disciples didn't really believe it, or that it was tacked onto their ideas by some later group of people. That is tampering with the facts in an illegitimate way. One who says that the resurrection faith is a delusion must have the honesty to grant that the first Christians were so deluded, and that it is this delusion which is the foundation of the Christian religion.

It's either delusion or sober fact. You can't steer a middle course in between.

Turning a Terrorizer Topsy-turvy

(How Does Jesus "Change" People?)

It all boils down to this: in the first century a handful of people made the astounding claim that the Messiah for whom the Jews had been looking for hundreds of years had arrived upon the scene.

The rest of the people thought it was nonsense.

Ask an intelligent man why he thought it was nonsense, and you'd get an answer like this:

INTELLIGENT MAN (*patiently*): Look. The real Messiah is going to be a great leader. And the Messiah the "Christians" are offering is nothing of the sort. I know about his being put to death with a couple of crooks. You can't keep that sort of thing quiet. But believe me, a real Messiah won't get crucified—he'll be a leader. What's that? Oh, I know as well as you do that they're noising around this incredible notion that their Jesus isn't dead. What do they mean, isn't dead? I saw the soldiers seal the tomb with the body inside. That's good enough for me.

Eavesdropping on a Preacher

Even so, a persistent, stubborn little group of people did believe "this incredible notion," quite tenaciously, without compromise and without fear. They began to preach about it and they began to convince other people that it was the truth. Let us eavesdrop on a couple of their sermons. We are inquisitive outsiders. We want to know what the Christians are shouting about, so we follow Peter around and take notes on his sermons. The notes we accumulate turn out to be similar to the outlines of some of the sermons in the book of The Acts, which scholars tell us go back to a very early date in the life of the Christian Church. (They are found in Acts 2: 14-39; 3: 13-26; 4: 10-12; 10: 36-43.) They represent the general pattern of preaching which was probably followed. First of all, the preacher "proclaims" the good news. He tells us what it is that he believes, what the heart of his Christian faith really is. Only after that does he deal with the question, If this faith is true, what are we to do about it? So the pattern becomes, first the preaching, then the teaching; or, first the proclamation of the good news, then some advice on "what to do about it."

Taking Notes on the Sermon

Preparing pad and pencil, then, or more properly stylus and papyrus, we jot down our notes, take them home with us, and by dint of a little homework emerge with a rough outline of what the early Christians preached about:

1. Prophets spoke of "one who would come." Those hopes + aspirations now being fulfilled. "New age" has started —

2. This (see above) made clear thru impact of Jesus. (nb - center of message always about J.) Diff. attempts to show how this true:

  a. His Davidic descent - occasional efforts to link J. with King David

b. his ministry - mention of various things J.
did in lifetime. "Mighty works", etc.

c. his death - always stressed. Impt. (Why?)

d. his resurrection - what makes _everything_
diff. Done by God. (Preachers always happy
at this point in sermon. claim to have seen J.
also. not just theory for them.)

3 J. exalted. Sure he is "at rt. hand of God." (means God
has honored and recognized him. J. is the Savior)

4. J. present in church thru "Holy Spirit." Preachers say
God is at work _in them_ thru "H.S." (!) Gives p_ower._

5. J. will return. Age of fulfillment (see #1) not only
begun (see #2) but will reach consummation when J.
comes again as Lord of all life.

* Therefore. (since all this is true, e.g. # 1-5)

6. Turn about + get fresh start! (stressed in every sermon) Admit our wrongdoing. If do so, God will forgive. new life, new person. Become member of group
by being baptized → transformed life (sounds
exciting).

What Then?

It _was_ exciting. On any interpretation, these were not
things that could be tossed off lightly. If they were true, they
demanded the most radical reorganization of life. If God had
in fact made himself known in a particular life on earth, then
it was important to know as much about that life as possible.
If the one who lived that life had not been held by the grave,
then it would be necessary to adopt a wholly new attitude
toward death as well as life. If this same Jesus was active in the
Church right now, then the Church must be a particularly important part of God's whole concern for man. If the work of

God in Christ was to be completed later on, then it would be important to be preparing for that event.

So every sermon led up to the question, What shall we do because of this? And it was in answer to this question that the concluding part of the sermon was always geared, the exhortation or "teaching" (point No. 6 in the notes above). "What are you to do? You are to repent," Peter would say. "That is, you are to turn about, shift the direction of your life—for this is what 'repentance' means. Your life is now to have a new center: no longer yourself, but God, the God you have come to know in Jesus Christ."

A break with the past, a new beginning. That, in fact, is what had happened to Peter himself. Peter had repudiated Jesus publicly, and denied that he had ever known him. And then Jesus had been put to death. It was too late ever to make amends. But it was *not* too late, for the risen Christ appeared to Peter and forgave him. So Peter had a fresh start. His life was remade. No wonder he could talk this way!

Getting Down to Cases

But Peter wasn't alone in this experience. The business of being "remade" was pretty common among all the early Christians. The best way to see it at work is to look at someone both "before" and "after" his life has been turned topsy-turvy by the impact of Jesus. There is one individual who is pre-eminently a candidate for such a case study. This is Paul, the terror of the Christians, the man who had a passion for putting them to death, and then became Paul the servant of Jesus Christ, willing to die himself in the service of the Jesus he had once hated. Here is a man, in other words, who undergoes a "reversal" of the most unexpected sort, so that the villain of the piece becomes the hero. We see in Paul an example of what can happen to a man when the living Christ gets ahold of him.

We can often learn more about a person by reading his informal letters than by reading an "official" biography by some admirer. Paul, fortunately, was an avid letter writer, dashing off a note here, a scribble there, a long letter when he had time, dictating to whoever could keep up with his tumultuous flow of words, and even then occasionally inserting a sentence of greeting in his own handwriting. He would probably have been astonished to know that some of his letters (though by no means all) have been preserved through nineteen centuries and are collected together as the earliest writings in our New Testament. He didn't pretend to write formal theology (with the possible exception of a letter to Christians in Rome); he simply dealt with specific issues as they arose. One of his most astonishing characteristics is his ability to "shift gears" from the very practical to the most exalted matters, or vice versa. His classic description of the meaning of the Lord's Supper (I Cor. 11:23-26) comes tumbling out on the heels of a vigorous "bawling out" he gave the Corinthians because they were getting drunk on Communion wine! And after his lofty treatment of the life everlasting (I Cor., ch. 15) he turns immediately to the very practical matter of taking up a special offering for the poor.

We need to remember these things about Paul's letters if we are to get the most out of them.

Sizing Paul Up

What about the man's credentials? Who was he? People sometimes think of Paul as a sort of "weak sister," since he apparently was ill a good deal of the time and had to have a doctor with him. (This was Dr. Lukas, who wrote the book of The Acts.) But the more you examine Paul's life the more you see that for a healthy man to have done what Paul did would be quite a record; whereas for a sick man to have done it is little short of a miracle. We can safely conclude that there was nothing "weak" or lukewarm about Paul.

He was always in the thick of a fight. If he wasn't speaking out of turn in the king's court, he was breaking out of jail. If he wasn't getting whipped with a lash, he was getting stoned. He'd go on a long sea voyage and be in a shipwreck. He'd go on another voyage and be in another shipwreck. When he went to a new town, the chances were pretty good that he'd be run out of town a few days later. Wherever he went he seemed to incite, as someone has said, either a riot or a revival. You couldn't keep him down. Put him in jail and he'd go you one better by converting the jailer. Try to trap him in a walled city by guarding all the exit gates, and he'd escape at night by being lowered over the wall in a basket.

This "stormy petrel" was born in Tarsus, which was "no mean city," as he tells us proudly. He was a Roman citizen, a fact of which he was also proud. He worked for a living, being a tentmaker by trade. He was a Jew through and through, he tells us, "circumcised on the eighth day, of the people of Israel, of the tribe of Benjamin, a Hebrew born of Hebrews; as to the law a Pharisee, as to zeal a persecutor of the church, as to righteousness under the law blameless" (Phil. 3: 5, 6). Such a person had no use for the nonsensical claims of the Christians. So, in characteristically direct fashion, Paul acted. "I persecuted the church of God violently and tried to destroy it," he says with utmost candor to his friends (Gal. 1: 13). He is first mentioned in the New Testament at the time when a Christian named Stephen was being stoned to death for his views (Acts 7: 57; 8: 1).

Paul thought it was a splendid idea. He helped.

Paul's Predicament

He was, then, a stern, tough little man, thoroughly dedicated to the proposition that Christianity is a lot of nonsense, and that any individual worth his salt will try to wipe it out. That is Paul "on the outside," the man who "laid waste the church, and . . . dragged off men and women and committed them to prison" (Acts 8: 3).

But there was a Paul "on the inside" too. He was a man at war with himself. Underneath this frenzied activity, he was mixed up. Perhaps he was disturbed at the glad, gay way in which the miserable Christians were dying, because when they died they didn't appear miserable. Take this same Stephen. He hadn't groveled before his persecutors, begging to be let off. Not for a moment. He had asked God to forgive his persecutors. Tie that! And a tiny voice inside Paul kept asking, "Could there possibly be something to this Christian nonsense after all?"

Something else worried Paul. He took the Jewish law very seriously. The law told him just what he must do to be in right relationship with God. But the law didn't make Paul feel "right" with God. On the contrary, it made him feel more wrong than ever. And the more he studied what the law told him *not* to do, so he reports, the more he wanted to do the very things that were forbidden. This was a rough situation! Even though he could call himself "blameless" in terms of the law, he didn't feel that he was in the right relationship with God which was so desperately important to him. Rather than freeing him, the law only enslaved him more deeply.

Here, then, is how Paul describes his predicament. He is a prisoner of the law. He feels that he must fulfill all the legal requirements, do everything the law demands, before he can be worthy of God's love. He must "earn" the right to fellowship with God. And that sounds all right on the surface: live a good life, using the law as a guide, and thus become righteous in God's sight. But there was a catch. Living up to the law did not bring Paul this fellowship with God. He was frustrated and disappointed by his inability to do enough to feel that he had *truly* earned the right to God's love. Rather than saving him, the law only condemned him more thoroughly. It could show him where he fell short, but it couldn't give him the power to rise above his inadequacies. "I can will what is right," he acknowledged, "but I cannot do it" (Rom. 7: 18).

A Terrorizer Transformed

It was a Paul in this kind of seething turmoil who set out one day to go from Jerusalem to Damascus. He had a very specific purpose in mind. It was to capture as many Christians as he could, take them back to Jerusalem in chains, and see that they met the same fate as Stephen.

And then something happened. It is described on three different occasions in the book of The Acts (chs. 9: 3-6; 22: 6-10; 26: 13-16), and fundamentally the accounts are the same, differing only on minor details. Paul found himself confronted by the Jesus whom he had been persecuting.

This overturned his entire world.

The risen Christ, he stoutly affirmed, had appeared to him. To Paul's question, "Who are you, Lord?" he got the disconcerting answer, "I am Jesus, whom you are persecuting." And Paul began to see that he had been following the wrong track and going in the wrong direction. He must turn about in the most radical sense of the word; rather than being a killer of Christians he must become a lover of Christians; rather than denying the God of the Christians, he must commit himself to the God of the Christians. In short, Paul, the notorious anti-Christian, must become a Christian himself! An astonishing suggestion. The only thing more astonishing is that he did precisely that!

Some people argue that this dramatic change in Paul occurred immediately. One moment he hated Christ; the next moment he loved him. Others will suggest that Paul had been moving in this direction for a long time, even though the decision "clicked" at one specific moment. Imagine that you are listening to a symphonic recording. You know the music pretty well, and you like the way the violins play the main theme. Then there comes a section that isn't too clear, after which the violins play the theme again. But one day, perhaps all of a sudden on the fifteenth hearing or perhaps only gradually in the next few hearings, you hear in that middle section the same theme, this time played very slowly by the cellos. Of course! No wonder the other parts sounded a little strange. They were merely accompaniment. If you discover this at one particular moment, it is still true that the discovery would not have come without hearing the music fourteen times before. In the same way, although many people seem to "get religion" in spectacular ways, it may be the result of a long previous spiritual pilgrimage. Furthermore, just as your awareness of the cello theme may come only gradually, and the beauty of the passage increase with each rehearing, so our real awareness of God may come very unspectacularly, and continue to deepen throughout the rest of our lives. The person who has had no sudden moment of clarification need not feel that he has been denied an authentic experience of the presence of God in his life. Not even Paul claimed that the whole story had been written on the way to Damascus; years later he wrote, "Not that I . . . am already perfect; but I press on" (Phil. 3: 12).

What happened after this event? Press on he did, for the rest of his life, determined not to be "disobedient to the heavenly vision" (Acts 26: 19). After a period of preparation, he embarked on one of the most vigorous lives of which there is any record. He literally tramped up and down Asia Minor and Europe, spreading this "good news" and demonstrating what a difference it made. It is an understatement to say that there was never a dull moment. Paul has left an accounting:

Five times I have received at the hands of the Jews the forty lashes less one. [Forty lashes was supposed to kill a person.] Three times I have been beaten with rods; once I was stoned. Three times I have been shipwrecked; a night and a day I have been adrift at sea; on frequent journeys, in danger from rivers, danger from robbers, danger from my own people, danger from Gentiles, danger in the city, danger in the wilderness, danger at sea, danger from false brethren; . . . in hunger and thirst, often without food, in cold and exposure (II Cor. 11: 24-27).

Not an easy life! Why live this way? Why not "play it safe"?

A Brand-new Situation

Because, as Paul put it, "Life means Christ to me" (Phil.
1: 21, Moffatt's translation). How did Christ change Paul's
situation? Remember that before all this he had been frantically trying to *do enough* to earn God's love, by following
the law to the letter. And now Christ has come as the revolutionary word that this is not necessary. It is not even possible.
Christ has laid down his life, not for the worthy but for the
unworthy, not for the deserving but for the undeserving. He
has bridged the great gulf between God and man. Paul can't
contain his wonder at the fact:

Why, one will hardly die for a righteous man—though perhaps
for a good man one will dare even to die. But God shows his love
for us in that *while we were yet sinners* Christ died for us (Rom.
5: 7, 8, italics added).

Talk about unexpected news!
So Christ is God's way of acting out his freely given love.
The law has been set aside. The situation is not, Be good
enough to earn God's love, but rather, God loves you even
though you *can't* be good enough to earn his love. For Paul,
everything else flows from that amazing fact.

From Death to Life

The difference, for Paul, is the difference between being
dead and being alive. A more dramatic contrast is hardly possible. Before this new life was a possibility for him, he tells
us, the old life had to be killed. Just as Christ was killed and
rose again, so Paul has to undergo his own kind of crucifixion
and resurrection. "I have been crucified with Christ," he tells
us; "it is no longer I who live, but Christ who lives in me"
(Gal. 2: 20). Paul's former self has gone, and a "new" Paul
has come, a Paul whose life is directed by the Christ who
dwells in him. He is starting out all over again.

The contrast can, if possible, be made even more dramatic. In a symbolic way, Paul tells us, we must share Christ's death and resurrection. Here is how he interprets baptism:

To be submerged = your death = Christ being placed
in the grave.

To emerge = a new life = Christ's resurrection
from the grave.

No death, no resurrection. But as you identify yourself with Christ's death, so you share in his resurrection.

Do you not know that all of us who have been baptized into Christ Jesus were baptized into his death? We were buried therefore with him by baptism into death, so that as Christ was raised from the dead by the glory of the Father, we too might walk in newness of life (Rom. 6: 3, 4).

Newness of life! That's what happens. There we have it in three words.

What difference does this newness of life make to the way you live? Listen to Paul describe how life looks *now*, even in the face of swords, stones, shipwrecks, and soldiers:

Who shall separate us from the love of Christ? Shall tribulation, or distress, or persecution, or famine, or nakedness, or peril, or sword? . . . No, in all these things we are more than conquerors through him who loved us. For I am sure that neither death, nor life, nor angels, nor principalities, nor things present, nor things to come, nor powers, nor height, nor depth, nor anything else in all creation, will be able to separate us from the love of God in Christ Jesus our Lord (Rom. 8: 35, 37-39).

It is because he believes this, that Paul is willing to "stick his neck out." He is one with God in Christ. Who needs to fear the sword when such a thing is true? How can a little thing like death destroy such a relationship?

Good News—from Prison

Fine in principle, you say. But did this sort of thing hold true when the chips were down? Suppose, for example, Paul

had been in prison. How would he have reacted in that kind
of situation? Wouldn't his nice little theory have gotten a
pretty rough challenge?

A fair question. And we can give a fair answer. For, as a
matter of fact, Paul spent a great deal of time in prison. And
some of his "prison letters" have been preserved. A look at
one of them (Philippians) can tell us how Paul reacted to
real hardship.

Is Paul discouraged at finding himself behind bars? No, he
can even rejoice over the fact, because it means that the gospel
can be made known to the guards. He realizes that what
happens to him is unimportant, so long as Christ is being
preached. Even the matter of whether he lives or dies becomes
incidental—he would like to depart and be with Christ, but
he realizes that he has work to do now, and that he should remain in the flesh. It is a glory, he says, to suffer on behalf of
Christ. The Philippians themselves must not be anxious;
they are to make their requests known to God and trust in
him, since "the peace of God, which passes all understanding,
will keep your hearts and your minds in Christ Jesus" (Phil.
4: 7). Paul does not grumble about being where he is. He is
more than equal to the occasion:

I have learned, in whatever state I am, to be content. I know how
to be abased, and I know how to abound; in any and all circumstances I have learned the secret of facing plenty and hunger,
abundance and want. *I can do all things in him who strengthens
me* (Phil. 4: 11-13, italics added).

This is how Jesus "changed" Paul. In the midst of trying circumstances Paul could be serene. When things were rough,
Paul could rejoice. Not only that, he could call on others to
be serene and to rejoice also.

Shifting Gears to Our Own Situation

It all sounds rather thrilling when applied to Paul. He
seems to cruise along in a sort of spiritual "overdrive," while

we painfully make our way in low low, sometimes not quite sure that we're moving at all. And yet, Paul's experience is not all that "strange" to us. To be sure, we do not need to be converted from Jewish legalism. But we may need to be converted from a kind of Christian legalism, a religion that tells us that we must be good boys and girls and do the following eight things without fail if we want God to love us. We may even need to be converted from a kind of conventional Christianity which is dull, drab, and dreary. And whether we go through the kind of spectacular experience of conversion Paul did or not isn't very important. What is important is that somehow or other we come to the place of being able to say with Paul, "Life means Christ to me." For when that begins to happen, then life can get just as exciting for us in our day as it did for Paul in his.

When God Took a Chance

(Why Did People Want to Kill Jesus?)

In a way, it was the lions' fault. They were so hungry, and the Christians were so delicious. And as time went on, more and more lions ate more and more Christians, for the state did its best to stamp out this dangerous new sect. Of course, most of the people who had known Jesus just plain died. Others were sentenced to the mines in Sardinia. Others went underground. But for whatever reasons, the fact remained that the generation that had known Jesus "in the flesh" was disappearing, and there was need to get some of the scattered little collections of stories about him into permanent form.

Some Literary Detective Work

Let's start off with a little private sleuthing. Anyone who reads the first three books of the New Testament (Matthew, Mark, and Luke) will recognize that they are the end product of the attempt to "get down in writing" the important things about Jesus. We call them the "Synoptic Gospels" because when we study them synoptically, that is in parallel columns, we can see their similarities and relationships more clearly.

So let us imaginatively do just that. What do we find? We find that Mark is much the shortest of the three, and that both Matthew and Luke follow its basic outline. When one of them departs from Mark's account to bring in new material of his own, he inevitably returns to Mark at the point where he left off, and continues to follow Mark again. At many points, the words are identical in all three accounts. Matthew helps himself to over 90 per cent of Mark's exact words, and Luke uses over 50 per cent. The scholars conclude that Matthew and Luke must have had Mark's account before them as they wrote.

Now let us cut out and throw away all the places where the three accounts are identical. (This pretty much disposes of Mark.) We make the interesting discovery that there is still a good deal of Matthew and Luke which is word for word the same. Apparently they used another common source in addition to Mark. No copy of this source has ever been found, and the scholars simply call it "Q," for the German word "*Quelle*" meaning (can you guess?) "source." "Q" seems to have been a collection of Jesus' sayings. The Sermon on the Mount is an example of material from "Q."

If you now scratch off all the places where Matthew and Luke agree, each book still has a sizable number of verses left, and the scholars conclude that the authors must have had further private sources of information.

This means that our present Synoptic Gospels are based on four basic sources of information:

1. Mark's account—also used by Matthew and Luke
2. "Q"—used extensively by Matthew and Luke
3. Luke's special source
4. Matthew's special source.

John Mark (and Some Others) Get to Work

The thing that got the writing started was a great fire in Rome about A.D. 64. Much of the city was destroyed. Nero, the emperor, needed a scapegoat, so he blamed the Christians. As a result many of them were killed. A man named John Mark escaped. He was a companion of Paul and a friend of Peter, and he decided that before this kind of thing happened again, he would write down all the information he could gather about Jesus. Shortly afterward his little book appeared, "The Gospel of Jesus Christ." It was not a "biography" or "thumbnail sketch" of Jesus; it was an attempt to show that he was indeed the promised Messiah. John Mark shared with his readers a collection of more or less disconnected incidents, all of which underlined and proclaimed the "good news" of God's activity in Jesus Christ.

This may have been as early as A.D. 65. Within the next twenty or thirty years a number of other accounts of the "good news" appeared, two of which have survived. One of these was by a Gentile convert, Dr. Lukas, apparently the physician who took care of Paul. Dr. Lukas not only wrote the volume to which we referred in the last chapter, The Acts of the Apostles, but also an earlier volume in which he too collected important things that should be remembered about Jesus. As we have seen, he made free use of Mark, "Q," and his own special source of information. He put particular stress on the fact that Jesus is "good news" for all men, of whatever race, nationality, or station in economic life.

About the same time, another book appeared, this one by a Jew named Matthew, who made a strong appeal to his fellow Jews to embrace Christian faith. He took special pains to show how Jesus is the fulfillment of the Old Testament prophecies, and he also included much material from Jesus' teachings. He too made copious use of Mark, "Q," and his own private source of information.

Probably a little later than the "Synoptic Gospels," a fourth Gospel appeared. Rather than using the crisp narrative style of the Synoptics, the author of the Fourth Gospel lingered over a few events and examined their inner meaning. In a few places he made important changes (probably for the better) in the chronology of Jesus' life. Who wrote this Fourth Gospel is not clear. Nowhere did the author identify himself. Many people claim that he was the apostle John, but others feel it more likely that he was another "John," perhaps John the Elder, who lived at Ephesus. At all events, he was a man who had meditated very deeply upon the meaning of Jesus' life, and he put the fruits of these reflections into a masterpiece of devotional meditation.

Religious Propaganda

These, then, are the four accounts that give us specific information about Jesus' life. But they are not just "collections of information." They do not attempt to be objective, impartial biographies, but rather testimonies, frankly "biased" accounts written by people who believe Jesus to be the Son of God. This is why they are called "gospels," or "good news," rather than biographies. We may freely call them "religious propaganda," so long as we remember that "propaganda" is not necessarily a bad word. It can also describe an attempt to convince us of something that is good.

"A Child Is Born"

We are given little information about Jesus' early life. Mark, the earliest account, starts in briskly with the mission of John the Baptizer, and within nine verses, Jesus, as a full-grown man, has appeared upon the scene. John, the latest account, has a very important (and difficult) "prologue" on the significance of Jesus' birth, but of the birth itself and the early life of Jesus he too says nothing. In Luke and Matthew, on the other hand, we have beautiful stories about the birth of Jesus. What do these narratives tell us about the significance of Jesus? We learn a great deal, for example, about the significance of Jesus from the story in Luke that when God chose to make Jesus' birth known to men, he did not proclaim it in the palaces of the Palestinian rulers or to the mayors of the big cities. Rather, the news was first told to a group of shepherds, people of quite insignificant social standing. The birth of Jesus shows God's concern with the lowliest. Likewise, the story of the Wise Men in Matthew shows that the message was not *just* for poor and humble folk, but for all men everywhere, not only in Palestine, but in the far corners of the earth, rich as well as poor, wise as well as simple, foreign as well as native. And when Luke tells us that Jesus was born in a stable, we are reminded that he did not come as a high and mighty prince, but as one who did not have a place to lay his head. The one for whom there was "no room in the inn" will be the one who is "despised and rejected of men."

It is important not to become too sentimental about the birth narratives. It is easy to gush over "the baby Jesus" and what a sweet picture the stable scene makes on a Christmas card with "cute little angels" flying about overhead. We must not forget that the baby whom everyone helps to adore will grow up to be the man everyone helps to crucify. The birth is not the beginning of a human "success story"; it is the beginning of a story in which the hero will be rejected as the villain, and good religious people will be only too glad to have him put to death.

The "Hidden Years"

The first thirty years of Jesus' life are practically a blank in our sources, so that they are often called the "hidden years." Luke includes the only direct story, a tale of Jesus going to the Temple in Jerusalem at the age of twelve, a quite likely occurrence in the life of a young Jewish boy. Further than this, we do know that Jesus was a member of a large family, with four brothers and at least two sisters (Mark 6: 3; Matt. 13: 55, 56). We know that it was his custom to attend services on the Sabbath (Luke 4: 16). And since he later displays such an intimate knowledge of the Old Testament, we can infer that he went to a synagogue school as a boy in Nazareth. We know that Jesus' father was a carpenter and it appears likely that Jesus was a village carpenter until he was about thirty. If, as is sometimes presumed, Joseph died when Jesus was young, Jesus was probably the breadwinner for a large family.

About our only other source of even indirect information for this period is found in Jesus' stories or parables, which give us a picture of what his early life may have been like. He undoubtedly saw children playing in the market place (Luke 7: 31-35), or women sewing patches on old clothes (ch. 5: 36), or men attempting to put new wine in old wineskins and having the wineskins burst (vs. 37-39), or a woman who had found a lost coin calling her friends in to rejoice (ch. 15: 8-10), or a shepherd telling how he had gotten back to the sheepfold and had found one sheep missing and had gone out into the night to find it (vs. 1-7).

Stage Directions: Enter John

But now the real drama gets underway. Things come into clear focus with the arrival on the scene of a young man named John. John was a fiery orator—what today might be called a "rabble rouser"—and he preached in the bleak area down near the Dead Sea. People came out to hear him. John brought them small comfort. He was blunt and outspoken. He was not one to pull his punches. When King Herod Antipas committed adultery, for example, John told him he was wrong. It cost John his head. John told the people that the Day of Judgment was coming and that they had better prepare for it. He said that very soon God would send his Messiah to bring in this day. He said that they couldn't get by on the lame excuse that they were the "chosen people"; God could raise up a people from the very stones about them. He said that they had better repent and believe, and that they should show that they meant it by being baptized. Thus he was called John the Baptizer.

Stage Directions: Enter Jesus

One day when John was preaching, Jesus, then a young man of about thirty, appeared in the crowd and asked to be baptized. He may have wanted to show that he believed in John, or he may have wanted to identify himself with the sinful humanity he was going to serve. At any rate, John (who felt unworthy of doing so) did baptize Jesus in the River Jordan. The moment had tremendous significance for Jesus, for he seems to have received unmistakable confirmation that he had a special vocation to which God had called him.

Jesus was therefore immediately faced with the question, "If I have been called by God, if I am to be the Messiah, what kind of Messiah does he call me to be?" Jesus struggles with this problem alone. Various tempting short cuts are offered to him:

He sees the loaf-shaped stones around him. Why not change them into bread? A Messiah has that power. What a capital idea! Give the poor downtrodden Palestinians food for their hungry stomachs, and there is nothing they will not do for him. Fill their stomachs, and then fill their souls. Splendid! They will surely listen to anyone who alters their economic condition. And isn't this, after all, the kind of thing the people were hoping for from a Messiah? Someone who would relieve their dreadful poverty? Isn't this really the way to show his compassion toward them?

But another voice intervenes, the voice of the true Jesus, who finds in his Jewish heritage a more important truth, "Man shall not live by bread alone, but by every word that proceeds from the mouth of God" (Deut. 8: 3). He does not say that bread is unnecessary, but simply that bread is not sufficient. There is a more fundamental need in man.

Another picture appears. Instead of using bread as a lure, why not use religion itself as a lure, by posing as a wonder-worker? Climb to the very top of the Temple and then jump off; use the power of God so as to land unhurt? This will be a spectacular proof of his Messianic calling. By challenging God's power, Jesus will prove God's power. Then people will pay attention. Isn't this also what the people have deeply yearned for? A Messiah whose claims are so clear-cut that the people can rally around him without any qualms or questions? Doesn't he owe this much to them if he is to be their leader?

But another word comes: "You shall not tempt the Lord your God" (Deut. 6: 16). And Jesus rejects the notion of winning followers by spectacular means. (Remember this when we discuss Jesus' miracles.)

A third short cut is offered. Jesus sees all the kingdoms spread out before him. By worshiping evil, he can gain political control of them all. Then people would listen. What an opportunity! Doesn't he really owe this to his people? To free them from bondage to Rome? To be a political leader around whom they can rally? Isn't this worth a few compromises?

But Jesus turns this one down too. He is not to serve evil. "You shall worship the Lord your God, and him only shall you serve" (Deut. 6: 13).

Jesus thus refuses the kind of Messiahship that would be a worship of the power of evil rather than a giving of himself to the true God. God, not Satan, is the object of his loyalty. Nor will he be simply the kind of Messiah the people want. He must be Messiah on God's terms, not theirs.

Stage Directions: Shift Scene to Galilee

The bulk of Jesus' ministry was spent near the Sea of Galilee in northern Palestine. For perhaps as little as a few months, certainly for no longer than two or three years, Jesus was engaged in an active ministry. What did he do?

First of all, Jesus *preached,* sometimes in Capernaum (which seems to have been a sort of "headquarters"), sometimes in the synagogues, and sometimes along country roads or on hillsides. Mark gives us a capsule summary of what he was preaching: "The time is fulfilled, and the kingdom of God is at hand; repent, and believe in the gospel" (Mark 1: 15) That time of which the prophets had spoken is now here, Jesus says. The time of preparation is over. The Kingdom of God is at hand. (We will examine the idea of the "Kingdom of God" in Chapter 16.) What are people to do because of this? They are to "repent," turn about, begin again. Life must be different now, if these things are so. The "good news" makes all the difference.

Jesus also *taught.* He spent a great deal of time trying to make clear just how you were supposed to live after you had committed yourself to him and his Kingdom. (Chapters 18 to 23 will deal with Jesus' teachings.)

Then too, Jesus gathered a group of *followers* around him. A few people were convinced not only that Jesus was speaking the truth, but that he himself was the truth. They helped him in all that he did. The "inner circle" were called *apostles,* from a Greek word meaning "messenger" or one who speaks with authorization. There were all sorts and kinds—fishermen from Galilee, a member of the fanatical Zealot party, two sets of brothers, a tax collector (the most despised profession in Palestine), a lone individual from Judea named Judas, and a few others. That Jesus was able to mold such diverse characters into a real community is a telling tribute to him. In addition to the apostles were many *disciples,* "learners" or apprentices, who were eager to know more about Jesus. Some of them may originally have been followers of John the Baptizer. Jesus instructed them and sometimes sent them out in small groups to preach, so that his message could be proclaimed more widely.

Query from Audience: What About Those Miracles?

During his ministry Jesus also performed many "mighty works" or *miracles.* Here we must pause, since these same miracles are a real stumbling block for many people.

We must be clear about one thing: The miracles are not "late additions" to the accounts about Jesus. They are present in the very earliest material we have. To omit them is to do unwarranted violence to the accounts. They are central to the whole purpose of the Gospel writers. For example, Jesus comes with the message of the Kingdom of God, a Kingdom that is now a reality in the lives of men. He *tells* people what the Kingdom of God is like, by stories and teachings. But he not only describes it; he *enacts* or *dramatizes* what life in the Kingdom of God is like. In this sense, some of the miracles are "enacted parables." In those days sickness was interpreted as a result of human sin. Jesus cures a sick man by touching him and taking the defilement upon himself. By his action, Jesus is dramatically representing himself as the "sin bearer," the one who takes upon himself the sins of others. This is one of the characteristics of life in the Kingdom of God, that sins are forgiven. (This gives special meaning to the significance of Jesus' death, as we shall see in the next chapter.) On another occasion Jesus says, "If it is by the finger of God that I cast out demons, then the kingdom of God has come upon you" (Luke 11: 20). He says this after he has in fact "cast out the demon," that is, cured a man. So this action also dramatizes what the Kingdom of God is like. In it, evil is subdued and overcome by the power of God. Such miracles as these are demonstrations of God's forgiveness in action, and of God's conquest of the forces of evil.

In addition to this approach to the miracles, think for two or three minutes about each of the following points, and see if together they can bring you to a fuller understanding of Jesus' miracles:

1. The fundamental miracle (as we saw in the last chapter) is Jesus himself. That God should be concerned enough about us to send his Son to effect his forgiving love is, if you please, the most "incredible" thing imaginable. This miracle of forgiving love is basic to the New Testament. If it is a false conception, everything else in the New Testament falls to pieces. If it is a true conception, there is nothing else quite so amazing in the rest of the New Testament.

2. If this is truly God's world, and Jesus is truly God's Son, there is no reason why Jesus might not be empowered by God to do certain things that seem highly unusual to us but would be enactments of God's power and the reality of his Kingdom.

3. Jesus does not claim "credit" for the miracles. They are a manifestation of *God's* power. The early Christians likewise recognized this fact, and refer to the "mighty works and wonders and signs which *God* did through him" (Acts 2: 22). God is not letting Jesus "break the rules"; he is rather manifesting through Jesus the reality of his Kingdom.

4. Jesus does not, in the Synoptic Gospels at least, perform miracles to "win" adherents. He specifically repudiates this notion during his temptation. He tells people again and again not to talk about the miracles he has performed. In one place, even, he can do no miracles because of their lack of faith (Mark 6: 5). Those who *do* believe can see in the miracles a demonstration of what life in the Kingdom of God is like, and can see the Kingdom of God already in operation, in the activity of Jesus.

Stage Directions: Prepare "Opposition" Both Off Stage and On

Various kinds of activities, then, characterize Jesus' Galilean ministry: preaching, teaching, gathering followers, performing mighty works. A splendid program, we react, calculated to win boundless support from all sorts of people. But did it? We get far off the track if we take a verse such as "the common people heard him gladly" (Mark 12: 37) and infer from it that Jesus made enthusiastic converts everywhere. An enthusiastic following there was, to be sure, but there was also, apparently from the very beginning, tremendous opposition. People didn't like the sort of thing he was saying and doing. It made them uncomfortable. If some were attracted, many were repelled. If some were pleased, many were offended.

Even those who became followers could be offended. When Jesus first approached Peter, Peter was not attracted by Jesus' "magnetic personality." Not at all. "Get away from me," he said in effect, "I don't want to have anything to do with you." (See Luke 5: 8.) A sinful man, confronted by sheer goodness, feels uncomfortable; more than that, he feels awestruck and overwhelmed. This is too strange a business. Much easier to shut such a person out of your life than to surrender to him. Peter, of course, did surrender finally, but it was a struggle for him all the way.

There was opposition from other quarters as well. The neighbors in Nazareth had very mixed reactions when he came back home and preached in the synagogue.

LOCAL BOY RETURNS, BIG CROWD HEARS HIM, the papers might have said, but they would have had to add:

INHABITANTS SHOCKED, TRY TO KILL SPEAKER

For Jesus didn't give them a nice conventional talk about contributing to the synagogue budget. He read from the prophet Isaiah and then suggested that he—he!—was the fulfillment of the sacred Scriptures. The local people, of course, knew better. They had grown up with him. He was only the carpenter's son. What blasphemy!

So they tried to throw him over a cliff.

Suppose you asked a typical Pharisee, a good upright citizen, what he thought about Jesus. The answer would be emphatic.

PHARISEE (*belligerently*): Him? He's a madman. Why, he doesn't even take our Jewish law seriously! You know what he did last Sabbath? He and his disciples were walking through the fields and he let them pluck grains of corn to eat. On the Sabbath! When it is *expressly* forbidden by the law. I can show you the exact place if you doubt my word. Not only that, he healed a man on the Sabbath. Broke the law right under my very nose!

But that's nothing compared to what he did the other afternoon. You know Joses' house up the street there? Well, I wasn't there myself, but I have this on *very* good authority, because my brother was there and saw the whole thing. Four men let a paralytic down through the roof and Jesus looked at him and told him that his sins were forgiven! Sins forgiven? Who is this Jesus to go around forgiving sins? Nobody but God can forgive sins. The man thinks he's God.

And you know what that means to me? It means he's crazy, deluded, and must be gotten out of the way. Dead, buried, and forgotten.

Others might be offended by the company Jesus kept. *Their* Messiah wouldn't associate with riffraff. He would mingle with the people of influence and position. But Jesus? He was always hobnobbing with the hated tax collectors, and with "sinners"; people even circulated the story that he was a "glutton and a drunkard" (Luke 7: 34)—a "party boy," no less!

We can at least infer from all this criticism that when Jesus was around things were never dull. Whatever else Jesus did, he emphatically stirred people up. And this, in turn, made him fair game for the rulers and politicians, who never like to have people "stirred up." Herod Antipas, of Galilee, found Jesus quite a political nuisance and wanted to get rid of him. Even Pilate, procurator of Judea, though he could find no real fault with Jesus, finally succumbed to pressure because of the threat that it might be politically dangerous to leave Jesus alive. All this—supreme irony—about a person who said, "My kingship is not of this world" (John 18: 36).

Stage Directions: Prepare for Catastrophe

We have discussed (in Chapter 7) the event at Caesarea-Philippi, when the disciples became aware that Jesus was not only the Messiah, but a Messiah (strange notion!) who would suffer.

The upshot of this was that Jesus took them to Jerusalem, to the very center of the organized opposition. The most significant event on the way was an amazing sight seen by Peter and James and John. They went with Jesus up a mountain and there, in a kind of vision, saw him transfigured, present before them in the glory he would one day have. The significance of this event is undoubtedly Messianic. Elijah, so the Jews felt, would return before the Messiah came, and here was Jesus conversing with Elijah, and a voice saying, "This is my beloved Son; listen to him" (Mark 9: 7). It was all very strange and mystifying, but it was clearly seen as a sort of divine stamp of approval on the understanding Jesus had of his vocation.

Three times, so it is recorded, Jesus told the disciples clearly that he must suffer and die, and that he would be raised from the dead. Three times, so it is recorded, the disciples were unable to understand what this strange talk was all about.

And so they came to Jerusalem. The events of the week in Jerusalem are recorded in full detail in the Gospels. We have more information about that week than about any other part of Jesus' life, so we need not recount all the details here. A glance at a few will show how the net was closing in.

What was the meaning of the strange entry? Jesus rode into Jerusalem upon the back of a donkey, with crowds waving and cheering, a sort of first century equivalent of a ticker-tape parade up Broadway. He did not enter on a white charger as a great military hero would have done; he came on a lowly beast of burden. Matthew's account of the event gives us a clue: Jesus was consciously fulfilling a Messianic prophecy from Zech. 9: 9, that the "king" would come "lowly, and riding upon an ass." Not a warlike Messiah, in other words, but one who would be servant of all. The people spectacularly failed to get the point, with the result that in a few days those who had been shouting "Hurrah!" were shouting "Kill him!"

During the hectic days in Jerusalem, Jesus was besieged by questioners, who tried to back him into a corner so that he would make a damaging statement which could be used against him. Jesus met these questioners with astonishing adroitness, parried the thrusts of the questioners skillfully, and left them to retire befuddled from the scene. Behind the scene, however, the stage was being set, and the alliances against Jesus were forming a stronger coalition. They even had a "fifth column" at work within Jesus' band itself, in the person of Judas, the treasurer of the organization. Why Judas turned traitor is no easy question to answer. He may have become genuinely convinced, after a period of intense devotion, that Jesus was a fraud and should be put out of the way. At all events, he went over to the opposition and helped them keep track of Jesus' movements so that when the moment was ripe they could pounce.

While the final plans of the enemy were forming, Jesus was having a last meal with his disciples, probably the traditional preparatory meal for the coming of the Jewish Passover. (We shall examine the significance of what was said and done at this meal in Chapter 15.)

Soon they left the upper room where they had been eating and went to a hill on the edge of the city. And Jesus, apparently the only one who realized how imminent was his capture, went apart to pray. He did not want to die, and he told God so. But he added to that prayer some of the most significant words he ever spoke, "Not what I will, but what thou wilt" (Mark 14: 36). He was willing to make his will one with that of his Father.

And then, suddenly, the garden was full of clanking swords, cursing men, shouts, lanterns, and jeers. Jesus was surrounded by those who hated him. His friends fled in the darkness. He was a prisoner.

He was alone, and his doom was sure.

The Place of the Skull

(What Is the Cross All About?)

. . . His doom was sure? But certainly *someone* would intervene—his inner circle of followers; people interested in fair play; failing that, God himself!

But no one did. This was not just a moment of "suspense" before the author of the drama provided a swift and happy ending. To be sure, there was an ending, swift indeed, but scarcely happy, for everybody walked out on Jesus. Even Peter got scared, cursing and crying out in a frenzy of fear, "I don't even know the man."

"Cloak and Dagger" Episodes

If anyone had kept a check list of the progress toward getting rid of Jesus during those last days and hours, it might have gone like this:

- Sound out Judas. Get him to keep us posted on Jesus' whereabouts.
- Check with priests about bribe money for Judas.
- Alert guards to be ready to follow Judas at a moment's notice.
- Arrange for half a dozen people to meet with Eli. Have him drill them on charges to make against Jesus at the trial.
- Requisition funds from Caiaphas to pay off the "witnesses."

✔ Hire messenger to call members of high court (Sanhedrin) together at a moment's notice. (Impress on him that we've *got* to pull this thing off before the Passover, since no one can be put to death during the Passover.)

✔ Send representatives to Pilate to point out that he had better condemn Jesus too, unless he wants bad reports sent back to Rome.

Things worked out pretty well. The trial was held. The proceedings were illegal. The witnesses were bribed. The court ruled that the "evidence" was overwhelming. The death sentence was passed. All that remained was for Pontius Pilate, the representative of the Roman Government, to ratify it.

At the crack of dawn, Pilate was approached. He seems to have been justly troubled. What was wrong with Jesus? Nothing—and yet—there was a mob outside, screaming for blood. If he turned Jesus loose, he would have a riot on his hands. Word about riots got back to Rome, and Rome was displeased about riots in the outlying provinces. Rome, in fact, recalled procurators who allowed situations to get out of hand. And those procurators, once recalled, were put to death for incurring Caesar's displeasure. It was Pilate's neck or Jesus'. So Pilate ratified the death sentence. He made arrangements for his Roman soldiers to nail Jesus to an upright post and crossbeam, and leave him to die. It was the accepted way.

It was not a pleasant way to die. The victim was exposed to the Oriental sun, to the agonizing thirst, to the dust, and to the flies. Since life might linger on for days, it was considered a merciful act for a Roman soldier to bash in the victim's legs with a club, breaking them so that he would die more quickly.

And so they took Jesus as a common criminal, along with two other criminals, and crucified him on a hill outside Jerusalem called Golgotha, "the place of the skull." This is what men did to one who, on a modest estimate, was the best man who ever lived. This is what men did to one who, on a Christian estimate, was God incarnate in human life.

Was Jesus "Forsaken" by God?

You can learn a great deal about a person by seeing how he dies. Putting together the four accounts of Jesus' death, we find seven "words," or statements, that he made during the six hours he hung on the cross. When he says, "I thirst" (John 19: 28), we realize with a pang that he is *actually* suffering, going the long, hard road of full identification with us. When he says, "Father, forgive them; for they know not what they do" (Luke 23: 34), we stand amazed that at the very moment of his torment he can ask forgiveness for his tormentors.

But there is one "word" that causes us perplexity. It is that stark cry, the only "word" recorded in Matthew and Mark, "My God, my God, why hast thou forsaken me?" (Matt. 27: 46; Mark 15: 34). Could Jesus, of all people, have felt a sense of utter Godforsakenness? There are at least two ways of seeking to understand these difficult words. Jesus may have seen in a moment of terrible clarity what life is like apart from God. To that extent he has identified himself with us as fully and completely as it could be done, and has tasted the very dregs of human "lostness." He may have then recovered from this moment of piercing clarity to a feeling of complete trust in God: "Father, into thy hands I commit my spirit!" (Luke 23: 46).

A second interpretation is sometimes put upon the cry. Any Jew in trouble knew his heritage well enough to say the Twenty-second Psalm. The opening words are "My God, my God, why hast thou forsaken me?" The psalmist goes on to tell how he is scorned, despised, his bones are out of joint, his tongue cleaves to his jaws, his hands and feet have been pierced, his garments are being divided by his malefactors and they are casting lots for his raiment. But God comes to the aid of the psalmist. And the psalm which begins on a note of despair ends on a note of triumph. The psalmist not only praises God himself, but calls upon his fellow men to praise him also, because God heard him when he cried out. Many people believe that Jesus began to recite this psalm as an affirmation of his trust in God. Perhaps he was too exhausted to finish it; perhaps Matthew and Mark merely recorded the first verse, knowing that their readers would recognize it. At all events, there are so many similarities between this psalm and the crucifixion that it seems clear that it was in the minds of the Gospel writers.

Be that as it may, within about six hours Jesus was dead. His body was taken down and laid in a borrowed tomb. The tomb was sealed.

"Out of the Way at Last"

A roving reporter, interviewing people the day after, would have gotten reactions like this:

A "RELIGIOUS" PERSON: It's a good thing he's safely out of the way. Far too much a fanatic for my way of thinking. Why, his ideas would have blown our religion sky-high!

A PASSER-BY: He cured my son. He used to visit our home. We loved him very much. I'll miss him.

A MEMBER OF THE SANHEDRIN: Praise be to God that a blasphemer has been killed! This man's dangerous notions, and his claims to be Messiah were lunacy, pure and simple. It's a lucky thing we were able to get rid of him when we did.

PILATE (*the official viewpoint of a man who has rationalized a guilty conscience*): Peace has been preserved! Justice has triumphed! The power of Rome is secure! All hail to Caesar!

PILATE (*the inner thoughts*): I wonder. . . . Couldn't see anything so bad about him. He seemed, in fact, rather like a king. . . . There *can't* be any truth to what his followers believed about him. . . . Still, I wonder.

A DISCIPLE: Well, this is the end. I never really thought they could do him in. I was sure God would come to his aid. But we'll just have to face it. He had a beautiful dream, but it was only a dream, and I was foolish to think it was reality. My best move is to get back to Galilee and start up my fishing business again. I've learned my lesson.

It is supremely ironic that the day when men were surest that they were rid of Jesus was the day before his resurrection.

The Cross and the Resurrection

Crucifixion is a horrible thing. Why, then, does the New Testament seem so strangely fascinated by the cross? Why does it keep appearing on page after page? Why do people sing, to this day, in a startlingly illogical fashion, "In the cross of Christ I *glory*"?

It must be stressed immediately that the story of the cross, by itself, is no "success story." It is a story of defeat. The New Testament writers look at the darkness of the cross from the light cast upon it by the resurrection. They believe in a risen Lord; and it is for this reason that they are able to look with steady eyes at the moment when that risen Lord seems to be defeated, and find his triumph even there. We have looked at the significance of resurrection faith (in Chapter 7). Let us now look at the light that faith shed upon the cross, disentangling four strands of a total answer. No one of these is a complete answer in itself, but each strand is important.

1. The Cross as Example

Suppose you were one of the early Christians. Things were tough, no doubt about it. When you became a Christian, you lost your property. Your father was arrested. You knew that if you were caught, it might be the lions or worse. Whatever happened, being a Christian involved suffering. How did you bear up under this?

Well, for one thing, you remembered that you were being called upon to undergo nothing that Jesus himself had not undergone. He had set an example for you of the way to bear suffering creatively. You could remember him upon the cross and gain strength to bear your own cross. One of the letters you heard read in church might remind you of this: "Christ also suffered for you, leaving you an example, that you should follow in his steps" (I Peter 2: 20, 21). And you could remember the words of Jesus himself, telling you that to follow him wouldn't be easy: "If any man would come after me, let him deny himself and take up his cross and follow me" (Mark 8: 34).

Or, the cross might be an example to you of the extent to which you were called upon to love. You might think to yourself: "Here is an example of God's love. He has come to me and all men and loved us even when we put him to death. This is what it costs him to love us. We must try to be worthy of such love by loving each other just as much." And then you might surprise yourself (and everyone else) by sharing a meal with that hateful Aquila, or going to jail to shield Publius from the Roman soldiers.

Suppose you are one of the twentieth century Christians. If you live behind the Iron Curtain, or in occupied territory, or in fear of a firing squad, the parallels are obvious. But there are "crosses" in life no matter where it is lived, kinds of suffering that touch life everywhere, difficult decisions that have to be made, no matter how little you want to make them. And the cross remains an example, now as much as then, saying: "Christ himself has gone through pain and anguish. See if you can bear it as he did."

And, even more significantly, the cross remains an example to you of God's love for men, a love that you, even in the twentieth century, must imitate. As you think about it, you realize that this is the stuff of which modern saints are made—men who give themselves unstintingly to those in need, just as Jesus did by his unparalleled love. You recall Saint Francis in the thirteenth century, giving himself to the leper no one else would even go near; John Woolman, in the seventeenth century, appealing to hardhearted slave owners to free their slaves; Toyohiko Kagawa in the twentieth century, working for years in the slums of Japan. For such men as these, and for a host of others, the cross has been an example of the extent of

God's love, and they have sought to be worthy of that love by loving in return. And you realize, possibly with some dismay, that the same thing is asked of you.

But there is a catch. It is not necessarily true that the cross will inspire us by its example. We may not "love the highest when we see it." We may hate it. The "good" men in Jesus' time certainly did; they hated the highest so much that they put him to death. And for every soldier at the crucifixion who said, "Truly this was a son of God!" (Matt. 27: 54), there were a dozen who were interested only in winning the Son of God's castoff clothing by a lucky throw of the dice. The example of love, even the highest love, does not necessarily produce a response of love. It may produce scorn and repudiation. We can refuse to love. We can say: "I am not impressed. That's not for me." So to speak of the cross as example is to speak of a part of the New Testament faith but not the whole of it. We must go deeper.

2. The Cross as Judgment

The early Christians did go deeper. They also saw the cross as a judgment upon themselves and all men. Suppose, once more, that you are one of those early Christians. As you gaze at the cross, you discover in a new way what evil really is. You see the consequences, for example, of falsehood and treachery. For Jesus was placed on the cross by lies, conspiracy, secret plottings, refusal to grant fair hearings, bribed witnesses, and all the rest. Perhaps you cringe a little when Peter reminds you in a sermon that Jesus was "crucified and killed by the hands of lawless men" (Acts 2: 23).

But, far deeper than that, the cross shows you how evil your "good" can be. It is a judgment upon all the things you have come to think of as decent and worth-while. For who are the people who have put Jesus on that cross? The criminals, the dregs of society, the scum of the earth? No, they are up there getting crucified with him. The people who have put Jesus on the cross are the "good" people, the upholders of Roman law and order, the leaders of the best religious movements of the time, the respectable, law-abiding citizens.

People like you!

And you realize that you and your kind, with perhaps the best of intentions, are responsible for the man who is dying up there. Of course it's hard to take. You rebel when Peter says to the "religious" people, "*You* denied the Holy and Righteous One, . . . and killed the Author of life" (Acts 3: 14, 15). And when Stephen takes up the same tune and says, "You have now betrayed and murdered [the Righteous One]" (ch. 7: 52), it is too much for the "decent" people in the crowd, so they kill him too. Maybe you were there. At all events, the fact you cannot escape is that *evil is most powerful when it pretends to be good.* And in the light of this disturbing fact nobody receives a clean bill of health. And no matter how far removed you may have been from the actual crucifixion, you, Mr. First Century Christian, feel judged by the event.

Suppose now that you are a twentieth century Christian once again. You are clearly a great distance away from the actual crucifixion, and you heave a sigh of relief. But the relief turns out to have been premature. For you find yourself unable to avoid the unpleasant conclusion that the things that sent Jesus to the cross in the first century are things that are still being done—by you—and that they must disturb God just as much now as they did then. If falsehood and treachery did that to Christ in the first century, they are doing it to him in the twentieth. If the "good" people were responsible for his death in the first century, they continue to crucify him in the twentieth. Your easy dismissals of Christ ("impractical . . . too visionary . . . sure, sure, but you gotta be realistic . . . too idealistic . . ."), your refusal to take him quite seriously enough —these things keep him on that cross. His cross is a judgment on you in the twentieth century, just as it was on you in the first century. It tells you that your sin is not just sin against

another man, but sin against God. Just as sin and evil crucified
Christ in the first century, they combine to do so in the
twentieth. The cross is judgment, no matter who you are, no
matter where you stand.

3. The Cross as Reconciliation

But all is not darkness. The early Christians saw something
more. If the cross drove home to them with terrible acuteness
what men do to God, it also drove home to them with burning
clarity what God does to men. He reconciles them to himself.
The cross is reconciliation. And this time, let us reverse our
procedure. Let us first try to see what is involved in this difficult notion of "reconciliation" as it applies to our situation,
and after that look at the way it was understood by the early
Christians.

"Reconciliation" is not a word we ordinarily use in the high
school corridor, the business office, or the living room. And yet
the idea of reconciliation is important to the high school corridor, the business office, the living room. We have all seen the
"lone wolf," the boss-nobody-likes, the wallflower. These are
people who are isolated, separated from other people, and this
is wrong. What is needed in such situations is to have the broken relationship restored. And this restoring of a broken relationship is reconciliation.

Now let's be more specific:

You and Joe have had a fight.
Furthermore, it was clearly your fault. And your problem is,
how can you get back on good terms with Joe? How, in other
words, can reconciliation be brought about? Clearly it cannot be
"bought" by you. It will not be enough to give Joe an expensive
gift (though such a gesture may not be out of place). It will not
even be enough to go "all out" and be nicer to Joe than you nor-
mally are, since "being nicer than you need to be" is a contradiction in terms when friends are involved.

The fact of the matter is that the broken relationship will never
be healed just from your end. Even to throw yourself on Joe's

mercy and ask his forgiveness is not quite the whole story. For the decisive action must come from the one who has been wronged —from Joe. He must be willing to forgive, and so bridge the gap which your wrongdoing has created.

This may be a hard thing for him to do. He will have to humble himself, swallow his pride, and perhaps even suffer in order to demonstrate actively that he bears you no ill will and desires only your friendship.

This does no more than give us a faint hint and clue about the broken relationship between God and ourselves and how it is restored. You should be able to make the necessary connection. We are likewise separated from God, and it is the result of our wrongdoing, not his. We cannot amass credits before God by doing "more than we ought to," since there is no limit to the extent to which we ought to love God. The decisive action must be by him. And the Bible tells us that the decisive action has been taken by him, that he comes to meet us in Jesus Christ in an act of outgoing, reconciling love. And the cross, quite specifically and quite concretely, shows us that love "costs," that God loves enough to pay the price of the cross that we may be restored to one another. Our job is to accept this gift which we do not deserve.

Suppose, now, that you are a first century Christian. You need, as you see it, to be reconciled with God. The broken relationship needs restoring. And you discover that Paul has compressed the whole thing into one burning statement: "In Christ, God was reconciling the world to himself" (II Cor. 5: 19). And this speaks to your situation! For you know that *you* can't do the reconciling. Nothing you can do is enough to "make up" to God for the wrong you have done. And now you know that *God* does the reconciling, and that he does it "in Christ." And as you are aware of Christ, and see him now as God's mighty act of reconciliation, something else becomes apparent to you.

You come to see that reconciling love of this sort will be *suffering* love, suffering love endured on behalf of someone else—what is called "vicarious suffering." And then you recall those "Suffering Servant" poems in the latter part of Isaiah. You remember that in them a servant, who was not clearly identified, took upon himself voluntarily the suffering that should have been meted out to his tormentors. They came to realize what he had done, and they said:

> Surely he has borne our griefs
>   and carried our sorrows;
> yet we esteemed him stricken,
>   smitten by God, and afflicted.
> But he was wounded for our transgressions,
>   he was bruised for our iniquities;
> upon him was the chastisement that made us whole,
>   and with his stripes we are healed.
> All we like sheep have gone astray;
>   we have turned every one to his own way;
> and the Lord has laid on him
>   the iniquity of us all.   (Isa. 53: 4-6)

That's it! As you ponder this message, you find in it a wonderful description of what is true for you as you gaze at the cross of Christ. This same thing is true of him: he has suffered on your behalf. He has been willing to pay the cost of your wrongdoing, and he has done this voluntarily—out of love. He has broken down the barriers between himself and you, barriers that you erected. He has done the reconciling, and it is up to you simply to accept it.

We can never penetrate fully into the mystery of the reconciliation between God and man. But we can at least see that at the very heart of all things is a God of suffering love. We can have the overpowering realization that God has paid us the almost intolerable compliment of loving us *that* much. He has offered us himself.

4. The Cross as Victory

Suppose (for the last time in this chapter) that you are one of the early Christians. Not for a moment do you look upon the cross as "the defeat of God" or any such thing. For you, the cross seen in the light of the resurrection is the stunning victory of God—the "unexpected news" that changes everything. You nod your head in agreement as you hear read in the Sunday service Paul's summary of the things of central importance to your faith (Col. 2: 8-15), ending with the words, "He [God] disarmed the principalities and powers and made a public example of them, *triumphing over them* in him [Jesus]" (v. 15, italics added). You realize in a very poignant way that this is just what happened on the cross. There, you reflect, the "principalities and powers" (by which Paul means the forces of evil) were in mortal combat with God's power, and God "triumphed over them."

In other words, you see that something of lasting significance was taking place on that hill outside Jerusalem. And while it is hard to describe, you somehow have the feeling that here is the most important thing of all. You see the cross as a battlefield. On one side are the forces of evil, sin, and death, sure that now they've "got God cornered" since he has been foolish enough to play into their hands by becoming man. (In Jesus, Paul says, was "the whole fulness of deity," Col. 2: 9.) And on the other side is God. If he can withstand *this* assault upon his power, nothing else can defeat him.

And you are a little breathless as you think about the staggering importance of this conflict, until you remember that, as Paul put it, God "triumphed over them." You see that the crown of thorns is a real crown—the only crown such a "king" as Jesus could wear—and that he triumphs through and not in spite of the "weakness" that crown represents. And you, looking at the cross through the resurrection, share in the victory which has been so dearly won. You live in a world that is God's world, now and forever. His victory is sure.

Suppose (also for the last time in this chapter) that you are now a twentieth century Christian. Can this strange kind of talk and stranger kind of notion make any sense to you? The more you think about it, the more it does. For you remember that you live in a world where evil is an awful reality, and where it does seem to challenge God. And you become very sure that it matters a great deal whether God conquers or whether evil conquers. As you think about it, it occurs to you that there comes a point in a war, *before* all the fighting is over, when it is clear which side will win. In World War II, so you have been told, it was clear after the Allies got a secure beachhead on the European continent, that they would defeat the Nazis. The decisive battle had been won, even though months of fighting were still ahead.

And this helps you to see how the cross is still a victory, after nineteen hundred years, in a world where the contest between God and evil is not yet over, in which the fighting is still going on. For the cross is the decisive victory, the established beachhead, the one that makes plain who has already won the final victory. For here, so you continue to believe, evil had its supreme chance to defeat God—and could not. This is the faith that sustains you in dark times, that summons you to action when the odds seem overwhelmingly against you, that keeps you confident and hopeful. For you believe in the ultimate triumph of God.

No wonder, then, if this is true, that Christians in all ages have seen in the cross, not a symbol of degradation and despair, but a symbol of exaltation and victory. There has been a triumph. It is God's triumph. Christ is victor. He rules as the Lord of life.

The place of the skull has become a throne.

A Threat to the Whole Business

(Why Is There Evil?)

We have been hearing about a good God.

A God who is all-powerful.

A God who loves his children.

And it looks as though, with a God like this, the world should be a pretty fine place to live in. But there is a problem. . . .

Seeing Our Situation Clearly

It is important to see this problem in all its starkness. Perhaps the following exhibit can drive the point home:

> ## 43 Children Lose Lives in School Bus Accident
>
> All hope was abandoned today for the lives of 43 children whose school bus plummeted into the Yellow River last night when the middle span of the south bridge gave way under the weight of the bus. Divers have recovered all but 5 of the bodies.

Why should God let that happen to innocent children?

142

TELEGRAM

THE WAR DEPARTMENT REGRETS TO INFORM YOU THAT
YOUR HUSBAND CORPORAL RALPH BLANK 0021311729
WAS KILLED IN ACTION APRIL 23 STOP HIS HEROISM IN
DEFENDING HILL 203 WILL ALWAYS BE REMEMBERED
BY THE MEMBERS OF HIS COMPANY STOP FURTHER IN-
FORMATION BEING FORWARDED BY MAIL STOP

Can that wife and her two children believe in a loving God?

(*Fade out music*) And now for the six o'clock news. Here's a
recent dispatch just received over our wires from India. The
worst famine in India's history is now a grim reality. Officials
are unable to quell rioters who are storming local granaries
demanding food for families. In several localities police have
been forced to fire on the mobs.

Have you tried Kleeno, the new all-purpose cleanser that
makes *everything* whiter?

Can the Indians believe that God is the Father of all men?

-87-

*end. We were thirty-nine months in the con-
centration camp. During this period my father
died of starvation, and my mother was put to
death in a gas chamber. Fortunately my
brother had been shot to death during our
capture and thus escaped these horrors. I was
slated for the firing squad on Tuesday, and
only because our liberation came on Monday
did I escape. I don't see how one can really*

Why does God permit such things to happen?

No God, No Problem

Any Christian worth his salt must come to grips with the fact that these things happen—in God's world. They make it difficult, if not impossible, for many people to believe in God.

At the same time, there is a counterproblem which must be faced by those who refuse to believe in God because of the problem of evil. If there is no God, there is no "problem" of evil. That is, if we live in a purposeless and meaningless universe, we have no right to expect that decency and right and truth should prevail, and that baseness, suffering, and evil should not. There may be things that we do not "like," but we cannot claim that they "ought" not to be, or that they constitute a "problem." They are simply "the way things are," in a morally neutral universe.

Notice, therefore—and this is what makes it really tough for the Christians—that the more firmly you believe in a good, loving, and powerful God, the more vexing does the problem of evil become. If there is really such a God, why is evil so powerful? And if you take the New Testament seriously, you have the even worse situation that the very Son of God himself seems powerless against evil. Evil executes him. The higher your conception of God, the worse the problem. If there is no God, the problem ceases to exist as a "problem"; if there is a God, the situation seems intolerable.

Clearing Away the Underbrush

It is very important, in dealing with this perplexity, to get rid of some of the false answers, if we are to understand the true ones.

The Book of Job deals in a special way with this problem. In the prologue to this religious drama, God agrees that Job may be tested to see whether his faith will hold up in the pinch. The test proceeds:

1. Job receives word that his vast flocks of cattle have been captured or killed.
2. Then word comes that the same fate has befallen his servants.
3. A messenger reports that his sons and daughters are all dead.
4. He has no sooner learned these things than his body breaks out in ugly, painful sores.

Will he not now "curse God, and die," his wife asks. (His wife, incidentally, is so nasty that her survival, when all the rest of the family have been killed, is perhaps the greatest test that Job faces.)

The problems are not new problems, nor are they old problems. A modern version of Job could be written, in which Job heard within ten minutes (a) that his house had burned down, (b) that his bank had failed, (c) that his son had been killed in battle, (d) that his daughter had died in an auto accident, and who in the midst of all this (e) found that he had polio. He too would ask the question Job asks: "Why has this happened to me?"

Three "friends" (the quotation marks are used advisedly) come to give Job the straight answer. Most of the book is devoted to their discussion with Job, in the course of which it becomes clear that the author wants to show the inadequacy of the "friends'" answers. Let us look at two of the rejected solutions.

1. The "friends'" main theme is that *all suffering is the consequence of sin.* If you are "good," everything will be fine. But if you are "bad," you will be punished. Each of the "friends" gets an oar in for this one.

> ELIPHAZ: Who ever perished, being innocent?
> Or where were the righteous cut off?
> Even as I have seen, they that plow iniquity,
> And sow wickedness, reap the same.
>
> (Job 4: 7, 8)

BILDAD: God will not cast away a perfect man,
           Neither will he help the evildoers.
                              (Job 8: 20)
ZOPHAR: The triumphing of the wicked is short,
           And the joy of the hypocrite but for a moment.
                              (Job 20: 5)

Now this is a nice formula. It looks well on paper.

Goodness = Prosperity.
Badness = Suffering.

Only one question remains to be asked: Is it true? The Book
of Job shows that it is not true. The problem is precisely that
Job is a "good" man whose lot is *not* prosperity, but suffering.
The "friends" can solve the problem only by denying that it
exists. Since badness = suffering, Job must be bad. Period.
Case dismissed. But the book presents Job as an upright, righteous man. The formula, in other words, doesn't always work.
To put it in modern terms, the fact that a man is rich doesn't
necessarily mean that the Lord has blessed him. It may mean
that he has found ways to evade his income tax. The fact that
a person is poor doesn't necessarily mean that he is evil. It
may mean that he is too honest to accept bribes. The formula
doesn't always work.

But the thing that really undercuts the argument of Job's
"friends" is the suffering of "innocent" people. Is a starving
baby in India more "sinful" than a well-fed American baby
whose father makes $10,000 a year? Were the children killed
in the Korean war more "sinful" than children in America
who are alive simply because the actual fighting took place
there rather than here?

Furthermore, if you take this position seriously, you run the
risk of making religion nothing but a gigantic celestial fire
insurance policy: "Be good so God will reward you, for if you
are not good, he will surely punish you—and you don't want
to be punished, *do* you?"

2. Another answer that Job's "friends" try out is that *God sends suffering to help us "grow."* Suffering is a good thing, since it teaches us to rely on God, and we should never question his ways.

> ELIPHAZ: Happy is the man whom God correcteth:
>   Therefore despise not thou the chastening of the
>   Almighty.
>
> (Job 5: 17)

The view is suggested elsewhere in the Bible: "The Lord reproves him whom he loves, as a father the son in whom he delights" (Prov. 3: 12, and see Heb. 12: 7).

Now there is clearly more point to this argument than to the other one. It *is* true that a father may have to discipline a son out of love, so that the son can grow and mature. Such a position, however, accepted as an adequate answer to the problem of evil, can become a device for "excusing" evil and ceasing to be concerned about it. Notice the extremes to which such a view could lead us.

"O. K., so he broke his leg. Don't set it. The pain will help to build his character."

"There's no need to have a hospital here. People 'grow' by enduring suffering."

"Why bother to clear out that slum? The children will have more character if they grow up in a tough neighborhood."

No thoughtful person would agree with those statements. And yet they follow with fatal ease if you assent too glibly to the view that suffering builds character and is thereby justified.

Thus in both these answers of Job's "friends" there is just enough truth to make them risky propositions. It must certainly be true that some suffering is punishment for sin, and that some suffering is disciplinary in character.

It's when you substitute "all" for "some" that you run into trouble.

Some More Underbrush

There are other ways of dealing with the problem of evil on the market today. Most of these are even less satisfactory than those of Job's "friends." We must be careful not to be sold a false bill of goods on such items as the following.

There are those who claim that *all suffering comes from God*. This is simply a crueler version of the notion that all suffering is punishment for sin. If we say that all suffering comes from God, we thereby succeed in making him responsible for evil in a way that transforms him into a frightful kind of demon, bent simply on destroying rather than creating. We also provide ourselves with a nice way of escaping responsibility:

JUDGE (*at conclusion of murder trial*) : For deliberately and willfully strangling this person to death, in an act of premeditated crime, you are hereby sentenced to die in the electric chair. Have you anything further to say in your defense?

PRISONER: Sure. God made that person suffer, not me. It's his world, not mine. I can't be held responsible for what he made me do. Who are you to question God? I didn't do anything wrong. I ought to go free.

(*Exit prisoner, struggling with guards, unaware of the fact that to be consistent he would have to grant that God had ordained his suffering as well.*)

If you were the judge, you would hardly let the argument that "all suffering comes from God" pass unchallenged.

Occasionally, people will suggest that *evil is an illusion*—that it doesn't really exist at all. Obviously only a superficial sophisticate can make such a statement seriously. A trip to a casualty ward, or a battlefield, or a mental hospital, should be enough to dispel the illusion that evil is an illusion. Or, in a lighter vein, the well-known limerick may serve:

> There was a faith healer from Deal
> Who said, "Although pain isn't real,

> When I sit on a pin
> And it punctures my skin,
> I dislike what I fancy I feel."

Another sophisticated argument is that *evil is necessary to the "good of the whole."* A jarring discord in a symphony may be very irritating if heard in isolation, but when heard at the proper point in the symphony it contributes a contrast to the beautiful passage about to be heard, making the latter more beautiful than ever. If this view is true, there is no real incentive to get rid of evil. To remove the discord would spoil the symphony; to remove the evil would spoil the greater balance of the whole. This is a view that takes no account of people as people. Could you honestly suggest that someone dying of tuberculosis was simply contributing to the "good of the whole"?

Finally, some people will justify evil on the ground that *everything will come out all right in the end.* Those who suffer will get their reward in heaven. Here again, religion becomes simply a reward offered to "nice" people, and here again, the argument makes it possible to be supremely unconcerned with evil here on earth. ("Let 'em suffer a few years; they've got all eternity to be happy in.") But more on this in Chapter 17.

A Few Common Sense Answers

So far it might appear as though everything that people have thought about the problem of evil was wrong. But as a matter of fact, people have thought a good many sensible things about the problem of evil as well. Before we turn, in the next chapter, to some of the specifically Biblical answers to the problem, it will be worth-while to take note of some of the things that common sense has had to say. Here, then, are four factors that, taken together, will cast some light at least on our problem.

1. *The existence of dependable laws.* If the law of gravity were suddenly "repealed," this book might fly up to the ceiling

while the chair you are sitting in slid out the window. You might be unable to get up after you fell down. The bus outside might refuse to budge or it might only go backward. Everything would be chaotic. Nothing would be stable, dependable, or predictable.

The fact that these things do not happen, that there are dependable laws, helps to make human life possible. And it means that some kinds of evil can be partially explained as instances in which we have disregarded these laws or put ourselves in situations where they work against us rather than for us. It would be sheer chaos for everybody else if God were to suspend the law of gravitation for five minutes because a window washer on the sixty-fourth floor got dizzy and fell off the ledge.

There is a hint of this approach in the words of Jesus, that God "sends rain on the just and on the unjust" (Matt. 5: 45). The universe in which we live is ordered by God in a certain way, and we have no right to expect him to tidy things up for us if we happen to cross his purposes or break his established laws.

2. *The necessity of risk.* Almost every joy in life involves the fact of risk. You have to accept the risks in order to experience the joys.

If you make a good friend, you run the risk that the friend may be false to you. But you have to run that risk in order to have a friend at all.

If you fall in love, you run the risk that you may be hurt. Your beloved may not love you in return, or she may jilt you at the last moment for someone else. But people seem to agree that falling in love is worth the risks.

If you marry and have children, you have to take the risk that your child may hate you, or may grow up to be a thug who robs banks. But parents take those risks in having children, because they would rather have children, with the risks, than forego the joy of children.

The more deeply we love, the more deeply we can be hurt,

and yet we would not forego the joys of love to avoid the possible risks of hurt.

3. *Values in suffering.* If we don't try to press it too far, we can see that there are sometimes provisional values in suffering. In some cases, suffering can be a means of developing responsibility. An individual who sees human misery, poverty, or unemployment, may be moved to do something positive and constructive about righting those wrongs. And there are many instances where suffering has deepened the compassion and understanding of those who have endured it. The woman, for example, who has had polio, and has struggled through pain to a new kind of self-mastery and God-given compassion, can usually do more to help other people in similar situations than someone who has never really known that kind of pain at first hand. She can do this precisely *because* she has suffered herself, in a very extreme way.

4. *The fact of human freedom and sin.* It is important to remember that much evil and suffering are due to our own abuse of our freedom, and cannot therefore be chalked up directly to God. God has given us the freedom to choose him or to reject him, the freedom to live as he wishes or to defy his wishes and live unto ourselves. The fact of our freedom has within it the possible fact of our sin, and the fact of our sin has within it the disruption of the way God intends life to be lived. If we did not have this freedom, however, we should be mere puppets dangling on a string, or robots controlled by a mechanism—absolutely powerless to have any say about what we did or what became of us. But since we have this freedom, there is no way of avoiding responsibility and saying that it is God's fault if we choose wrongly and get into trouble. This is the price we have to be willing to pay for the gift of freedom. (See further, Chapter 13.)

These four facts, taken together, give us *some* light on the question, Why is there evil in God's world? But we must now attempt a more complete "answer" by looking directly at the Biblical treatment of the problem.

Meeting Ugly Facts Head On

(What Does God Do About Evil?)

Jeremiah was not a very cautious man. When people uttered pious phrases that didn't make sense, he called them on the carpet. When he felt God was being unfair, he said so. It was the "correct" thing in Jeremiah's time to believe that God rewarded the good and punished the evil. (Remember Job's "friends" in the last chapter.) But Jeremiah wasn't convinced. He saw that the "good" people were getting a raw deal, while the "evil" people were getting along very well. And so he took his case directly to God:

> Why does the way of the wicked prosper?
> Why do all who are treacherous thrive?
>
> (Jer. 12: 1)

Next time a seasoned skeptic tells you that the Bible is a lot of sentimental moonshine, remember that question. The Bible doesn't censor embarrassing questions. It asks them bluntly. And it does more than that (which is all the seasoned skeptic usually does). It answers them. In this chapter we must try to see how the Bible answers the question which the Jeremiahs in every age feel compelled to ask.

God's Justice and the Nations

We must not completely disregard the viewpoint that Jeremiah, along with Job, attacked. For the "correct" view makes some sense when nations are involved, even though it may look absurd when related to individuals. We saw (in Chapter 6) that the prophets believed in a kind of "rough justice" in the long sweep of history. They believed that if a nation consistently went against the will of the righteous God, that nation would ultimately perish. The nation couldn't "get away with it" forever.

Fine, you say, so long as you are top dog and not getting trampled on.

But a nation being trampled on would hardly talk like that. . . .

And the whole spectacular point of the prophets is that their country got trampled on and they *did* talk like that. *Just* like that. This was the way they interpreted *their own* suffering, not somebody else's. Micah, for example, speaks to his own people, and says:

> Your rich men are full of violence;
>   your inhabitants speak lies,
>   and their tongue is deceitful in their mouth.
> Therefore I have begun to smite you,
>   making you desolate because of your sins.
>   (Micah 6: 12, 13)

The nation *is* smitten, the lands *are* despoiled—almost everybody gets carried off into exile. And perhaps the most amazing fact of Old Testament history is that instead of interpreting their national disaster as a proof of the fact that God had deserted them, they could see it as an example of the fact that God *did* care for them, and was using these means to "bring them to their senses," so that they would give up their evil ways and return to him. A lesson was taught to them as an entire nation.

As an entire nation, yes. But if you try to say that good *individuals* are always rewarded, and bad *individuals* are always punished, then you are saddled with the vigorous protests of Job and Jeremiah.

The Problem of the Individual

What, then, about the individual? Here's Habakkuk's question:

> Why dost thou look on faithless men,
>   and art silent when the wicked swallows up
>   the man more righteous than he?
>   (Hab. 1: 13)

Habakkuk is told, in effect, to wait. In God's good time righteousness will be vindicated. It seems now as though this were not true, but his vision is limited and he must have faith that, in the end, God's purposes and his righteousness will win.

> And the Lord answered me:
> "Write the vision;
>   make it plain upon tablets,
>   so he may run who reads it.
> For still the vision awaits its time;
>   it hastens to the end—it will not lie.
> If it seems slow, wait for it;
>   it will surely come, it will not delay.
> Behold, he whose soul is not upright in him shall fail,
>   but the righteous shall live by his faith."
>   (Hab. 2: 2-4)

Let us also remind ourselves of the experience of Hosea (which we examined in some detail in Chapter 5). Hosea came to realize that suffering can have a healing and redemptive quality about it. Although there must be punishment for wrongdoing, it is punishment with a purpose. For the other side of punishment is restoration. God punishes for the purpose of winning his people back to him. And this is as true for the individual as for the nation. Hosea knew very well from his personal experience that suffering is not just God's vengeance; it has a real redeeming purpose.

The "Suffering Servant"

Hosea's experience suggests that suffering itself can be redemptive, and this belief comes to its sharpest definition in

passages in the latter part of Isaiah, which are called the "Suffering Servant" poems, and which we examined briefly in
Chapter 10. In these poems, you remember, a "servant" who
is innocent voluntarily assumes the punishment that should
be meted out to the guilty. This is an exceedingly high kind of
love—love which is willing to suffer the consequences of someone else's wrongdoing. It is as though you were to drive an ice
pick through your rival's heart and then his brother were to go
to the electric chair in your place. This is "vicarious" suffering—the innocent suffering on behalf of the guilty.

Here is an example of one level of "vicarious" suffering:

When the Panama Canal was being built, there was a tremendously high mortality rate among the workers because of yellow
fever. It finally seemed certain that yellow fever was being carried
by the mosquito, but it was necessary to study the nature of the
disease in order to be able to deal with it effectively. So a group
of men volunteered to be bitten by the deadly mosquitoes, so that
the disease could be carefully studied as it spread through their
bodies. Several of these men died. However, as a result of their
suffering and death, an effective serum was developed, and the
lives of thousands of workers were saved. The suffering of a few
became a benefit for the many, and it was thereby given meaning
and purpose.

That is the sort of idea that the "Servant Songs" stress. The
servant himself "had no form or comeliness . . . , and no
beauty." In fact, "he was despised and rejected by men; a man
of sorrows, and acquainted with grief." People hid their faces
from him. And yet, they came to see a very important thing as
they observed his suffering—he was suffering *for them.* Their
attitude changed to wonder and amazement, and they ex-
claimed,

> *He* was wounded for *our* transgressions,
>   *he* was bruised for *our* iniquities;
> upon *him* was the chastisement that made *us* whole,
>   and with *his* stripes *we* are healed.
>   (Isa. 53: 5, italics added)

This is one of the high points of the Old Testament. Suffering that is redemptive for others is suffering that itself has been redeemed. Pain and scourging voluntarily assumed can bring peace and healing to those for whom they are borne. It may even be true that the suffering of the innocent can be a kind of "shock treatment." If I see that something I have done has caused suffering to an innocent person, this may have a real effect on whether I do it again. It may cause me to act very differently, as I become drastically aware of how I have hurt someone else.

The Answer to Job

In the last chapter we left Job saddled with a problem. (Turn back to page 145 if you forget what it was.) What kind of answer does he get? It is not an "intellectually satisfying" answer; if we want a rational explanation which wraps up the whole problem of evil in a nice tidy package, we had better look elsewhere. Nevertheless, the answer (Job, chs. 38 to 41), together with Job's reply (Job 40: 3-5; 42: 1-6), constitutes an important part of a true answer. God begins by questioning Job. (Question after question.) He confronts him with the mystery of creation: "Where were you when I laid the foundation of the earth?" (Job 38: 4). He goes on to describe the wonder of creation, and asks Job questions about it. (Question after question.) And the force of the questions is to remind Job that he is only a small part of creation, and yet he is presuming to pass judgment on the Creator. How can the creature expect to know all that is known to the Creator? (Question after question.)

In reply to this devastating onslaught (the full force of which can be gained only by reading chs. 38 to 41 at one sitting), Job tries once to interrupt, remarking,

> Behold, I am of small account; what shall I answer thee?
> I lay my hand upon my mouth.
> (Job 40: 3, 4)

But the main burden of his response comes later:

> I know that thou canst do all things,
>> and that no purpose of thine can be thwarted. ....
> Therefore I have uttered what I did not understand,
>> things too wonderful for me, which I did not know. ....
> *I had heard of thee by the hearing of the ear,*
>> *but now my eye sees thee;*
> therefore I despise myself,
>> and repent in dust and ashes.
>
>> (Job 42: 2-6, italics added)

On the face of it this seems like a disappointing "answer." There is no clever twist of logic that solves the problem once and for all. But there is something infinitely more important than a clever twist of logic. For Job has had a firsthand experience of the presence of God. Before this, Job had heard *of* God; he had secondhand evidence. But now he *himself* knows God— he has firsthand evidence. He has come into a personal relationship with the living God. Beside that fact, everything else is insignificant. What makes the difference to Job is not that God has won an argument, but that God has become real for him. For the first time in his life Job can say, "Now my eye sees thee." And the upshot of the matter is that he can now trust God for everything. There is no need for an "answer" to his problem. The problem has been resolved by the fact that the all-powerful God who can "do all things" is in intimate fellowship with Job, who is "of small account."

And so Job repents. He realizes that in the final analysis it is presumptuous to make God "defend" himself. And Job, rather than being a bitter critic, is now at peace—a man of faith who is no longer crying at God to "justify himself," but worshiping the living Lord of his life. His problem has led him to the very heart of a living religious experience of God. And to one for whom that is real no "problem" remains.

What Has the New Testament to Say?

Such light we can get from the Old Testament with regard to the problem of suffering. What further clarification do we get from the "good news" contained in the New Testament? What difference does it make that Jesus Christ was born, lived, died, and rose from the dead? Here are four insights that the New Testament helps us to clarify:

1. God is involved in evil with us.
2. God conquers evil.
3. God conquers death.
4. God gives us the power to conquer.

Each of these deserves some comment.

1. *God is involved in evil with us.* A strange notion, this! God involved in evil? Surely God is beyond good and evil, off in heaven somewhere, free from the kinds of cares and sorrows that plague the lot of ordinary mortals. So the coal miner in "Caliban in the Coal Mines" thought, when he said,

> "God, You don't know what it is—
> You, in Your well-lighted sky—"

But the very heart of the gospel, the "good news," is that God *does* know what it is, that God is not far off and remote, but that in Jesus Christ he became man and dwelt among us. God has, so to speak, "invaded" our human life and taken part in it. (See Chapters 7 to 10.) This means, quite simply, that God is involved in evil with us; that he did not permit evil to exist in the same world and then stay as far away from it as he could, but that on the contrary he came to that very place where evil was—human life—to do battle with it, in human life, as a human being. You could almost say that God was "willing to take his own medicine," that he did not stay aloof from the unpleasant experiences through which his children were going. Biblical faith finds this claim most clearly focused in the crucifixion of Christ. Here we see God, present in Jesus Christ, being subjected to the very worst evils that men can devise. He does not bypass suffering and evil but accepts them.

He is involved.

Any notion that God "doesn't care" is promptly scotched by a little reflection upon the fact that men did not crucify just a nice man, but the very Son of God himself. The coal miner in the poem was too modest in his request. All he asked for was "a handful of stars." God didn't send a handful of stars. He sent his own Son.

Notice how this brings God into relationship with our suffering:

Item: A father and mother have a son who grows up and then dies almost at the beginning of his adult life. Those parents can know that God too has experienced some of the pain that they are experiencing, and that he understands.

Item: A man with great vision and concern for his fellow men begins to put his plans into concrete action, and people simply laugh at him and refuse to help him and utterly destroy him. That man can realize that his failure (if indeed it is a failure) is not an experience that puts him "out of touch" with God, but that on the contrary it brings him closer to what God, in Christ, has himself experienced.

To such people there comes not only the conviction that God understands, but also the conviction that God, being God, can help them in their time of trouble. The letter to the Hebrews sees this:

For we have not a high priest who is unable to sympathize with our weaknesses, but one who in every respect has been tempted as we are, yet without sinning. Let us then with confidence draw near to the throne of grace, that we may receive mercy and find grace to help in time of need (Heb. 4: 15, 16).

2. *God conquers evil.* Just to say that God is involved in evil with us wouldn't be "good news." It might mean only that God was "caught" in the same predicament we are, and that he couldn't escape either. So the New Testament makes an-

other startling claim at this point. It says that God is not only involved in evil, but that he does battle with evil and conquers it.

(Explosive retort by incredulous reader: Now *wait* a minute! How can you talk that way? If evil was defeated by Christ nineteen hundred years ago, it's doing a pretty good job of pretending to be alive today.)

This is a fair enough reaction, and to meet it we must remind ourselves of the inner significance of the crucifixion-resurrection event. If the Gospels ended with the death of Jesus, we should have tragedy pure and simple. God would be involved with evil, all right, and it would conquer him. But, as we have seen, the New Testament makes the point that the death of Jesus was not the end. Evil *did* crucify the Son of God and kill him, but it was not able to win the day, for God raised Jesus from the dead, thus making plain the true meaning of the cross, which was that the power of evil had been defeated by the power of God. Here was God, in the person of Christ, weak and defenseless and powerless, assaulted by evil men and evil forces. If God could conquer in *this* encounter with evil, it would be clear that he could conquer any further assaults upon him by the powers of evil. And the New Testament says that God did precisely that—that in this struggle he emerged the victor. (The section on "The Cross as Victory" in Chapter 10 should be reread in this connection.)

What does this mean for us? It means that we can be quite confident that no other display of the powers of evil is strong enough to defeat God. It means that we live in a world where his victory has been won.

(Grudging concession by incredulous reader: But even if God won on *that* day, he seems to have been losing ever since. How can you believe that evil has been conquered in the twentieth century world?)

There is no easy answer to this question. The only final answer the Christian can give is that he sees in the event of crucifixion-resurrection *enough* of an indication of God's power over evil to be willing to believe that the victory is sure. Perhaps an example can make this point clear:

As you read a detective story (*The Case of the Bloody Hand,* say, or *No Corpse, No Murder*) the plot seems very confused, and you are not at all sure what the outcome will be. But in the last chapter the detective summons all the suspects into a room, proceeds to unravel the mystery, shows the pattern running through it, and reveals how he knew the guilty man. It is only in the light of that final chapter that the rest of the book hangs together. After you have read it, you can say: "Oh, yes! Now I see why the butler in Chapter Three threw the knife down the well *without* erasing his fingerprints." Now you can understand the plots, the counterplots, the "red herrings," and the carefully planted hints and clues.

Suppose for a moment that you had read that final chapter first, and *then* had read the rest of the detective story. . . .

You would be able to make a good deal more sense out of the story! You would see something of the meaning and significance of the events as they took place. You would understand a little better the relationship of the knife, the fingerprints, the unmailed letter, the midnight visitor—while to others the same events would still be a hopeless chaos. Because you knew what happened in that final chapter you would have a clearer picture of the meaning of the story as a whole.

Now don't press that one too far; don't ask too much of it. But let it stand as a way of saying that you, as a Christian, are in a position *somewhat* like the reader. As you look at the mysterious tangle of events known as human life and history, you can see some meaning and direction in them because you know what the final outcome is. You know that God will be victorious in the ongoing struggle with evil, because he already is victorious in the event of crucifixion-resurrection. You have, so to speak, already seen the final chapter. And so you can live your life in the assurance that there the decisive battle has been fought, and that the outcome is certain victory for God. Of course you cannot "prove" this. You still walk by faith (which means "trust") rather than by sight. But you see enough to believe and trust in God.

Here we must underline more vividly a point that was made in Chapter 10. When we speak of God's conquering evil in Christ, we cannot do this fully without seeing the way in which the "Suffering Servant" passages (especially Isa. 52: 13 to 53: 12) illumine the event of the cross. Look again at the quotation earlier in this chapter. Here is another dimension of the cross as victory. We have sinned, we have disobeyed God's will, but rather than making us bear the full brunt of the penalty for sin, God in Christ bears it himself. (This is why, at various times in Christian history, Christ has been referred to as the "sin bearer.") *He* carries the weight of the burden that should be ours; he takes upon himself the punishment that should be meted out to us. He is "wounded for *our* transgressions"; he is "bruised for *our* iniquities."

Just why God should do this, we do not know. It is a mystery. But it is a mystery of his *love* and we see in this divine activity the way in which love comes to grips with evil—by bearing it and thus conquering it. Paul makes the same point in a slightly different fashion. In Christ, he says, "God . . . canceled the bond which stood against us with its legal demands; this he set aside, nailing it to the cross" (Col. 2: 13, 14).

3. *God conquers death.* To most people the fact of death is what seems to destroy life's meaning. For them, the whole story can be put in the formula:

We live, struggle, and die.

Our children live, struggle, and die.

Their children live, struggle, and die.

Finally everybody is dead and there is nothing to show for it.

Over against this, the Bible affirms very positively the fact of "the life everlasting." Death is not the end of the human venture. The incompleteness of life is completed by God in a way that we cannot totally understand, but that stands as the crowning affirmation of the fulfillment of God's purposes for human life. (Since Chapter 17 will try to spell this out more fully, here we will simply relate this claim to the problem of evil.)

We must not let the fact of life after death solve the problem of evil too simply. Too often, for example, people have been told not to worry about evil here on earth because "everything will be all right in heaven." But we must also see that Biblical faith in life after death cuts across the meaningless cycle of live-struggle-die-live-struggle-die-live-struggle-die generation after generation. We live, struggle, and die, yes—but God is able to raise us up, refashion us, and use us for his purposes in ways beyond our imagining, so that our incompleteness is completed by him, our unfulfilled lives are fulfilled by him. The Biblical claim is that nothing that threatens our lives can finally separate us from God in Christ, since God in Christ is the Lord of life *and* death. Paul put it most clearly:

For I am sure that neither death, nor life, nor angels, nor principalities, nor things present, nor things to come, nor powers, nor height, nor depth, nor anything else in all creation, will be able to separate us from the love of God in Christ Jesus our Lord (Rom. 8: 38, 39).

These words are the heart and center of the New Testament. They are worth reading again:

For I am sure that neither death, nor life, nor angels, nor principalities, nor things present, nor things to come, nor powers, nor height, nor depth, nor anything else in all creation, will be able to separate us from the love of God in Christ Jesus our Lord (Rom. 8: 38, 39).

4. *God gives us the power to conquer.* One thing more must be stressed: God gives us the power to conquer evil. This does not mean that we can avoid evil and suffering. It does mean that God gives us the resources with which to meet evil and suffering head on—and conquer them.

The Bible does not promise that by "being good" we shall escape evil and suffering; but it does make evident on almost every page that when evil and suffering come to us, as they inevitably will, we need not succumb to them but can live through them in such fashion that we are the conquerors, not they. We can face them with the resources that so far have been made available to us by the "good news": the confidence that God is involved in evil with us, that he conquers evil, and that he conquers death. Believing these things, we can face evil unafraid.

But we have a further obligation. It is expected that we will share whatever power we have acquired, with others. Once again, Paul can help us to understand:

> Blessed be the God and Father of our Lord Jesus Christ, the Father of mercies and God of all comfort, who comforts us in all our affliction, *so that we may be able to comfort those who are in any affliction, with the comfort with which we ourselves are comforted by God* (II Cor. 1: 3, 4, italics added).

Paul is saying that God gives him strength (comfort = con + fortis = with strength) so that he in his turn may give strength to those who are in trouble. It is not enough for him to receive strength and assurance from God; he must pass the strength and assurance on to others. And this constitutes the real victory over evil, that even "as we share abundantly in Christ's sufferings," as Paul goes on, "so through Christ we share abundantly in comfort too" (II Cor. 1: 5). To those who turn to God in trust, Paul assures us, God does give strength to meet whatever life may bring, and the job then becomes one of giving that same God-given strength to others.

This means that the most creative use of suffering is achieved when through it you are able to minister to the sufferings of others. The real question should not be, "Why did this happen to me?" but rather, "How can I use what has happened to me as a means of serving God more fully?"

The Only Real "Answer"

It is clear now that there is no simple, one-two-three answer to the parents of the children killed in the bus accident, the wife of the corporal, the rioting Indian families, or the victim of the concentration camp. But it should also be clear that there are resources within Biblical faith for meeting these situations, facing up to them, living with them, and transforming them by faith, rather than being transformed by them into despair. The job of the Christian is not to have a "ready answer" for every situation, but to have a total approach to life, gained from encounter with God, that enables him to live with, and conquer, every situation.

On the One Hand
... On the Other Hand

(Who Am I?)

When the hall of philosophy in a large university was being built, there was a controversy over the inscription to be carved above the main entrance. One group wanted the statement of Protagoras, "Man is the measure of all things." Another group held out for the words of the Eighth Psalm, addressed to God, "What is man that thou art mindful of him?"

There is all the difference in the world between those two conceptions of man. In the first, man is the center of everything. In the second, God is the center of everything. Who is right? What *is* man?

A Question You Can't Avoid

Don't think that the question "What is man?" is academic or unimportant. It is a question you ask all the time, and can't help asking. Each of the following questions is no more than a specialized way of asking: "What is man? Who am I? What makes us all tick?"

"Is it O.K. to neck on a date?"
"How can I be happy?"
"Why can't I do as I please?"

"How can we avoid World War III?"

"Why is it so hard to do the 'right' thing?"

"Why do I have to go to school?"

"What's wrong with Communism?"

"Why does my geometry teacher dislike me so much?"

Since we can't avoid this question, here is our "plan of attack" for coming to grips with it. First, we will take a sampling of answers to the question that are on the market today. Then for the rest of this chapter we will look at two parts of the Biblical answer, and in the next chapter we will look at a third part, which is so important that it must have a chapter all to itself. Finally, we will look at man-in-community, in the church. In this way we can see whether the Biblical answer makes sense or not, and also how it stacks up with other answers.

Some Current Answers — a Dime a Dozen

One very popular answer these days is that *we are made for the State.* It is only as we serve the State that we achieve our destiny. This is the Hitler-Mussolini-Stalin answer to the question, and since the Kremlin has forced it on millions of people in our lifetime, we cannot simply laugh it off. There is, of course, truth in the idea that we cannot live simply to ourselves, and must give our allegiance to something greater than ourselves. Where the answer is open to serious question, however, is in its assertion that the State is to be our highest object of loyalty. (We shall push this a little farther in Chapter 22.)

Some people claim that *we are made for happiness.* We are created to have a good time, the best possible time we can. People who believe this aren't necessarily selfish, since they can argue that the best way to have a good time is to help other people have a good time—that by bringing pleasure to others, you will find happiness yourself. The chief problem here is,

What do you mean by "happiness"? And for a great many people it will mean physical comfort—a nice house, good clothes, a 21-inch TV, and a new car. And we must ask whether people's lives necessarily have deeper and fuller meaning just because they have nice houses, good clothes, 21-inch TV's, and new cars. Their lives may be emptier than ever.

Other people answer the question by saying, "We're only human"—by which they seem to mean that *we are highly developed animals,* but nothing more. Ideas about love, or God, or self-sacrifice, are only wishful thinking—attempts to escape from the unpleasant fact that we are "earthbound." Much better, the argument goes, to face up to the fact and make the best of it. Notice that this answer is as dogmatic as that of the most unyielding theology. And we must surely ask whether there is not, after all, a basic difference between an animal's shelter and a cathedral; between the beast's cry of fear and a symphony; between the meal of an animal and the sacrament of the Lord's Supper.

The thing that is significant about these and other answers to the question "What is man?" is not that they are totally false, but that they are incomplete. We owe some allegiance to the State—but we owe other allegiances as well. "Happiness" may be a part of that for which we are created—but we are created for self-sacrifice as well. We are part animal, and must have food and drink and sleep to stay alive—but food and drink and sleep and nothing else would soon bore us to tears, because there is more to us than merely animal desire. And so we could continue with other current answers.

Let us therefore look at the Biblical answer and see if it does not give us a more fully satisfactory description of our human situation.

The First Part of the Biblical Answer

On the one hand, the Bible tells us that *God has created us for fellowship with him.* This idea is most clearly developed in the early portions of Genesis. In Chapter 4 we discussed the interpretation of these Creation stories. We saw that they are not accounts of our great-great-great-great-great-great (to the nth degree) grandparents. These stories, set in a particular point in time, are stories that are true about every point in time. Whatever they may tell us about someone else's ancient past, they tell us infinitely more about our own living present. They describe *us*. The Hebrew word *ad-ham*, for example, from which we get "Adam," is not a proper name for an individual. It is simply the word for "man"—every man—just as "Eve" simply means "woman"—every woman. What is true of Adam and Eve (of "man" and "woman") is true of us all as well. We are not reading ancient history. We are reading "our" story as it is put in pictorial form.

What Is the "Image of God"?

What do we learn about ourselves from these stories? We learn, first of all, that we have been created "in the image of God." This is a difficult thing to understand, but we must shed as much light on it as we can. It does not mean that we *are* God. That would be an intolerable notion to the Biblical writers. We are, however, made in God's "image" or "likeness." We are *something* like God, even though we are not *just* like God.

For example, God is creative. He makes and sustains the world. He makes and sustains us. And we too are creative. We create everything from poetry and music and democratic forms of government to mosquito netting, typewriters, and double fudge sundaes with nuts on top. Furthermore, men and women have a responsible part in the creation of new human life, as they marry and have children. As we look at creativity in human life we can see, as a kind of blurred image, something of what creativity is for God—with this significant difference, that we create because the creative impulse has been planted in us by God and is dependent upon him, whereas God creates because it is his nature to create, and he is dependent upon no one.

Another way of interpreting the "image of God" is to think of a *reflection*, such as you see in a mirror. When you look at your reflection in a mirror, it is something *like* you, and yet it is not truly *you*, even though it can give you a pretty good idea of what you look like. Furthermore, the image is completely dependent upon you. If you move away from the mirror—no more image. It cannot exist independently. This reminds us of an important fact about our relationship with God. We are dependent upon him, just as the image in the mirror is dependent upon us. If God were to depart completely from us, we would cease to be, just as the image in the mirror ceases to be if you go into another room.

Some Consequences

The notion that we are created in the image of God underlines both our greatness and our littleness. It underlines our *greatness*, since according to this view we occupy a unique place in God's creation. Only man has been created in the image of God. All else is to be in his control, to be used by him for the glory of God (Ps. 8: 6, 7). Man has a special significance because God is "mindful of him" and has "made him little less than God," and "dost crown him with glory and honor" (vs. 4, 5). There is something unique about being a human being. At the same time, the belief underlines our *littleness*, for it reminds us that we are dependent upon God for our very life itself. (Remember the mirror.) We did not make ourselves. We cannot completely rule ourselves. We can understand ourselves only as we admit that we are dependent upon our Creator—and this is something that it is difficult and unpleasant to admit.

Notice one other thing about being created in the image of God. It means that we are *responsible* beings. We can decide what we will do. And if the Bible is right, God places us here, and gives us the freedom to choose him or reject him. There is nothing automatic about it. We are not "guided missiles," completely under the whim of the person sitting at the control switch. We make our own decisions.

We have the terrible gift of freedom.

Terrible—because although we can choose to love God, we can also choose to reject God. We can say "No" as well as "Yes." And even though God has created us to enter into fellowship with him, he will not force this upon us, because love cannot be forced. It must be freely given. We have the chance, then, to fulfill our destiny by loving God and living as his children (which is the purpose of our creation). Or, we have the chance to repudiate our destiny by saying: "No, it's too hard. I don't want it that way. I'd rather love myself. I'll shut God out."

The Second Part of the Biblical Answer

Which brings us to the second thing the Bible says about us —that although on the one hand we are created by God for fellowship with him, on the other hand *we have rejected that fellowship*. We have had the chance to say yes to God's offer of love and fellowship, and we have chosen to say no. Instead of making God the center of our lives, we have chosen to make ourselves the center of our lives.

This is a roundabout way of describing what the Bible bluntly calls "sin." "Sin" is a rather unpopular word these days. Part of the trouble arises because our conventional notion of "sin" is very different from the Biblical notion. A typical list of "Sunday school sins" might go something like this:

smoking
drinking
playing cards
going to the movies on Sunday
being too interested in sex.

We shall discover that from the Biblical viewpoint this is a superficial analysis, and doesn't get to the heart of the matter at all.

What Sin Is

How, then, does the Bible understand sin? Once again, the Genesis story, which is "our" story, gives us our best clue. Moving ahead to Gen., ch. 3, we find that man is tempted. And what is the temptation? It is the temptation to play the part of God:

You will be like God, knowing good and evil (Gen. 3: 5).

"You will be like God"—there is the fundamental temptation. We are created to live as God's children and make him the center of our life, and instead we want to play the part of God ourselves. Sin, in other words, is centered in an act of *rebellion*. We rebel against submitting to God. We want to run the show.

Let's translate that idea into our language, and see if this is not, indeed, "our" story:

"My life's my own; nobody's going to tell me how to behave."

"What's in it for me?"

"I'll do as I darn well please."

"You gotta look out for Number One."

"I know just what I want to get out of life, and I'm jolly well going to get it."

When I say such things, I make it plain that the center of my life is "I." This is what sin is—making "I" the center of life rather than God. It is insisting upon *my* will rather than God's will; it is thinking primarily about myself. But I was not created to think primarily about myself. I was created to love and serve God. And rather than doing this, I say: "I will play the part of God in my life. I will be the center of things."

And even if I get sanctimonious about it (look that word up sometime) and assert that I am only trying to do God's will, I find that I have an uncanny ability to make God's will coincide with what I wanted to do all along. I am still at the center.

This is something that is uniquely possible to me as a man, because I have a freedom which can be abused. A tree does not "sin"; neither does a tiger or a turtle or a tomtit. But I do, because I have potentialities that the tree and tiger and turtle and tomtit do not have, and I rebel against using them as I should. Having a chance to love God, I choose to love myself. And in so doing, I separate myself from God.

Now the unhappy consequence of separating myself from God is that I thereby separate myself from my fellow men as well. If I do not accept the fact that I am created for the high destiny of fellowship with God, I am not likely to feel that Bill Jones is created for that destiny either. If he is not a child of God, but a child of dust, then I do not need to worry too much about him, or about what happens to him. If the opportunity arises, I will try to "use" him—manipulate him to my own advantage. He becomes a "thing." I am separated from Bill Jones, just as I am separated from Fred Smith and John Brown, and just as (by the same token) all the Joneses, Smiths, and Browns are separated from each other. We are all trying to "play the part of God" against each other, to "lord it over" each other, and we turn out to be pretty poor at playing God's role.

And the result is disaster.

Once more, the story in Genesis underlines "our" story. The consequence of rebellion in Genesis was expulsion from the "Garden of Eden." In our day the consequence of rebellion is the whole dislocation of human life. Our earth, which could be an Eden, is for great numbers of people a living hell.

I look at life in terms of my own interests.	This nation looks after its own interests.
You look at life in terms of yours.	So does that nation.
We clash.	They clash.

All the way up and down the scale we find that the same difficulty is at the root of our trouble.

Supplying Some Documentation

Now this is not a particularly pleasant conclusion. We don't like the notion that there is something radically wrong with us. We would much prefer to believe that the difficulty can be cured with a little tinkering. Surely the Bible isn't so pessimistic! But the Bible gives us little comfort if we try to escape from this conclusion. Take a brief run down.

Isaiah not only recognizes that he is a man of unclean lips, but acknowledges that he dwells among a people of unclean lips (Isa. 6: 5). A later prophet points out that "all our righteous deeds are like a polluted garment" (Isa. 64:6). Jeremiah reminds us that "the heart is deceitful above all things, and desperately corrupt" (Jer. 17: 9). Nor is Jesus any easier on us. He reminds us that "out of the heart of man, come evil thoughts, fornication, theft, murder, adultery, coveting, wickedness, deceit, licentiousness, envy, slander, pride, foolishness" (Mark 7: 21, 22). The words he speaks to the Pharisees are addressed to all of us: "You are like whitewashed tombs, which outwardly appear beautiful, but within they are full of dead men's bones and all uncleanness" (Matt. 23: 27). He tells us, "When you have done all that is commanded you, say, 'We are unworthy servants'" (Luke 17: 10). Paul picks up the refrain, "None is righteous, no, not one" (Rom. 3: 10; see Ps. 14: 1, 2). Over and over again we are told that *even our highest achievements* are corrupted.

This is only a sampling. And it strikes a harsh note which we do not like. And yet this is the Biblical reading of our plight. Notice that it is not the case that we are as bad as we can be, for in that case we should not even know that we were bad. It is rather that we are something good that has been spoiled. So although we are made in the image of God, the "image" has become very badly distorted.

We can clarify this by a final insight from our mirror analogy. Rather than seeing our reflection in a perfect mirror, we now see our reflection as it appears in one of the mirrors at an amusement park. In such mirrors the glass is bent and the image is distorted. In one mirror we are two feet tall and three feet wide. In another we are nine feet tall and six inches wide. In a third we are just a blob of face, and mostly nose at that. The image has been distorted, twisted and spoiled, almost beyond recognition. That is the way we now stand in relation to God. The image of God in us has been distorted, twisted and spoiled, almost beyond recognition.

What Sin Is Not

On the basis of this understanding of sin as
   rebellion
      against God
         which separates us
            from God
               and man
                  and defaces the "image of God" within us, we can see the inadequacy of some of the more conventional interpretations of sin.

Sin is not simply ignorance. Against those who assert that we do the wrong because we don't know any better, and that once we know what is right we will do it, must be set the more profound assertion of Paul:

I can will what is right, but I cannot do it. For I do not do the good I want, but the evil I do not want is what I do (Rom. 7: 18, 19).

The problem is precisely that we so often choose the evil when we know very well what is good.

Sin is not simply the legacy of our "animal" origins. As Dostoevsky points out, that's an insult to the animals. Animals may kill other animals, but they never nail people up by the ears or cremate them in concentration camps while they are still alive. Man can be much more fiendishly clever in his wickedness than an animal can ever be.

Sin is not simply our "physical" impulses conquering our "spiritual" impulses. This is the commonest misunderstanding of the Biblical view. The Bible does not make the distinction between "body" and "soul" that we are inclined to do. In Biblical thought, man is a complex *unity*—not, say, a soul inhabiting a body. (See further Chapter 17.) When Paul talks about the "flesh," he does not mean evil physical impulses that stand opposed to good spiritual impulses. He means rather our *total humanity* as such, our moral and religious life just as much as our sensual passions. The point is well brought out in one of his lists of the "works of the flesh." He includes things like

> idolatry,
> strife,
> enmity,
> jealousy,
> anger,
> selfishness,
> dissension,
> party spirit,
> envy, and the like,

as well as the more obvious "sins" of

> immorality,
> impurity,
> drunkenness,
> licentiousness,
> carousing, and the like.
>   (Gal. 5: 19-21)

Perhaps now we can see why the "Sunday school sins" are superficial. In the Bible sin is a fundamental dislocation of the *whole* of life. At its very center life is wrenched apart in such a way that all of it is affected and distorted. Sin, rather than being a series of specific acts, is a condition of life on all its levels. Getting drunk, for example, is not so much a sin in itself as it is an indication that something has gone wrong and that life has become profoundly disrupted at its very center.

The person who cannot handle his relationships with other people, or who is afraid to face himself as he really is, may get drunk to escape from the harsh real world which he feels unequipped to handle, into a pleasant make-believe world of his own creation where he is king of all he surveys. His getting drunk, in that case, is only a symptom of a more profound disorder.

The source of our sin, then, is not found in our ignorance, or in a "carry-over" from our animal origins, or in our physical impulses. It is found in the fact that we abuse the freedom which God has given us. The thing that ought to make us great—the fact that we are free, responsible creatures—is the very thing that makes us such a problem to ourselves. We use our freedom in the wrong way. We say no to God, rather than yes.

As a result, we are so enmeshed in wrongdoing that we can't set the situation right ourselves.

Getting Straightened Out

To say this usually evokes a vigorous response.

VIGOROUS RESPONDER: Did you say, "We can't set the situation right ourselves"? What defeatist talk! Certainly we can set the situation right, if we are just determined enough. We will try specially hard to do what we should. We will do *more* than we usually do. If pride is our problem, we will be very, very humble before God. And in time the surplus of good will overcome the deficit of evil from the past. Don't tell us that we're powerless. We're going to lick this thing ourselves!

Actually, this only makes the situation worse. Our problem is that we "think more highly of ourselves than we ought to think." We must stop being proud and arrogant, and become humble. When we recognize this, we say to ourselves, "We will strive with all our might to be humble." And what happens? To the extent that we succeed, we become aware of how humble we are, and, try as we will, we are unable to avoid the conclusion that it is pretty grand of us to be so humble. We really have been *very* good about it—much better than a lot of people we know. God must be pleased at the splendid character of our humility.

What has happened? We have become proud of being humble. But does recognition of this solve our problem? No, even as we become aware of this fact, we are in danger of being proud of the fact that we recognized that we were proud of being humble.

We are caught, and we seem doomed to remain caught. We cannot escape.

Unless, of course, God should decide to help us.

A Full Scale
Reconstruction Job

(How Can I Be Changed?)

... The Bible says that God *has* decided to help us.

It says that where we are powerless to save ourselves, God saves us.

It says that when we cannot set ourselves right, God sets us right. If you are clear on all that, you can skip this chapter.

Budding Angel or Hopeless Sinner?

Let us review our situation. On the one hand the Bible claims that man is made in the image of God, for fellowship with him. We have great possibilities. This is the "optimistic" side of the picture. On the other hand, the Bible claims that we have spoiled these possibilities. We have defaced the image of God. We are sinners. This is the "pessimistic" side of the picture.

Many people grab ahold of one of these affirmations and act as if it were the whole truth. Thus you will hear some people talk about man in a way that would make you think we are already sprouting wings. And you will hear others talk so exclusively about sin that you will think Christianity consists of reminding us (rather gleefully) that we are bad as we can be, period. It is important, therefore, to remember that the Bible recognizes both the optimistic and the pessimistic side. Neither one stands by itself. Both are needed.

But even that is not the whole story. That would be saying, "We have tremendous possibilities, but we have lost them, and cannot recover them." And that would leave the last word on the side of pessimism. We need to remember that the last word, from the Biblical perspective, is not a bleak pessimism any more than it is a naïve optimism. The Bible indeed affirms "the sinfulness of sin," but not as the end of the story. For if the Bible seems to be pessimistic about man, it is never pessimistic about God, and what God can do with man, and make of man. Just as a doctor needs to know what the illness is before he attempts a cure, and just as the kind of cure will be determined by the nature of the illness, so it has been important for us to see the nature of our human "illness" in order that we could understand the radical "cure" which Biblical faith says is possible.

The Third Part of the Biblical Answer

Consequently, there is a third affirmation about man which the Bible stresses. If we are created for fellowship with God, and if we have rejected that fellowship, it is also true that *God has provided a way for the fellowship to be restored.* This is what makes the Christian faith "good" news. Without this, it would only be "bad" news. The "good" news is that the separation between God and ourselves which we cannot overcome has been overcome for us by God, and that he freely offers us a brand-new relationship with him.

This is a roundabout way of describing such Biblical words as "salvation," "redemption," "reconciliation," and "grace." While these are not precisely identical in meaning, they all describe the same fundamental experience, and represent the heart and core of Biblical faith. We must try to understand what is at stake here, for in one way or another all of us ask the question to which these words offer an answer. We ask it in different ways:

How can I be changed?

How can I stop being so self-centered?

What must I do to be saved?

Who will deliver me from this body of death?

How can I find some meaning for my life?

The First Step

In John's teaching, Jesus' teaching, Paul's letters, Peter's sermons, we find again and again the word "repent." As we have seen previously, the word means to "turn about," "begin again," "make a fresh start." This is a pretty universal starting point in the process of being changed. It is not pleasant, for it involves admitting that we have been wrong, and nobody likes to do that. (And even if we have been "a little bit wrong," we certainly haven't been as wrong as *some* people we could mention. Why should *we* be the ones to admit that we've been wrong? Why doesn't somebody else do it first?) We shy away from this first step, and invent reasons to postpone it. It is something like going to the dentist; we snatch at any fleeting excuse for postponing the evil day.

As long as we do this, of course, we shall still be involved in our plight. As long as we refuse to admit that there is anything wrong with us, it is impossible for us to be made well. Repentance, then, involves our willingness to *admit our need*. It involves saying in effect: "I have made a botch of things. I need help."

After the First Step

What happens then? The amazing thing, the totally unexpected thing, is that even though we are "in the wrong" before God, he forgives us and empowers us to live new lives. He accepts us as we are. He does not say, "Go out and prove how good you can be, and then come back, and perhaps we'll reconsider your case." No, he says: "Right now, just as you are, I accept you. There is no longer any barrier between us. I will enter into as close a relationship with you as you will let me."

How does the Christian know that this astounding claim is true? How can he "bank on it"? Because this is what the New Testament is all about. For there we do not find simply a statement about this kind of love, but an enactment of it. Looking at Christ from the point of our need, we see in him the embodiment of this kind of love. We see in him God's outgoing love coming to us when we could not get to him, entering into our experience, refusing to hate people even when people hated him, loving them to the bitter end, even death upon the cross. And so Christian faith says: "*That* is God's love, coming to you just as you are, not waiting till you are worthy, but meeting you precisely at the point of your unworthiness. Simply believe that God is like that. Simply believe that God has taken the initiative in seeking you, that you are already forgiven if you will accept the gift of forgiveness which he offers you."

This accepting us as we are makes a tremendous difference. It makes, in fact, all the difference, because it now means that relationship is possible. I can enter into relationship with God *now*. I do not have to wait until some distant day when I become "good enough." We can see the significance of this in the relationship between parents and children. If your parents never entered into relationship with you except when you were "being good," you wouldn't have very much to do with each other. The thing that is most significant about parental love (at its highest and best) is that it is not a love that is dependent upon being deserved. It is strongest just at those times when there is least "reason" for it:

> ... when you have smashed the left fender and headlight of the family car the day before you were all going to the lake, and you feel absolutely sick about it;

... or when you are a mass of ugly blotches (chicken pox) and want to crawl away and hide forever;

... or when you get home after striking out in the ninth inning with the winning run on third, and can never go back to school again.

These are the times when you think: How can anybody love me? I'm a total flop. And these are the times when you find that your parents love you—at the unexpected times, when it is clear that they love you, not because you have done something to deserve their love, but simply because you are you and they love you just as you are—in all your misery and unhappiness.

Well, the love of God is something like that. Infinitely more, of course, but of that sort. It is love that is undeserved, reaching out to you, right where you are, offering itself without reserve, to meet your need.

So the establishment of the new relationship is the work of God. C. S. Lewis puts the point graphically in his fairy story, *The Voyage of the Dawn Treader:*

A nasty specimen of humanity, called Eustace Scrubb, is so thoroughly nasty that he is changed into a dragon. After a while he discovers that it is not much fun being a dragon, and that it is actually not much fun being nasty to everyone else. So he begins to help rather than to hinder his shipmates (who are stranded on an island after a bad storm).

But he can't get rid of his dragon skin.

It just won't come off, no matter how hard he works at it. It is only possible for him to be changed back to his rightful form when he consents to let Aslan, the lion who is king of the beasts, use his claws to scratch off the terrible scales. Eustace the dragon cannot save himself. He can be saved only by something that the king of his creation can do for him. His emancipation is a gift— not something he was able to achieve himself.

So, too, in the Bible, the new relationship (which the Bible calls "salvation") is a sheer gift. It is not earned, it is not deserved, it is not anything that I can claim as a "right." I am brought into new relationship with God, not because I am good (which I am not), but because God loves me in spite of the fact that I am not good. It is the side of love that is so "new," so unexpected, in Christian faith. Paul points out that it would be quite astonishing for a man to die on behalf of a good man. That would be a real test of his love. But what an unprecedented kind of love, he goes on, when Christ dies for men who are not even good, who are unworthy. Christ dies for us while we are yet sinners (Rom. 5: 8: see also the end of Chapter 10 above), and that shows the lengths to which true love is ready to go. God loves the undeserving. Unexpected news, indeed!

The Heart of the Matter

Let us sum this up as briefly as we can. There is a phrase by Paul Tillich that puts the whole matter in two lines. It goes this way:

You are accepted. All you have to do is to accept the fact that you are accepted.

You are accepted, just as you are. You need not "prove" yourself, or strive frantically to achieve God's recognition. You are accepted right now. What, then, must you do? Merely accept this fact. Merely begin to live as though this were true.

This is another way of describing what the Bible means by "justification by faith." It is what Paul discovered, what Martin Luther rediscovered, what Christians in every age have found to be the transforming fact in their so-far unfulfilled lives. It is the gift of salvation, of new life.

Our Response

Where does all this lead? It leads to transformation:

If you are accepted by *God* just as you are, then you can accept *yourself* just as you are; and if you can accept yourself just as you are, then you can accept *other people* just as they are.

Relationship is once more a possibility. You are no longer isolated and separated (as you were in Chapter 13). You are now free to love, and that is what you were created for. This time we can sum up the whole matter in *one* line:

We love, because he first loved us (I John 4: 19).

How does this gift which has been given to us resolve our problem of self-centeredness and pride? We discover that this gift is of a kind that cannot possibly feed our pride. We do not deserve it, and yet God gives it to us. There is no possible ground for patting ourselves on the back. Our response can only be one of *gratitude*, gratitude to God for so great a gift of love. (See further, Chapter 18.) Our "righteousness" is the righteousness of Christ, who has broken down the barrier of our pride by becoming humble himself, in order that he may exalt us. (Remember Paul? "I live; yet not I, but Christ liveth in me.") And as long as we remain humble (which is not a fake attitude of thinking we're pretty good because we claim we aren't, but an honest recognition of how we stand in relation to God)—as long as we remain humble—God can constantly invade our lives, and continually become more real to us. A Biblical insight, which pops up in various places, can drive this fact home. It goes like this: "God opposes the proud, but gives grace to the humble" (James 4: 6; I Peter 5: 5; cf. Prov. 3: 34).

In our new situation, then, we must take seriously Paul's advice, "Let him who boasts, boast of the Lord" (I Cor. 1: 31). What we are we owe to him and to his love, not our own cleverness and goodness. He has worked the revolution in our lives. Let Jeremiah, finally, clinch our understanding of the attitude of the "new person" who has accepted God's gift of new life:

Let not the wise man glory in his wisdom, let not the mighty man glory in his might, let not the rich man glory in his riches; but let him who glories glory in this, that he understands and knows me, that I am the Lord who practice kindness, justice, and righteousness in the earth; for in these things I delight, says the Lord (Jer. 9: 23, 24).

Not Once and for All

Some people assume that this happens "just like that." (To get the effect, snap your fingers as you read "that.") For them the moment of clarification is sudden. Usually it takes people a long time. But for no one is the event or long series of events (usually called "conversion") the end of the road. It is simply the beginning of a new road. Paul talks about "pressing on." He recognizes, correctly, that we do not "arrive," that we do not reach (in this life at any rate) the *full* achievement of Christian living. That is why it is more correct to speak of "becoming" a Christian, than of "being" a Christian.

The Bible calls this ongoing process "sanctification." This sounds like a forbidding word, but it is not hard to understand if you have had a smattering of high school Latin. The word breaks down into *sanctus* (holy) and *ficare* (to make). "Sanctification" is thus the process of becoming more holy, or as Christians sometimes put it, "growing in grace." It doesn't happen overnight. It isn't easy. It can never be claimed as an achievement. But the thing that makes it supremely worth-while is that on this pilgrimage the Christian realizes that he isn't alone any more. He is being helped.

Some Hints for Growing—Tried and Tested

How does one "grow in grace"? How does one become more "holy"? There are no spectacular answers, no "seven rules for success," no simple formulas for "being good," regardless of what "popular" books on religion may tell you. But there are certain things that have emerged out of the experience of the "people of God" which sooner or later should ring a bell for you. Here are a few of them.

1. It is the experience of Christians that as you live with the Bible, God does "step forth" from time to time, and meet you

in personal encounter. Perhaps that language is too spectacular at this stage of the game. Perhaps it should just be said that when Christians, perplexed about doing the will of God, live close to their Bibles, they find that God's will becomes clarified. This does not mean flipping through the pages looking for a magic proof text to tell you what to say in that dreadful interview next Tuesday. It means simply that the more you expose yourself to the way God acts and does things in the Bible, the more real God becomes, and the more chance there is for him to make his way into your heart. It is a fact—not just a pious hope—that the longer you live with the Bible the more possibility there is that the God of the Bible can become real in your life. This involves good, hard study, as you try to find out what a particular passage means. But just study will not be enough. You must always go on to ask the further question, "What does this passage say to me, right here and now?" (See further, Chapter 1.)

2. It is the experience of Christians that as you pray you are not merely talking to yourself, but that through prayer there can be a deepening of the relationship between yourself and God. Since God is truly interested in establishing personal relationship with you, prayer is not something "spooky." It follows naturally that prayer is a fruitful means for establishing this relationship more fully. This is true of the great men of the Bible who have been close to God. Abraham, Moses, David, Isaiah, Jeremiah, the psalmists—for none of these was God just an "idea" about which they had heard. He was the living God with whom they were able to enter into personal relationship. And "personal relationship" is just another way of describing what is suggested by the word "prayer." The preeminent example in the Bible is Jesus himself. He rises early in the morning to pray. He prays at mealtime, in the Garden of Gethsemane, upon the cross. He is at all times in the constant relationship with God that is the heart of true living. And no life can be full if this element is lacking.

3. It is the experience of Christians that faith and conviction grow and deepen as they are tested, as you "go out on a limb" for something you believe in. The promise is that when you take a stand in the name of your faith, you find that you are not alone, but that God is with you, reaching out to hold you up and give you courage sufficient for the occasion. This does not mean that life becomes a bed of roses, but that, whatever comes, there are resources available for coping with the situation.

4. Finally, it is the experience of Christians that to be part of a community of worship is to grow in grace. The Christian life is a particularly rocky road for the individual, and the path is made smoother by the knowledge that there are others walking it too. You would not think of trying to scale the Matterhorn by yourself. You try such a task as a member of a group. So it is in the Christian conquest. To share in the experience of corporate worship—to confess together our sins, to hear together the words of pardon, to praise God together in song, to listen together to the reading and expounding of the Word of God—to share these experiences is to have the lives of all who participate enriched. Particularly is this true in the service of the Lord's Supper, the high point of the life of the worshiping community. All these experiences indicate that the Christian life is not a life of isolation but a life of community and sharing. We have never fully answered the question "What is man?" until we have recognized this fact. Man in community —as a member of the worshiping fellowship—is the only *complete* picture of man that we can sketch. This is why our understanding of man will not be complete until we have taken another chapter to discuss this community, the Church, in which man finds his fulfillment.

A Final Warning

Before that, however, a final warning must be sounded. "Growing in grace" is not a path straight to perfection. Quite the contrary. The Christian is one who realizes that he *always* stands in need of God's forgiveness and grace, to the very last moment of his life. Paul has seen this clearly:

> For I delight in the law of God, in my inmost self, but I see in my members another law at war with the law of my mind and making me captive to the law of sin which dwells in my members. Wretched man that I am! Who will deliver me from this body of death? Thanks be to God through Jesus Christ our Lord! So then, I of myself serve the law of God with my mind, but with my flesh I serve the law of sin (Rom. 7: 22-25).

Notice that the quotation does *not* end when Paul is delivered from "this body of death." Even *after* his deliverance, Paul does wrong. He still serves "the law of sin." Paul is very perceptive about this. It would be too simple to say that the battle is won once and never needs to be waged again. It is a battle that is always being waged, a battle in which we cannot relax our defenses.

But it is a battle that is a glorious battle, because as Martin Luther put it in "A Mighty Fortress Is Our God," "the right Man [is] on our side, the Man of God's own choosing:

> "Dost ask who that may be?
> Christ Jesus, it is He."

"But Surely You Don't Go to Church!"

(Why Isn't "Individual Religion" Enough?)

Many people will go part way with the Bible. They would deal with a multiple choice test in this fashion:

Instructions: underscore appropriate answer

1. There is a God......................... <u>yes</u> no
2. God is concerned about man .... <u>yes</u> no
3. God is creator, judge, redeemer .... <u>yes</u> no
4. God is revealed in Jesus Christ .... <u>yes</u> no
5. God demands obedience .... <u>yes</u> no
6. One who believes these things must be active in the church .... yes <u>no</u>

At item 6, the protests would begin.

The Case Against the Church—
a Bagful of Objections

Why are so many people hostile to the church? Let us list some of the common objections, before we look at the Biblical understanding of the church. Then, at the end of the chapter, we can see the objections in perspective. Here is a starter.

I don't like the church because:

... the people in it are so hypocritical

... it's full of old maids of both sexes

... it doesn't *do* anything

... you have to be so pious to belong

... I don't believe God has "office hours" on Sunday
     morning

... the churches are always fighting among themselves

... I can't stand the horrible anthems the choir sings

... I'm more interested in this world than in heaven

... the church is always fifty years behind the times

... it's doing things that counts, not pulling a long face on
     Sunday

... religion is an individual matter

... ministers don't practice what they preach

(The space is left for objections of your own. If you
     need more room, write in the margin.)

Some of these objections are valid and some are foolish. But
every one of them is commonly heard.

When Did the Church Get Started?

Before we let the critics have the last word, let us turn to the
Bible and find out something about this maligned institution.
First of all, when did the Church get started? The conventional
answer goes:

Q. What is the birthday of the Church?

A. Pentecost.

Q. Very good. Next question . . .

Even when you look up "Pentecost" in the dictionary and find
that it refers to the occasion when the disciples were empowered by the Holy Spirit (Acts, ch. 2), you must refuse to
be completely satisfied. For who were these disciples? Before
the cross and resurrection, they were a community united by

their common commitment to Jesus of Nazareth. Do not the real roots of the church lie here? Yes and no, for this, in its turn, was not a brand-new community. All these men, Jesus included, belonged to various synagogue communities scattered across Palestine; they were already members of the worshiping community of the Jewish nation. So the beginning of the Church must be pushed back through the history of that Jewish nation, back to Old Testament times, to the formation of the "covenant relationship" (we'll get to that in a minute) between Israel and God, when the Jewish people became "the people of God." Their beginning lies on the very edge of recorded history, when Abraham, responding to the call of God, migrated from Ur to Canaan. Here is the beginning of "the people of God." The Christian community, the church, has its roots way back in the earliest history of the Jewish people.

Just What Is a "Covenant"?

The word "covenant" crept into the last paragraph. We must take a moment to understand this word, since it is very important. When the Bible talks of a covenant *between two people*, it means an "agreement" or a "binding." Each party promises to be faithful to his side of the bargain, and if party A is unfaithful, party B is released from his obligation.

But the Bible also talks of a covenant agreement *between God and his people Israel*. This is not an agreement between equals but between a superior (God) and an inferior (Israel). God takes the initiative and chooses Israel, and then Israel can respond, and in so doing is bound to God in a unique and inseparable way. The most significant instance of such a covenant agreement is the one made at Sinai (Ex. 24: 3-8), at which time the Israelites promise to give exclusive allegiance to God and to be obedient to his will while God promises that the Israelites will remain his chosen people. Later on, the covenant is renewed. (Josh., ch. 24, for example.) But it is also broken.

The people drift away from God, or they worship other gods. Thus Israel breaks its side of the covenant agreement.

But God does not! This is the astounding thing—God remains faithful. Choosing Israel out of sheer grace—for Israel was in no sense "worthy" of the privilege—God remains faithful to Israel even when Israel is faithless. God has set his heart on Israel. He cannot give it up. When he would have every right to throw Israel overboard, he says:

> My heart recoils within me,
> my compassion grows warm and tender.
> I will not execute my fierce anger,
> I will not again destroy Ephraim;
> for I am God and not man,
> the Holy One in your midst,
> and I will not come to destroy.
> (Hos. 11: 8, 9)

The "New Covenant" Becomes a Possibility

The prophet Jeremiah speaks of the future possibility of a new covenant. This covenant will not be based on keeping a set of rules, like the Sinai covenant and its subsequent renewals. Rather, in this new covenant, God will put his law "in their inward parts, and write it in their hearts." A new relationship with God will thus be possible, something brought about, not by man's goodness, but by God's action in reaching out toward man. It will be possible because God forgives:

They shall all know me, from the least of them unto the greatest of them, saith the Lord: for I will forgive their iniquity, and I will remember their sin no more (Jer. 31: 34).

The "New Covenant" Becomes a Reality

This remains, throughout the Old Testament, a future possibility. The New Testament claims that the Christian Church is the new covenant community in actuality. In the earliest account we have of the Last Supper, Jesus says, "This cup is the *new covenant* in my blood" (I Cor. 11: 25). And in the earliest of the Gospels, Jesus says, "This is my blood of the covenant, which is poured out for many" (Mark 14: 24). (A few early manuscripts have, "This is my blood of the *new* covenant. . . .")

Notice carefully what this implies. The new covenant is no longer way off in the future. It is right here, now, being realized. It will become a reality through Jesus' death, which the meal with the disciples is dramatizing in advance.

This is precisely what the early Christians found to be true. Through the death (and the resurrection) of Jesus a new relationship to God became a reality. A new covenant community came into being, consisting of those who gave their allegiance to this Jesus Christ. For them, the old Israel was continued in this new community. Christians referred to themselves as the "new Israel" or "true Israel of God" (Gal. 6: 16; I Peter 2: 9; Rom. 9: 27, 28; Heb. 8: 1-12; Eph. 2: 4-10). Paul expressly links up the purpose of the Church with the new covenant:

> Not that we are sufficient of ourselves to claim anything as coming from us; our sufficiency is from God, who has qualified us to be ministers of a *new covenant*, not in written code but in the Spirit; for the written code kills, but the Spirit gives life (II Cor. 3: 5, 6; italics added).

From first to last, then, the Bible is a book about community. Those who enter into relationship with God do so as part of a community, not simply as individuals. Biblical religion finds its highest expression in corporate community life.

Those Words of Jesus to Peter

What is Jesus' relationship to the new Christian community? Did he leave any provision for its development? To answer these questions we must look at one of the most controversial verses in the New Testament. Jesus says, at Caesarea Philippi:

> I tell you, you are Peter, and on this rock I will build my church, and the powers of death shall not prevail against it (Matt. 16: 18).

One of the most fundamental differences between Protestants and Roman Catholics hinges on how this verse is interpreted. The Roman Catholic says: Here Jesus gives Peter unique power as the head of the Church; Peter is the rock on which it is built. Peter transmits this power to his successor, and that successor to his successor, and so on in unbroken succession, right down to the present pope. Only where the pope is honored as the vicar of Christ on earth does Christ's Church truly exist. Any Church that does not so honor the pope is not part of the true Church.

The Protestant way of putting it will take a little longer:

1. Some Protestants feel that the words did not come from the lips of Jesus, but were added later. It seems clear to them that if the whole future of Christendom depended on the idea this verse expresses, it would have been mentioned more than once (the other Gospels all omit the verse). This, of course, is only negative reasoning from silence and is not conclusive by itself.

2. Many more Protestant scholars will grant that Jesus spoke the words. But remember, they go on, the context of the statement. Jesus has asked, "Who do you say that I am?" and Peter has replied, "You are the Christ." So the crucial question is: What is the "rock" upon which the Church is to be built? The Protestant holds that the "rock" is Peter's declaration that "Jesus is the Christ." Where that faith is present, there is the Church. Thus the verse is to be interpreted, "You are Peter, and on this rock [of your faith in me] I will build my church."

Note to the careful reader: This interpretation was the common one in the Early Church. Among the Early Church Fathers, 44 understood the verse in this way, and only 17 took the "rock" to be Peter himself. After the fourth century and during the Middle Ages, the predominant interpretation shifted, but the Reformation helped bring about a return to the original view.

3. But even, the Protestant continues, if the meaning *were* that Peter himself were the rock, there would be no ground for assuming that Peter's power was passed on to his "successors." The Protestant claims that the apostles, rather than bequeathing some unusual powers to their successors, bequeathed their testimony, their witness, which was contained in the pages of the New Testament. The Church is thus found where men maintain fidelity to the truth proclaimed in the New Testament that "Jesus is the Christ." It is that faith which distinguishes the Church today, just as it distinguished the Church nineteen hundred years ago.

Those "Upsetters of the World"

What was it like, this Church that the New Testament tells us about? Why were these obstreperous Christians able to make such a noise that not all the bellowings of Nero or his lions could drown them out? Rather than being academic about it, we will let a few vignettes tell the story.

SCENARIO FOR A SILENT MOTION PICTURE

Long-distance shot of Oriental market place. Shift to middle-distance shots of different booths, occasional close-up of camel or donkey carrying produce for market day. Gradual close-up of a short, sad-faced merchant coming to market—a stranger in town. Shift to booth of tall merchant instructing others about arranging produce—a person at home in the district.

Long-distance shot of short merchant approaching booth of tall merchant. Gradual close-in on the two faces as men converse. A tentative recognition in eyes of tall man as he studies other's face. Shift to middle distance, lower camera to arm of tall man, stick in hand. Shift lower to dust, and focus on point of stick outlining a fish in the dust.

Shift to short man, his face watching the fish being drawn. As he sees what it is, his expression changes, face lights up, the sadness disappears. He looks at tall man happily and nods vigorously. Shift to middle distance, men embrace in Oriental fashion and depart together. Fade out on figure of fish gradually being obliterated by passing feet.

Puzzle: Why did the drawing of a fish in the dirt unite two strangers who had never seen one another before?

(Solution to the Puzzle appears on page 198.)

A LETTER FROM AN AMAZED PUBLICAN

Publius to Romanus, hail!

I write you in haste, to tell you of my amazing experience yesterday. As you know, I arrived only two days ago in Jerusalem from Cappadocia, a complete stranger. I chanced to go to a public place where a number of people were gathered. They seemed to be waiting for something and I was intrigued. All of a sudden something quite amazing happened. I don't know how to explain it, but the air seemed to be full of sound—like those winds which whip over the Cappadocian plains—and the men were transfixed. They seemed almost "on fire" with something they had to share. Then a number of them started talking, and I'll swear (you'll think this is crazy, Romanus) I could distinguish a number of words in my own language.

The man next me shrugged it off with the words, "They're drunk." One of the leaders overheard him and said: "These men are not drunk. After all, it's only nine o'clock in the morning." (That got a laugh.) Then he gave an explanation, in the common Greek all of us speak.

These men, he said, himself included, had received the Spirit of God. And then he went on to tell some of the things they believed. There had been a man named Jesus who had just recently been killed. But he had been raised from the dead and was with them and in their midst. Things like that. When the man finished, I found myself blurting out, "What must we do about it?" And he said, "Get a new start, be baptized, and you will receive the Holy Spirit too."

And, Romanus, I did just that. I have found the God I have always been seeking—only really he has found me. Hurry to Jerusalem so I can share this with you.

FRAGMENT OF A CONVERSATION IN CORINTH

LEADER *(reading from a letter):* "On the first day of the every week, each of you is to put something aside and save, as he may prosper, so that contributions need not be made when I come. And when I arrive, I will send those whom you accredit by letter to carry your gift to Jerusalem." (*Rolls up the scroll.*)

That is the portion of Paul's letter we must now discuss. The rest of it is mostly personal greetings. (*To young man*) Yes?

YOUNG MAN: I don't get it. I admit I'm only a recent convert, but I don't see why we Greek Christians in Corinth should be giving up our hard-earned money for Jewish Christians in Jerusalem we've never even seen.

ANOTHER MAN (*jumping in*): Well, for one thing, the Jerusalem church is sort of our "mother church." We should never have heard the "good news" if men from there hadn't begun to spread it in Antioch, and then in Galatia, and finally clear over here in Greece.

STILL ANOTHER MAN: Yes, and don't forget that we aren't a lot of different "churches." We are all part of the one Church. We are the church of Christ in Corinth; that same church of Christ is in Ephesus, *and* in Jerusalem. It doesn't make any difference whether we know each other or not. Christ died for all of us. If he gave his life for us, surely we can give a little money for his children, wherever they are.

Solution to the puzzle on page 197:

The tall man, a Christian, wondered if the stranger was a Christian. Since at this time Christians were being persecuted, it would not do to shout the accusing word "Christian?" at a friend, or a possible enemy. So a secret sign language was used. The Greek word "fish" (*ichthus*) was used as an acrostic. That is, each letter was the first letter of a word in the Christian statement of faith, "Jesus Christ, Son of God, Savior." Like this:

$$I=i=Iesous=Jesus$$
$$X=ch=Christos=Christ$$
$$\Theta=th=Theou=of\ God$$
$$Y=u=(h)Uios=son$$
$$\Sigma=s=Soter=savior$$

To draw a fish, then, was to indicate that you were a believing Christian. No one but another Christian would understand the sign. Thus the two men were saying: We both worship the same Christ, and this unites our hearts in love, even though we have never seen one another before.

AND STILL ANOTHER MAN: Besides, we have to remember that there are no differences between people in the Church. I admit it's hard to believe, but just because Christians in Jerusalem are a different nationality from us doesn't matter to God—and it shouldn't matter to us either.

FIRST YOUNG MAN: Well, it still seems strange to me, but if the rest of you take this so seriously, I guess I can too.

FRAGMENT OF A CONVERSATION IN SAN FRANCISCO

STUDENT: But why was worship in the Early Church that important?

TEACHER (*making a supreme effort to understand*) : Let's look at it another way. Let's put their experience into modern clothing and pretend it happened today.

STUDENT: O.K.

TEACHER: Imagine yourself a clerk in a San Francisco supermarket. Very early on Sunday morning you went to a big house on Jackson Street. You slipped along the driveway and entered through the back door. In the living room the "church" was gathering. There were all sorts of people. Some you knew, some you didn't. You looked the place over carefully for Government spies. But the deacons seemed to have things in hand. In front of the room, seated on the far side of the living room table, were the presbyters, and one of them, the chief presbyter, finally called you all to order. After you had all warmly greeted one another, a tablecloth was spread on the table, and on it were placed a silver plate and goblet, from the owner's sideboard. As the familiar words of Jesus were repeated, a loaf of bread from the kitchen was broken, and some wine from the cellar was poured into the goblet. After there had been some prayers and responses, the bread and wine were passed around by the presbyters and you all partook. When it was finished, some of you got small pieces of the bread to take home. Then the chief presbyter said, "All right, time to break up," and everybody slipped out of the back door again.

STUDENT (*a bit disappointed*): You mean that's all there was to it?

TEACHER: On the surface, yes. The details would vary from place to place, and of course as time went on the service got more elaborate. To an outsider it would have almost no meaning. However, on the day we are talking about, there was a sequel.

STUDENT (*more hopeful*): Yes?

TEACHER: As you left the driveway, somebody looked at you queerly, put two and two together, and began to yell, "Hey, here's a bunch of Christians!" A crowd gathered, somebody got shoved, and pretty soon there was a street fight going on. Then you heard the wail of a siren and a police car drove up. "What's going on here?" the cop demanded, and when he heard people calling you "Christians," he clapped handcuffs on the lot of you, and when the police wagon arrived, he took seventeen people to the station.

It didn't take long for things to happen there. Everybody knew the law: "It is forbidden to be a Christian," just as, "It is forbidden to commit murder," and the procedure was about the same in both cases. You were all asked whether you were guilty or not guilty. Almost everyone admitted being a Christian, and when one fellow faltered, the police judge pointed to a picture of the President and said, "Kneel down before that picture and say, 'God forgive me for my sins.'" The fellow wouldn't do it because it was his faith that only God in Christ forgave sin, and not any human person.

There was nothing more for the police judge to do. You were all guilty. So they took you out to Alcatraz, and put you in the electric chair one by one, all morning long.

STUDENT (*rather impressed, now*): Why did they risk it?

TEACHER: Just because that little "meaningless ceremony" of worship was the very heart and center of their lives. It brought them into firsthand contact with their risen Lord and with each other. Everything else depended on that.

A Rebuttal of the Case Against the Church

People who "pan" the church need first to be told that their indictment is usually not severe enough! Those who love the church and live within it can offer a much stiffer condemnation than the outsider. As they know it better, they see its wretchedness better—but they also see its potential greatness better. And often this fact keeps them within the church, rather than going outside and throwing stones at the windows.

See how it works. The outside "critic" is doing some slippery thinking. When confronted by obvious weaknesses in American democracy, he does not say: "Democracy is rotten. Look at the graft and corruption. The whole thing's a mess. I won't even bother to vote." No, he says: "Democracy ought to be better than this. Let's get good candidates into office, so that democracy will work." The constructive critic on the inside is more realistic than the destructive critic on the outside. If this is true in terms of democracy, it is also true in terms of the church. But . . .

At one point, the analogy fails. It needs to be clear that the church is not just a voluntary association of good, earnest people who get together to form a club for raising the standards of community morality. The church is rather something that came into being because ordinary people found themselves in the midst of an experience of community quite different from anything they had ever experienced before, something that was not their doing at all, but something that proceeded from the power and love of God, as it was made known to them through Jesus Christ and the Holy Spirit. These people responded to God's outgoing love and recognized that this community (that is, the church) was God's doing and not theirs.

The critics need to remember that they often criticize the church as it *is,* by comparing it with the church as it *ought to be.* This is really a left-handed compliment. To say, "The church stands for racial equality but doesn't practice it," is an admission that the church's *principle* is right, and that only the *practice* is wrong. The inference is clear. People who believe in racial equality should work within the church to make practice conform more nearly to principle. They will find people within who are just as disturbed about the disparity and who are working hard to try to remove it.

Why the Church?

Why the church? Why isn't "individual religion" enough? Here are four suggestions as you attempt to formulate your own answer.

1. Christianity is first and last a religion of community.

Christianity without community is not Christianity; it is something else. "Individual Christianity" is a contradiction in terms. People who say, "I believe in Christianity but not churchianity" simply betray the fact that they haven't the foggiest notion what Christianity is all about.

2. The "Church" is not that ugly board building at the corner of First and Main, with those terrible windows, that terrible choir, and that even more terrible minister. Nor is it the beautiful Gothic vault downtown with lovely Gothic windows, a choir singing lovely Gothic music, a minister with a lovely Gothic voice, and a budget with a lovely Gothic debt. The Church is rather that great fellowship of men and women down through the ages, in heaven and on earth, the saints, the martyrs, the ordinary stumbling folk like us, who have committed themselves to God as he is made known in Jesus Christ, and try to live their lives in terms of that faith.

3. As a matter of historic fact, it is by means of the church that Christianity has lived and grown. Christianity could not survive in history without the ongoing community through which it is proclaimed, practiced (to a greater or lesser degree), and propagated. It is not isolated individuals who accomplish this; it is the fellowship of believers. Wherever the name of Christ is known and acknowledged today, it is because the Church has been there.

4. Christians find that their ethical concerns are strengthened by their corporate life together. As Christians do things together, they not only strengthen and undergird one another, but they also find that God himself strengthens and undergirds what they do. Gamaliel's statement to the Council in Jerusalem, when some of the first Christians were on trial, has been true ever since:

> If this plan or this undertaking is of men, it will fail;
> but if it is of God, you will not be able to overthrow it.
> (Acts 5: 38, 39)

Neither will the gates of hell be able to prevail against it.

A Strange New World

(Last Judgment? Second Coming?
What Do They Mean?)

A great temptation in reading the Bible is to skip over the parts that you don't understand—or at least refuse to take them seriously. This is particularly the case with ideas like "Last Judgment," "Second Coming," and so on. This whole side of Biblical thought is suggested by a covenient, though jaw-breaking, word: *eschatology.* This is a word you have never needed before, and you probably don't want to be bothered with it now. Nevertheless, it will be very convenient to use it in this chapter.

Your algebra book says, $A = \pi r^2$

> ... which means that the area of a circle can be found by multiplying the distance from the center to the periphery by itself and then multiplying the product by 3.14159265+. But what a space saver to put "$A = \pi r^2$"!

A box score has, Mays, cf.	ab	r	h	po	a	e
	5	2	3	8	2	0

> ... which means that Willie Mays played center field for the Giants, made the eight put-outs and two assists, while playing errorless ball, and that in five times at bat he made three hits, for an impressive .600 average. But what a space saver to put:

Mays, cf.	ab	r	h	po	a	e
	5	2	3	8	2	0!

In the same way, this book uses the word "eschatology,"
... which means "the last things" (from the Greek, *ta eschata*).
It represents an attempt to think about final things, about
fulfillment, about an area of life that transcends anything of
which we have any direct and firsthand experience. It reminds
us that time, the time in which we live, is not complete in
itself. Nor is our human history complete in itself. It is going
somewhere. Our "three score years and ten" are not the whole
story. Our life and experience, in other words, are surrounded
with something more ultimate, more fundamental, than what
we touch and feel from day to day. God has purposes that go
beyond anything that can be fully accomplished here. But
what a space saver to put "eschatology" for the rest of this
chapter!

The Inescapability of Eschatology

Notice that you can't escape eschatology. If you reject Christian eschatology, you only substitute some other version of
eschatology. The famous statement, "Eat, drink, and be merry,
for tomorrow you die," is an eschatological statement. It says:

There is something more ultimate than life.

The name of this something is death.

It is more powerful than life.

It conquers and defeats life. It is supreme.

Since death is going to catch you in the end, live your life
accordingly: enjoy yourself.

In a similar way, Christian faith is eschatological faith. It says,
in contrast to the pagan eschatology:

There is Someone more ultimate than life.

The name of this someone is the living God who has
visited man in Jesus Christ.

He is more powerful than life.

He transforms and renews life. He is supreme.

Since he confronts you in love and wants your love in return, live your life accordingly: love him and your fellow men.

Either way, you're involved in eschatology.

The Point of Biblical Eschatology: History Is Going Somewhere

The significance of Biblical eschatology can be seen by comparing it with its chief rival in the New Testament period. This was a belief that history did not move forward, but moved in a circle. As the Greeks looked at nature they saw endless repetition. Flowers bloom in the spring (tra la), live in the summer, die in the fall, disappear in the winter, bloom in the spring (tra la), live in the summer, die in the fall, disappear in the winter, bloom in the spring (tra la), live in the summer. . . . Always the same pattern. There seemed to be nothing new.

They applied the same pattern to their *own* existence. And it meant that there was no forward direction. History never got anyplace; it had no final purpose or meaning: it was simply the same monotonous round over and over again. Right now, I am writing a chapter on eschatology, on a hot afternoon, in a stuffy office. When history has gone full cycle, I shall again find myself writing the same chapter, on a hot afternoon, in a stuffy office, and later on I shall again find myself writing the same chapter, on a hot afternoon, in a stuffy office, on and on, over and over, time after time, never escaping from the pattern, with no more end in sight than this sentence has seemed to have until right now.

In contrast to that dreary picture, Biblical eschatology affirms that history is a series of unique events, which are significant because they point toward a time of fulfillment, which will be brought about by God. History is *going somewhere,* not just "round and round." It is the arena where God is active. (See Chapter 6.) Since God's activity is not limited just to history, this means that our history will have final significance because it is related to *all* of God's activity, both here and beyond. Our job in the rest of this chapter will be to "spell this out."

The Dangers of Literalism

"Will the Last Judgment come on a Tuesday?" "Will the Second Coming take place in the year 2000?" People are always trying to date these things. But next time someone tells you that Judgment Day is coming on October 24, at 7:32 A.M., remember Jesus' words, "Of that day and hour no one knows, not even the angels of heaven, nor the Son, but the Father only" (Matt. 24: 36). It is a little presumptuous to claim more knowledge than Jesus had himself.

Rather than claiming inside information on just *when* and *how* the fulfillment of God's purposes will come, it is more important to believe *that* the fulfillment will come, that history is moving in a significant direction, and that in God's own good time his purposes will be fulfilled, as his power expresses itself over human life and destiny. We can assert this kind of belief, furthermore, without worrying about heaven's geography and hell's temperature. Such notions are not our worry, and whether they even have any meaning can safely be left to God to determine.

How Biblical Eschatology Has Been Expressed

The Old Testament looks to the future. The present is ambiguous: God chooses a people and that people forsakes him; power in God's world goes to nations who do not acknowledge him; the way of the wicked prospers. Consequently, the Old Testament asserts, these ambiguities will finally be overcome. God will intervene to re-establish his righteousness. The writers describe this fact by such eschatological phrases as the "Day of the Lord," the "Age to Come," the "Last Days."

Sometimes this Day of the Lord is interpreted as a *judgment:* "It is darkness, and not light" (Amos 5: 18).

Sometimes it is interpreted as a *restoration:* rebellious nations will be trampled underfoot, and the people of God will be restored, after their experience of suffering.

Sometimes it is connected with the *hope of a Messiah* who will come to vindicate God and God's people. Then God will be all in all, the people will follow his will, and there will be a kind of earthly paradise:

The cow and the bear shall feed;
   their young shall lie down together;
   and the lion shall eat straw like the ox. . . .
They shall not hurt or destroy
   in all my holy mountain;
for the earth shall be full of the knowledge of the Lord
   as the waters cover the sea.

(Isa. 11: 7, 9)

Toward the end of the Old Testament period we see a shift in this thinking. In Daniel (the last Old Testament book to be written) the scene of the New Age seems to shift from earth to somewhere else. There will be violent interruption of the historical process, history itself will be transformed into something utterly different, and in an indescribable way God's rule will be manifested, not just on earth, but throughout the entire cosmos.

The New Testament atmosphere is somewhat different. It is claimed that the "end" *has* come, but in a way very different from what the Old Testament expected. With the sending of his Son, Jesus Christ, God *has* actively intervened in human life. Christ has come, and with him has come the beginning of the Day of the Lord. And very soon, the New Testament avers, the *full* consummation will take place, Christ will return again, and the "end" which has already broken into history, will be completed. In the interim, Christians are to live as citizens both of the present age and of the "age to come."

Exploring New Testament Eschatology

Let us look at the New Testament terms that describe the "end." Our job is to see the realities to which the eschatological terms point, rather than stopping with the terms themselves.

The Second Coming of Christ—What is significant about
the claim that Christ will "come again"? Just as the Creation
stories say, "In the beginning God," so statements about the
Second Coming affirm, "In the end Christ." History is encompassed before and after by God. God *is* the sovereign Lord
of history. History, in other words, moves *toward* Christ,
rather than *away* from Christ. It is in terms of him that our
history is to be understood. The first coming of Christ is our
present clue to what life is all about. The claim that he will
"come again" promises that what we now know of him in part
will be clarified in full.

The Antichrist—Certain New Testament books, Revelation in particular, speak of the Antichrist, the embodiment of
all that is evil. The Antichrist is revealed at the "end," along
with the true Christ. The figure of the Antichrist stands for
the fact that evil will continue up to the very end.

Before dismissing this as a fantastic bit of imagery, ask yourself if this is not an accurate description of our situation. The
world does not, in fact, get "better and better." Each new historical advance brings a new peril. The greater the advance,
the greater the peril. Today we stand on the brink of world
community, but we also stand on the brink of world destruction. The things that make world community possible are the
things that threaten world community.

> The airplane makes us all neighbors but it also makes it
> easier for us to kill our neighbors.
> World-wide communication binds us closer together, but
> as a propaganda medium it can drive us apart.
> Atomic power can make poverty unnecessary, but it can
> also make us extinct.

It is this kind of thing that the symbol of Antichrist makes
plain. Evil persists, right up to the end.

The Last Judgment—The notion of a time of taking stock,
of a judgment, means that *what happens in human life has
lasting consequences.* Right and wrong are significant and do

make a difference, and some kind of accounting will be made concerning them.

It is easy to get into trouble here. Some people think of the Last Judgment as similar to getting final report cards:

> Some people flunk ... and go to hell.
> Some get C+ ... and barely squeak into heaven.
> A few get *summa cum laude* ... and become saints.

This suggests (wrongly) that our relationship to God is based *strictly* on merit. A moment's thought will make it clear that on the basis of rewards-and-punishments nobody could claim the divine favor. ("If thou, O Lord, shouldst mark iniquities, Lord, who could stand?") Salvation, or eternal life, is a gift—not something earned. "By grace ye are saved," is the indisputable keynote in this regard. The symbol of the Last Judgment stands beside that keynote as a reminder that we are responsible before God for what we do with our lives.

Perhaps the fairest (and most terrifying) thing to say would be that we shall be seen by God as we truly are, with all our pretensions stripped away. This is a grim prospect at best. Peter got an inkling of it during the trial of Jesus. After his denial he saw Jesus once. Jesus looked at him—and Peter couldn't return the look. He was judged, seen as he truly was, and a terrible experience it was. But there was an ultimate redemption even for Peter, as Jesus (after the resurrection) forgave him and restored him to fellowship.

"But what about the Hottentots?" What, indeed, about those who are not saved? Or is everybody saved? There is certainly no "party line" answer here that satisfies all Christians. If the love of God is supreme, it is hard to believe that God would "give up" on a person who had refused to love him in return, but would keep trying, beyond this life, to win that person back to him. On the other hand, to say too easily that "everybody gets saved" is to suggest that moral distinctions really

don't matter—that Hitler is as close to God as Albert Schweit-
zer. We must allow people the moral right to say no to God on
and on, if they choose. God cannot "force" people to love him
or it is not true love, and part of the significance of human
freedom is that it gives us this awful privilege of refusing love.

We are dependent, no matter how good or bad we are, upon
the mercy and love of God. We must not build fences around
that love, or claim to know precisely how far it reaches out.
Our job is to commit our lives to God, and spread his love to
others, rather than passing judgment on the completeness or
incompleteness of somebody else's commitment.

The Kingdom of God

This Biblical notion is shot full of eschatological significance. The Kingdom of God is central to Jesus' ministry. He
preaches about it, he tells parables about it, he performs
"mighty works" which exhibit it. And yet—are you sure you
know what it means? It has been subject to a greater variety of
interpretations than almost any other Biblical idea.

A good Roman Catholic: The Roman Church is the gateway
   of entrance to the Kingdom of God. If you want to be in
   the Kingdom, you must be in the Roman Church.

A good Protestant sectarian: My sect is the gateway of entrance
   to the Kingdom of God. If you want to be in the Kingdom, you must be in my sect.

A rugged activist: The Kingdom of God is built by the intense
   effort of men of good will. If we band together, we can
   bring in the Kingdom here on earth.

A stern literalist: I have studied the Bible carefully and discover that the Kingdom of God will come on March 14,
   1987, slightly before 2 P.M. Woe to those who have not
   forsaken their evil ways before then!

A dedicated individualist: The Kingdom of God is in my heart.
   No matter what happens, the Kingdom is alive within me.

We have, then, such extreme interpretations as . . .

"Rise up, O men of God!	*Sit down, O men of God,*
His Kingdom tarries long;	*His Kingdom he will bring,*
Bring in the day of brotherhood	*Just as and when and where he will,*
And end the night of wrong." *	*You cannot do a thing.*

. . . and everything in between.

A Few Bits of Help

One reason for difficulty: the phrase "the Kingdom of God" does not clearly convey the meaning of the original Biblical words. The Biblical concept suggests not so much a geographical kingdom, with boundaries and so forth, as God's kingly rule, his Kingship, or his sovereignty. The "Kingdom of God" is God acting in his kingly power, or exerting his sovereignty over life. The notion of the Kingdom as a domain or area which men can enter is a secondary meaning.

Another source of confusion can be avoided by realizing that "the Kingdom of heaven," used in Matthew's Gospel, means just the same as "the Kingdom of God" in the other accounts. The Jews thought it was a blasphemy to use the divine name. "Matthew," the most Jewish of the Gospel writers, takes this seriously. By writing "the Kingdom of heaven," he avoids using the word "God" and thus feels more comfortable. But he means just the same thing.

The Kingdom Both Present and Future

In the Bible are three interpretations of the Kingdom.

There is *first* the understanding of the eternal and unending sovereignty of God. He exercises his Kingship over all creation "from everlasting to everlasting." God is Lord of all that is, both now and forevermore. His Kingdom is an everlasting Kingdom, whether we know about it or not.

---

* Used by permission of *The Presbyterian Tribune.*

In *addition* to this, it is plain that to a certain degree this ultimate rule of God is actually manifested in human history. It is partly realized by the Jews when they obey the Torah or Law. It is partly realized in the coming of Christ. After his coming it is spoken of as being "in your midst." It it "at hand"; it has "come upon you."

Finally, there are a number of passages that make it plain that the Kingdom, in all its fullness, is still off in the future. If it has partially come, it is also still coming. The consummation of the purpose of God has not yet been completely achieved, but is still to come.

These elements can be combined so as to bring out the distinctiveness of the Biblical position by saying that the Kingdom of God has "broken in" to human history in a decisive way in the coming of Jesus Christ, but that the completion and fulfillment of this mighty act of God still lie in the future. Look at the two sides of this statement.

The Kingdom is present; it has come. God's reign is here, and allegiance must be given to him. The Day of the Lord has dawned. That which was only a hope is now a reality. In his own presence and activity, Jesus says, "the kingdom of God has come upon you" (Luke 11: 20). In him, God's reign has actively begun on earth. The time is now fulfilled. The Kingdom is not just on its way. It is here.

And yet (and this must always be said in the very same breath), *the Kingdom is in the future; it is coming.* The Kingdom in its universal scope is not yet a reality. Jesus looks for this to come in the future. He bade his disciples pray for it: "Thy kingdom come . . . on earth as it is in heaven" (Matt. 6: 10). There will be a consummation in the future of what has already appeared in Christ.

To stress either one of these statements to the exclusion of the other is to distort the picture badly. To assume that the world as we now know it is identical with the Kingdom of God is a manifest absurdity. To assume that the Kingdom is simply

in the future is to write off the present as unimportant and irrelevant. In the Lord's Prayer we pray, "Thy kingdom *come*...
thine *is* the kingdom." We are asking God that the Kingdom
we see present in all its fullness in Christ may, when God so
wills it, be present in all its fullness throughout creation.

The Gift of God

The Kingdom is represented in the Bible as the *work of
God*. It is not something we can earn or "build"; it is only
something we can receive. The "coming" of the Kingdom is
not our doing. Jesus says, for example:

> "The kingdom of God is as if a man should scatter seed upon
> the ground, and should sleep and rise night and day, and the seed
> should sprout and grow, he knows not how. The earth produces
> of itself ..." (Mark 4: 26-28).

Man can take no credit for "building" the Kingdom of God.
It is God's Kingdom and not something we have achieved.

There is, however, a condition attached to our living under
God's sovereign sway. That condition is one that we have en-
countered many times before in this book. We are to repent.
Jesus' first recorded message concludes, "The kingdom of God
is at hand; repent, and believe in the gospel" (Mark 1: 15).
Nothing in life is more important than this. If your eye is a
hindrance to accepting the gift of the Kingdom, pluck it out!
It is like finding that there is treasure buried in a field. You
must sell everything you have in order to gain that treasure
(Matt. 13: 44). It is like seeing a pearl of surpassing beauty, for
which you give up everything you own in order that you may
possess it (Matt. 13: 45). There must be fixity of purpose about
life—to live as a citizen of the Kingdom of God.

Eschatology and "What I Do Today"

IMPATIENT INQUIRER (*who has been trying to get a word in for at
    least half a dozen pages*): This eschatology is all very well,
    and no doubt very true. But what gets me is what all this has

to do with my decisions right here and now. It seems to me that the more you get involved in all this "otherworldliness," the more irrelevant you become. If you are always concentrating on the "last things," or a Kingdom not of this world, aren't you bound to lose sight of the business of everyday living right here and now?

This is a fair query. We shall deal with it in three ways, each time showing how they "got at it" in the New Testament Church, and then relating their answer to "here and now."

1. The fact of the matter is that the concern of the early Christians with the "age to come" *made them live more responsibly in the present age.* This is a fact. We can document it. Take Paul; at the end of his first letter to Corinth he has a long discussion of resurrection—an eschatological symbol if there ever was one. From this he turns immediately to urge the Corinthians to take up a collection and send the money to the poor in Jerusalem. Not for a moment did he give his readers the option of thinking, "Eschatology is so important that we can forget our needy brethren." As a matter of fact, when some of his flock in Thessalonica did try to pull that line, saying that since the "end" was coming soon they wouldn't work any more but would expect free handouts from the church at mealtime, Paul dealt with this nonsense very sternly by writing to them, "If any one will not work, let him not eat" (II Thess. 3: 10). Whoever wrote the letter to the Hebrews made the same point in the familiar eleventh chapter. The author stresses that here we have no continuing city, and that we are strangers and pilgrims on earth, but does he go on from this to conclude that we are to sit back patiently and wait for the great day with folded hands? Not for a moment. "Therefore [i.e., because of our eschatological situation], . . . let us run with perseverance the race that is set before us" (Heb. 12: 1). "The race that is set before us" is right here and now. We have a job to do, and we are to get on with it, and no dillydallying around!

Now our situation is not exactly the same as that of the early

Christians. They were expecting an almost immediate return of Christ. We see now that this hope was misplaced—Christ did not return, at least not in anything like the way in which they had expected. In our situation we must take account of what may be a long historical future stretching before us. We can live in the belief that the meaning of our life will be made manifest by God in his own good time rather than ours. Consequently, the lesson we can learn from the early Christians is that we must act as responsibly toward *our* situation as they did toward *theirs*. Since our situation makes it necessary for us to take strict account of the historical future, we shall need to do more than give to the needy or take care of our Christian brethren. We shall need to see that our Christian social responsibility is immensely broadened, that *our* eschatological concern, as we work it out in the practical realm of action, may involve us in a local fight for decent housing, or a foreign policy that is based on something more than mere military might.

2. To be concerned about such things takes not only power and conviction, but courage as well. And here is a second thing which the Early Church shows us. *The Christian, secure in the eschatological hope, can live in this world with a kind of abandon or nonchalance.* Listen once again to the way Paul puts it:

If we live, we live to the Lord, and if we die, we die to the Lord; so then, whether we live or whether we die, we are the Lord's. For to this end Christ died and lived again, that he might be Lord both of the dead and of the living (Rom. 14: 8, 9).

These verses capture the mood of the early Christians perfectly. There was nothing to worry about. You could go about your activities in this world sure that nothing could harm you. If Caesar didn't like the way you were behaving, so much the worse for Caesar. He couldn't do you any real harm, for whether you lived, or whether you died, you were the Lord's and not Caesar's. Your ultimate allegiance to God freed you to live responsibly in the world and made it unnecessary for you to be frightened by "what might happen to you." Rather than dulling ethical responsibility, this kind of eschatological faith strengthened it.

There is perhaps no perspective more needed by people who will live during the last half of the twentieth century. This is an age that a novelist calls "The Age of Longing"; that a poet calls "The Age of Anxiety"; and a journalist calls "The Age of Suspicion." It is an age in which people are afraid to speak out for fear they will be branded as "subversive" or "red" or maybe only "pink," an age when people are afraid to join "causes"— an age, in short, when what is particularly needed is the kind of tough nonchalance that eschatological faith makes possible. To believe today, as the early Christians believed in their day, that "whether we live or whether we die, we are the Lord's," is to be freed and released for responsible, and courageous, living.

Note to the Careful Reader: If this seems to you only a theoretical problem, remember how tragically real the problem is for many of your fellow Christians behind the Iron Curtain today. Many accounts of heroic Christian resistance filter through that curtain, accounts that indicate that it is precisely because of their eschatological hope that Germans, Czechs, Hungarians, and others have had the courage and power to stand firm against diabolical attempts to make them betray, not only their own faith, but also their fellow Christians. That story is not yet fully written, but when someday it is, it will attest in an overpowering way to the fact that to believe that "here we have no lasting city, but we seek the city which is to come" is to have a faith that brings courage and power in quite unexpected proportions.

3. Christians are helped by this eschatological perspective *to see what things are really important and need doing.* A splendid sense of discrimination is developed. Paul saw, for

instance, that to take eschatology seriously meant that you must revise your attitude toward possessions:

If you buy anything, you should remember that you do not have it to keep. If you make use of this world's goods, remember that you have no chance to use them up, for the structure of this world is passing away (I Cor. 7: 30, 31).

And another early Christian writer saw that if eschatology has any real meaning it forces us into certain kinds of activities and concerns us rather than others. He makes it quite concrete and specific:

The end of all things is at hand; therefore, be sane and sober and say your prayers; above all, have intense love for one another; be hospitable; and use your gifts in the service of God that he may be glorified in everything (I Peter 4: 7-11, abridged).

These are the things that are important. It is precisely because the "end of all things is at hand" that we must "have intense love for one another." To see the direction in which life is moving is to see more clearly than ever what things are important and what things need doing.

Therefore, to take eschatology seriously is not to take ethical demands flippantly. The more seriously you regard your citizenship in the Kingdom that is not of this world, the more seriously do you find yourself engaged in the struggle within the kingdom of this world. Whether that makes sense on paper or not, the whole experience of the Early Church shows that it makes sense when lived.

The Facts of Life—and Death

(What Happens When I Die?)

At one point, Job isn't realistic enough. He asks what he thinks is a hard question: "If a man die, shall he live again?" (Job 14: 14). But the real question is, "*When* a man dies, shall he live again?" We know that we shall die, and unpleasant as that fact is, we cannot avoid it. So the question keeps cropping up, Is death the end, or shall I live again?

Scrapping Some False Answers

There are all sorts of inadequate answers to the question. And to appreciate the fullness of the Biblical answer, we must look first at some of the others.

1. *The stark, stern, "let's-face-it" response.* The easiest and dreariest way of answering the question is with a flat: "No. There is no eternal life. When you're dead, you're dead, period." When people give this answer, they usually do one of two things about it:

Some say: "O.K., we live only once, let's make the best of it. Let's have a full life, enjoying it; let's make the most of what we have, and no regrets when it's all over. Since we don't get another chance, we'll fill our cup to the brim and enjoy our lark

Others say: "O.K., we live only once, and it's a rotten trick that fate has played on us. Let's not kid ourselves that life is a happy business. We'll try to squeeze a little meaning from it while we're here, but we know there isn't any meaning. We can

218

before we're snuffed out. We won't buck the tide. We'll move along with the stream until the bubble of life bursts."

This can be called the "Row, row, row your boat" attitude. You remember how the rest of it goes: ". . . gently *down* the stream; merrily, merrily, merrily, merrily, life is but a dream."

try to buck the tide if we want to, but we know perfectly well it will engulf us in the end. We shall finally pass into nothingness just like everything and everybody else."

This can be called the "sound and fury" attitude. You remember how the rest of it goes: Life "is a tale told by an idiot, full of sound and fury, signifying nothing."

It is amazing how many people hold the "Row, row, row your boat" attitude without realizing that the boat goes down the stream until it topples over a waterfall and everybody gets killed. It is the realization of this fact that often pushes thoughtful people over into the "sound and fury" attitude.

There is something very honest about the "let's-face-it" response, when the people who hold it do not try to cover up the fact that it implies that we live in an alien, hostile universe, in which our most cherished ideals and values are ultimately of no significance. Work for a good world, if you wish, but do not expect your work to have any ultimate meaning, for even if your ideal lingers for a few generations after you die it will soon pass away, for in the end everybody dies and there is nothing left. This view of life has been compared to a road built of the ground-up bones of previous generations; soon your bones will be added to the road and it will be a little longer, but the time will come when there will be no more bones to add to it and the road will have no more travelers. Everything perishes along the way, until finally nothing is left. History is merely a row of tombstones.

2. *The "pie-in-the-sky-when-you-die" option.* A second false answer, adopted by many people who are afraid to be stark and stern, is characterized by the words of the old song: "You'll get pie in the sky when you die." In other words, things may get

pretty tough here on earth, but take heart because after you die you'll get your reward. Eternal life is like the lollipop Mummy promises little Junior if he sits in the nasty old dentist's chair without screaming while he has a tooth filled. Life is pretty grim and ugly, but everything will get smoothed out in the end, and "in the sky" everything will be peaches and cream (in case you don't like pie). There is, of course, a kind of minimal truth in this view, namely, the assumption that there is something more ultimate than the here and now, but the notions that living on earth is simply a process of gritting one's teeth (thus making things harder for the dentist) against unpleasant things, and that there is some sort of automatic reward for "being good"—these are highly dubious, as we shall later see more clearly.

3. *The "living-on-in-the-memories-of-others" evasion.* Other people say that eternal life is nothing more than the "immortality of influence." We do live on in the memories of others, because our influence, our ideas, our personality, are perpetuated in those who remember us. Abraham Lincoln, for example, is "as alive as he ever was" because his influence is still felt in America, and he lives "enshrined in the hearts of his countrymen."

True enough. We do live on in the memories of others.

But not true *enough*. For this notion fails to come to grips with the real fact of death—its finality and completeness. What happens to the people who are *not* remembered? Or suppose you are remembered for fifty or seventy-five years. What happens when everybody who ever remembered you is dead? What happens when the whole human race has passed away and there is nobody left to remember anybody? This is a pretty frail kind of immortality.

4. *The "wheel-of-existence" theory.* Some religions look upon eternal life as reincarnation, that is, being born again in another form or shape. If you are bad, you may be reborn

as a dog; if you are very bad, as a lizard. Then you have to work your way back up the scale by being a good dog or a *very* good lizard, and when you are gradually purified enough you will escape from this cycle of incessant rebirth and finally be relieved of the unhappy necessity of existing at all.

What does this add up to? It adds up to a very pessimistic view of life. The object is to escape from the cycle. Life is something to avoid—and you may be able to if you're lucky (which you probably won't be) or if you're good enough (which you probably won't be, either). There is also something depressing in the idea that the chicken you eat on Sunday may be your Aunt Gertrude, or that the mosquito you squashed may be your great-great-grandfather, who was evidently quite a scoundrel.

5. *Why not "immortality of the soul"?* One other inadequate answer must be examined before we look at the Biblical view. And be forewarned, this one is hard to understand, particularly because many people confuse it with the Christian answer.

This is called "immortality of the soul." It comes from the Greeks, and when Greek thought and Hebrew-Christian thought came into contact in the Early Church, the Greek view often seemed to predominate. This view says, in effect, that there is a portion of me, my soul, that will continue to exist. During my lifetime here on earth this immortal soul is lodged in my mortal body. What happens at death is that my body dies and turns to dust, while my immortal soul is released and made free so that it can continue its immortal existence without being hamstrung by confinement in a body.

Sounds pretty good, doesn't it? But wait a minute. This means that my body is a nuisance to my soul, something that confines it, limits it, hampers it, subjects it to temptation. As the Greeks themselves put it, "the body is the prison house of the soul." This means that life on earth in the body is a waste of time, an unpleasant interlude in the life of the soul, something to be over and done with as quickly as possible. The whole aim of life is to escape from life, get rid of the pesky body, in order to resume a free and unfettered existence in eternity. Human life on earth has no final significance.

How the Bible Approaches the Problem

The Bible takes it for granted that we have been created by God for fellowship with him. At first it is thought that we can enter into this fellowship during our lifetimes. But as the Old Testament writers wrestle with the problem they gradually come to see that this God, since he is beyond mere time and space, must open up the possibility for a relationship with his children that goes beyond mere time and space. The eternal God, in other words, must open up the possibility for us to enter into eternal relationship with him.

The Bible also takes it for granted that something has gone wrong. Our sin, that is, our persistent desire to place ourselves rather than God at the center of life, has disrupted the relationship and seriously hampered its fulfillment both as a present reality and as a future possibility. It is for this reason that the Biblical writers stress a notion that is difficult for us to understand—the connection between sin and death. Sin is a way of talking about the fact that our relationship with God has broken to pieces. Death is a way of talking about the fact that life itself has broken to pieces, life which was God-given. Both sin and death thus stand as threats to the relationship between man and God. There is a real connection between sin, a separation from God, and death as a further separation from God. Let us see how these notions develop in the Bible.

Sheol—Where God Is Not Present

The Old Testament writers felt at first that death brought total separation from God. Man cut himself off from God by his sin, and death completed the cutting-off process. Thus they took the fact of death very seriously, and did not try to avoid thinking about it; as a result, early Old Testament writers did not have a particularly pleasant view of the afterlife. They conceived of the dead person as going to Sheol (incorrectly translated as "hell"), a place called "the pit." Sheol was a sort of shadowy, underground cave, where people continued to live a vague and undesirable kind of existence. The significant thing about Sheol was that *God was not there.* This is what made it so vague and undesirable. Not only was God not there, but he took no account of those who were—they had passed beyond his concern. When the psalmist wants to describe a situation in which God is not present, he likens it to the experience of being in Sheol:

> For my soul is full of troubles,
>   and my life draws near to Sheol.
> I am reckoned among those who go down to the Pit;
>   I am a man who has no strength,
> like one forsaken among the dead,
>   like the slain that lie in the grave,
> like *those whom thou dost remember no more,*
>   for they are cut off from thy hand.
>   (Ps. 88: 3-5, italics added)

Sheol—Where God Is ~~Not~~ Present

However, at a later time they came to see that this was an incomplete picture. How futile to limit God in this way! How absurd to think that he could not reach out even unto Sheol! And so we find a very different note in another of the psalms: "God will redeem my soul from the power of Sheol, for he shall receive me" (Ps. 49: 15). And as you remember (from Chapter 4) the author of Ps. 139 got the shock of his life when he tried to go to Sheol to get away from God, and found that God was even there. Further positive affirmations of God's continued concern for man beyond the range of earthly life are heard:

Nevertheless I am continually with thee;
    thou dost hold my right hand.
Thou dost guide me with thy counsel,
    and afterward thou wilt receive me to glory . . . .
My flesh and my heart may fail,
    but God is the strength of my heart and my portion for ever.

(Ps. 73: 23-26)

Beyond Sheol

In two late portions of the Old Testament the idea of individual resurrection of the dead is mentioned. These passages do not refer to Sheol. On the contrary they hint that life after death involves a positive relationship with God. The earlier of these, probably the most important in the Old Testament, suggests the resurrection of the righteous.

Thy dead shall live, their bodies shall rise.
    O dwellers in the dust, awake and sing for joy!
For thy dew is a dew of light,
    and on the land of the shades thou wilt let it fall.

(Isa. 26: 19)

The other passage suggests a resurrection not only of the just but of the unjust, the just to their reward, the unjust to their punishment. "And many of those who sleep in the dust of the earth shall awake, some to everlasting life, and some to shame and everlasting contempt" (Dan. 12: 2).

There is little more in the Old Testament about eternal life. To see the full belief stressed as a joyous affirmation, we must turn to the New Testament.

The Community of the Resurrection

One of the earliest hymns in the Christian Church contained the lines

"Awake, O sleeper, and arise from the dead,
    and Christ shall give you light."

(Eph. 5: 14)

These lines sum up the attitude of the New Testament. From the first page of the New Testament to the last, the belief in eternal life with God is affirmed. The early Christians are in a real sense "the community of the resurrection." They know that God's power is greater than death's power, because God has conquered death by raising Christ from the dead (see Chapter 7). This is the charter for their existence. And it changes everything.

No more is the idea of God's power over death a pious hope. It is a hard-shelled fact. Christ has been raised from the dead, and those who believe in him can be "partakers of his resurrection." The New Testament, in other words, does not hotly debate and argue about this belief, because it is the backbone of every other belief.

Jesus takes it for granted, in an almost offhand comment, "You will be repaid at the resurrection of the just" (Luke 14: 14). He defends belief in eternal life in debate with the Sadducees (who denied it), although he makes clear that the resurrection is not just a reproduction of the conditions of this life. Eternal life is one of the recurring themes of the Fourth Gospel and the attitude there underlined is expressed by Jesus, "This is the will of my Father, that every one who sees the Son and believes in him should have eternal life" (John 6: 40).

Paul's Attempt to Describe the Christian Fact

Paul's letters, the earliest Christian documents, record the same belief. In the very first of them to be preserved, he is at special pains to point out that those who have died are not cut off from participating in the coming victory of God over the powers of evil (I Thess. 4: 13-18). But Paul's fullest discussion takes place in his answer to the Greeks, who thought the idea of the resurrection of the body was absurd. They wanted a "spiritual" salvation. All that the "body" stood for in their eyes was a limitation, a hindrance. It is to these people that Paul writes in I Cor., ch. 15.

The chapter is not easy reading, but Paul is not dealing with an easy subject. There is no "simple" answer to such questions as: "How are the dead raised? With what kind of body do they come?" (I Cor. 15: 35). Paul's answer is an analogy from nature. He reminds his skeptical readers that when they sow grain, it must first "die" if it is to burst forth in newness of life. The "body" that the unplanted seed has is very different from the "body" that the full-grown wheat has, and yet there is continuity between them. The seed is "raised" in a transformed fashion. What is reaped is different from what is sown, and yet it comes from what is sown.

Now the same kind of thing is true, Paul goes on, with regard to the resurrection from the dead. We are "sown" a physical body, he says, but we are "raised" a spiritual body. He makes this clear in a series of contrasts:

What is sown is perishable,	what is raised is imperishable.
It is sown in dishonor,	it is raised in glory.
It is sown in weakness,	it is raised in power.
It is sown a physical body,	it is raised a spiritual body.

(I Cor. 15: 42-44)

A "Spiritual Body"

Just what Paul means by a "spiritual body" is not easy to determine. It *is* clear that by the term "body" he means our total personality. He does not talk about "immortality of the soul" as though only part of us were significant to God. He talks about "resurrection of the body," suggesting that our bodies are important in God's sight. I am not a total personality without my body. Neither are you. The body is a part of what makes me me, and you you.

We shall not have, Paul avers, our weak earthly bodies, but we shall have new bodies, fashioned by God. There will be continuity between us now and us then (even though we shall be changed by God) just as there is continuity between the grain of wheat sown in the earth and the full-grown wheat a few months later.

We get a clear picture of this sense of *transformation* and *continuity* in another letter, where Paul describes the meaning of a spiritual body:

> But our commonwealth is in heaven, and from it we await a Savior, the Lord Jesus Christ, *who will change our lowly body to be like his glorious body,* by the power which enables him even to subject all things to himself (Phil. 3: 20, 21, italics added).

This is the clue: the body of "humiliation" will be refashioned, remodeled, by the power of God. There will be continuity in spite of transformation; my body will be refashioned, but it will still be *my* body, still myself. God is concerned with the whole of the created order, the physical as well as everything else. It is not junked by God as unimportant and worthless; it is transformed by him for his own purposes, so that it may be a more worthy vehicle for the doing of his will.

The analogy of the grain of wheat is about as far as Paul can "spell out" the idea of the resurrection body. In the last analysis it is something about which one can only offer an inspired guess. The matter remains beyond full human comprehension: "Lo! I tell you a mystery" (I Cor. 15: 51). The main fact for Paul is not the chemical composition of a spiritual body; the main fact is that God, in his own way and fashion, will remold and reshape us, so that we may continue to live in constant fellowship with him, doing his will and offering him praise. At the end of the chapter, giving up the attempt to give detailed answers to questions no man can answer, Paul puts the ultimate Christian assertion very clearly:

> "Death is swallowed up in victory."
> "O death, where is thy victory?
> O death, where is thy sting?"
> The sting of death is sin, and the power of sin is the law. But

thanks be to God, who gives us the victory through our Lord Jesus Christ (I Cor. 15: 55-57).

The Facts of the Case

Now let us pull our loose ends together.

Fact one. The Bible recognizes the reality and finality of death. It does not try to avoid the problem. It does not minimize the fact that we die and that our bodies decay. It looks this fact squarely in the face. Anything more that it has to say, then, will come not from an unrealistic evasion of the problem, but from a realistic facing of the problem, and a determined wrestling with it.

Fact two. The Bible does not try to "prove" eternal life. It is not something that can be demonstrated so convincingly that it must be believed. *Belief in eternal life is a consequence of belief in God.* If you believe in the God revealed in the Old Testament, eternal life becomes a possibility, and even a probability. If you believe in the God revealed in Jesus Christ, whom God raised from the dead, then you know for sure that death is not something that can frustrate God's purposes. God has conquered death, and is the Lord of life *and* death. This does not mean that the Christian has a blueprint of heaven, but he knows that eternal life will mean continuous fellowship with God—and that is enough.

Fact three. Eternal life is a *gift.* It is not something that is earned. Fellowship with God is not something of which we are "worthy." It is God's gift, bestowed upon us despite the fact that we are not worthy. We can refuse it, but not demand it. When Jesus tells a parable about the Last Judgment (Matt. 25: 31-46), the "righteous" ones, who shall enter into the joy of their Father in heaven, do not realize that they are righteous. They do not feel that they have earned any special privilege, that they have done "good deeds" that guarantee heaven to them. Paul makes it clear that fellowship with God is not achieved by "works," but that it is the result of faith that God in Christ has himself opened up new possibilities for fellowship, even though we do not deserve them. We are not "good" enough to deserve eternal life. It is God's gift.

Fact four. Eternal life can be described as *rebirth.* This lies behind Paul's image of the grain of wheat. It must die and be reborn. So with us. We die, and are reborn. This is, in fact, what Christian faith itself involves, and is at the heart of what Paul says so often about putting off the "old" man and putting on the "new" man. The Christian life is a perpetual dying to self and being raised to newness of life in Christ. It involves a break with the worship of self. Somewhere along the way, whether suddenly or gradually, the time must come when we cease to organize life around ourselves, and organize it around God. We must die to the life of self-concern, and begin a "new" life centered in God-concern. We must, in other words, be reborn. Jesus stresses this in his discussion with Nicodemus, "Unless one is born anew, he cannot see the kingdom of God" (John 3: 3). When one is reborn in this manner, he has begun to live eternally. Eternal life therefore is best described as a new life, in which the individual is born again to a different kind of existence. He is no longer trying to praise himself; he is trying to praise God.

Now the way in which the notion of rebirth is emphasized in the New Testament in connection with eternal life is by the idea of resurrection. Rather than speaking of immortality of the soul, the New Testament, as we have seen, speaks of eternal life as something that will be accomplished by the power of God, who will raise up and transform the total personality of the individual; not just the soul, but all that is distinctive about him. Both Old and New Testament agree that the body and soul cannot be split apart. They are not two very different ingredients, poorly fused together. They form a unity. We are "psychosomatic" persons (*psyche*=soul, *soma*= body). We are not just one or the other; we are both, together and indissolubly.

This means, then, that eternal life is a transforming, rather than a junking, of life on earth. The "body" stands for everything that we *do* and *are,* here on earth. Thus, to talk of the "resurrection of the body" is a way of saying that all that happens on earth concerns God, and that he will pick up, fulfill, and complete all our partial incomplete human efforts.

Fact five. This leads to one other point. Eternal life is not understood in the Bible simply as something that begins at the moment we die. Eternal life is *a possibility here and now.* This is particularly stressed in the Fourth Gospel and the letters written by John. To the degree that the life of the individual is oriented toward God in Christ, he is living eternally. He is experiencing in a fragmentary form that quality of life which is deathless, which, rather than being terminated by the moment of physical death, will be released at that moment to continue in a richness and fullness unimaginable to us. We can thus have foretastes, "hints and guesses," about eternal life, because eternal life is a partial reality here and now.

Theme and Variations

(I Try to Live a Good Life.
Why Isn't That Enough?)

Perhaps this paragraph should be called "By Way of Introduction." Its purpose is to point out that for the rest of this book we will be doing something rather different. So far we have been examining some weighty problems and questions—everything from the Trinity to tornadoes, from Eden to eschatology. But it is not enough just to look at problems and questions. We have to be sure that we relate problems and questions to where we are, right now. From now on we are going to be looking at the impact of all these Biblical beliefs upon the way we live and act today. We usually call this realm of personal and social conduct the realm of *ethics.*

The Bible has a good deal to say about ethics. It makes clear that our religious convictions—what we believe about God, about human nature, about history, about life and death— have a great deal to do with the way we act. It suggests, in fact, that we cannot separate religion and ethics from each other. They always go together.

That is the "theme" of this chapter. If you have listened to much music, you know that a popular form for a symphonic movement is the "theme and variations." The same theme is played several times, but each time in a way that is slightly different.

231

For example, the second movement of Beethoven's *Fifth Symphony* goes like this:

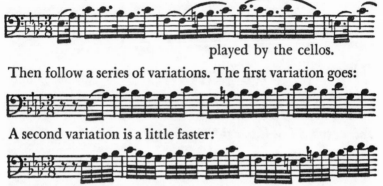

                    played by the cellos.

Then follow a series of variations. The first variation goes:

A second variation is a little faster:

The fourth is played (rather comically) by the double basses:

It's basically the same theme each time, but varied each time it reappears.

We shall follow a similar procedure in this chapter. The theme was stated in paragraph two. The rest of the chapter will consist of four variations on it, which should show more clearly how important it is.

An Objection to the Theme

DISGRUNTLED READER (*not the least hypnotized by the bass clef*): Now wait a minute. Wait just one minute. What makes you so sure the theme is a good one? I'm not at all sure I like it. I don't even believe it's true. I try to live a good life. I try to be decent to my neighbors. Why isn't that enough? If we all did that, this world would be a pretty fine place to live in. Why should you insist on dragging religion and God into this discussion? Why isn't ethics itself enough? Can't I lead a good life without believing in God?

In the light of this telling challenge, let us play our theme once more—a little more fully this time—and let it and the four variations upon it serve as an attempt to meet Disgruntled Reader's objections.

The out-and-out Biblical affirmation is that there is no sphere of life from which God is "cut off." There is no "sacred" realm of life that is unrelated to the "secular," no secular realm that can be understood apart from God. The whole Biblical approach prohibits us from dividing life into such watertight compartments. We see a clear-cut example of this in the covenant agreement made at Sinai. God's demands and concerns invade *every* area of life. It is not enough just to believe in God or worship God. Those who agree to believe in God and worship God must also bring their life *in its totality* under the divine will. A reading of Ex., chs. 20 to 23, will show this. Everything is to be made conformable to God's will,

from regulations concerning
> stealing,
> cursing,
> animal husbandry, and
> real estate transactions

to regulations concerning
> borrowing,
> sacrificing,
> courtesy to strangers, and
> telling the truth.

All of life belongs to God. We are accountable, not simply to our consciences or to society, but to the Giver and Sustainer of life. Religion and ethics can never be separated. They are two sides of the same coin.

Now let us get at the same thing in another way. What happens in point of fact when people *do* separate religion and ethics? We must acknowledge that many people who don't believe in God live selfless and devoted lives which are a challenge and a rebuke to professing Christians, and no self-righteous Christian should be allowed to forget this fact. However, it is fair to ask whether this "ethic without religion" can sustain and perpetuate itself for very long. Think of that large tree in the park near your house. If a disease attacks the tree and kills the roots, you may not know this for some time, because the branches and leaves will continue to live for a while after the roots are dead. But sooner or later the branches will dry up and the leaves will wither, for they cannot live long without the life and vitality that the roots furnish.

The same thing is true of the problem we are discussing. Historically, the roots of ethical concern and responsibility have been religious faith. To say that ethics should be cut off from religion is thus like saying that the branches and leaves can live without the roots. It just won't work. It may appear to work for a time, just as the tree lives for a little while after the roots die. But it won't work long. The rootless "ethic without religion" will finally succumb.

And even though the individual may do this for a while, it is doubly hard for society as a whole. As our culture tries to enhance this split between religion and ethics, we find that the ethics get more and more dubious. The notion that truth and honesty and justice are important is replaced by the notion that "business is business," which means, finally, that "anything goes." Put simply,

> If you can, be honest (it's safer).
> If you can't be honest, be legal.
> If you can't be legal, don't get caught.

The "Micah" Variation

Now for some "variations" on the theme that religion and ethics cannot be separated. The first one is short, and involves only a recognition of some ideas in a familiar verse:

> He has showed you, O man, what is good;
>   and what does the Lord require of you
> but to do justice, and to love kindness,
>   and to walk humbly with your God?
>
>   (Micah 6: 8)

Most people, whether "religious" or not, would agree that it is a good thing to "do justice" and to "love kindness" (though they might not agree to the walking-humbly-with-God part). "That's what we need," they would say, "more justice, more kindness."

But notice that the Biblical view is utterly different. Justice and kindness are not important merely in themselves, even though they are ethical demands of a high order. They are significant *because they are what God requires of us.* It is because he wills us to do justice and to love kindness that we must take them seriously.

Thus in the field of Biblical ethics, the important questions are not such abstract queries as, "What is the good?" or, "What is a reasonable way to live?" or, "Is this a wise thing to do?" The important question is the specific and concrete question, "What is the will of God?" Ethical questions do not stand alone; they are considered in the light of God's will, and how it can best be fulfilled. Religion and ethics go together.

The "Worship and Action" Variation

Many people try to draw a line between "worship" and "action," and make the choice an either/or. Something like this:

The most important thing in life is relationship with God. Nothing is as important as that. Prayer, meditation, Bible-reading—these are the really important things in the growth of the soul. Beside them, nothing else really matters. So let's stop arguing and continue steadfast in prayer.

The most important thing in life is doing the practical down-to-earth things that need to be done. Nothing is as important as that. Voting, legislation, action —these are the really important things in the betterment of humanity. Beside them, nothing else really matters. So let's stop arguing and get on with the job.

Each position has a certain appeal. The relationship to God *is* fundamental to human life, and the need to do things *is* important. The mistake comes in trying to separate the two, and the Bible points out again and again that this cannot be done without getting into trouble. Those who concentrate on worship alone get so involved in the niceties of ritual that they become blind to injustice. Those who are concerned only with "doing things" find that their sense of direction and purpose deteriorates. Worship leads to action, action must be grounded in worship—that is the truth which the Bible proclaims.

Let's be more specific. We can follow an individual through an experience of worship and see how it made him a "man of action." The individual is Isaiah. He remembers the experience very well, for it took place "in the year that King Uzziah died" (Isa. 6: 1). He was worshiping in the Temple, and he realized as he never had before that God was there. He realized that his first obligation was to worship and adore God, to affirm with the very angels themselves, "Holy, holy, holy is the Lord of hosts; the whole earth is full of his glory" (v. 3). He realized that God is, indeed, "holy," apart from men, and that before such a God men must always bow in reverence.

As Isaiah became aware of the majesty of God, he became aware that by contrast he was evil and impure, as were the people among whom he dwelt. Before such a God he could only cry out, "Woe is me! For I am lost; for I am a man of unclean lips, and I dwell in the midst of a people of unclean lips; for my eyes have seen the King, the Lord of hosts" (v. 5). This is a genuine reaction when God confronts men: God is worthy and I am unworthy; God is pure and I am impure; God is holy and I am debased.

If that were all, we could think of God as an evil tyrant, concerned only to condemn people. But that was not all. Isaiah went on in a very vivid way to point out that God did not leave him impure and sinful. His lips were unclean so his lips were cleansed. His sin was forgiven.

Even that was not the end. For then came the part of the experience that showed how intimately worship and action are related. For Isaiah heard the voice of God, calling for a messenger: "Whom shall I send, and who will go for us?" (v. 8). And Isaiah replied, "Here am I; send me." It was *because* of his experience of worship that Isaiah was prepared for his strenuous activity as a prophet. His intimate confrontation with God made it imperative that he go forth and confront his fellow men. Because he had worshiped, he was now ready to "act." This is the authentic Biblical note.

This does not mean that worship is only a device or "gimmick" to make people do a more "effective" job of social action. There is a real sense in which worship is an "end in itself," something we do simply because we are created to praise and worship God, and this is our highest activity as human beings. We worship God because he is "worshipful," not because it makes us better citizens. However, when worship is real, it is not an "escape from the world," but thrusts us back into the middle of that world more firmly than ever. In the Biblical view there is no real difference between "worship" and "action." They are simply parts of the same total experience of living all life as "under God." To pray for a sick neighbor and to help out in the sickroom are parts of the *same* fundamental concern. True worship does not leave us "wallowing in our own piety," but pushes us into those areas where the will of God needs to be done.

The "Therefore" Variation

Now let us look at a New Testament variation of the theme. The thing that you can't escape as you read the New Testament is the fact that these Christians were concerned about one another primarily because they believed that God was concerned about all of them. It was because of *God's* love, made known to them in Christ, that they felt impelled to love one another. "We love," one of them says, "because he first loved us" (I John 4: 19). God loves us, therefore we must love one another. It would be absurd to talk about loving God if you did not also love your brother:

If any one says, "I love God," and hates his brother, he is a liar;
for he who does not love his brother whom he has seen, cannot love
God whom he has not seen. And this commandment we have from
him, that he who loves God should love his brother also (I John
4: 20, 21).

Jesus observes the same order of priority. The first commandment is to love God. The second commandment—*just
like the first*, he tells us—is to love your neighbor. You are to
love Joe Doakes (against whom you may happen to have a
grudge at the moment) because:

a. God loves you, and you must "pass on" that love to
   others;
b. God loves Joe Doakes (even though you may find that
   hard to believe) and you must not refuse to love one
   whom God loves; and
c. If you love God and wish to do his will, his will is crystal-
   clear on this particular point.

There is no way of wriggling out from under that demand.

We now begin to see why New Testament ethics can be
called "therefore" ethics. Again and again we find that a long
passage about God will end with a "therefore," which goes on
to point out how the belief in God leaves you saddled with all
sorts of ethical demands. Here are a few examples.

In his letter to the Romans, Paul writes eleven long, difficult
"theological" chapters, explaining to the Romans what Christian faith is, who Jesus Christ is, what he has done for men,
and so on. Straight theology. And then what? Chapter 12 begins, "I appeal to you *therefore*, brethren," and Paul gives a
long list of attitudes, practices, and characteristics of the way
in which Christians are to act—things like:

Let love be genuine.
Hate what is evil.
Hold fast to what is good.
Love one another with brotherly affection.
Bless those who persecute you.

> Live in harmony with one another.
> Repay no one evil for evil.

And the word "therefore" is the pivot of the entire argument. Because all these things that I have been writing to you about (for eleven chapters!) are true, Paul is saying in effect, *therefore* this is the way in which you must act.

The same thing happens in the letter to the Ephesians. The first three chapters expound the work of Christ upon the cross. And the fourth chapter begins,

I *therefore*, a prisoner for the Lord, beg you to lead a life worthy of the calling to which you have been called, with all lowliness and meekness, with patience, forbearing one another in love, eager to maintain the unity of the Spirit in the bond of peace (Eph. 4: 1-3).

And the writer continues with advice about the way life is to be lived *because* of what God has done in Christ. The ethics are dependent upon the faith.

An even more striking example of placing ethics squarely in the context of what God has done is found in Paul's letter to the Philippians. He finds it impossible to separate religion and ethics, and they are woven together inextricably.

Do nothing from selfishness or conceit, but in humility count others better than yourselves. Let each of you look not only to his own interests, but also to the interests of others. Have this mind among yourselves, which you have in Christ Jesus, who, though he was in the form of God, did not count equality with God a thing to be grasped, but emptied himself, taking the form of a servant, being born in the likeness of men. And being found in human form he humbled himself and became obedient unto death, even death on a cross (Phil. 2: 3-8) .

You will notice that in this striking passage, Paul has been giving ethical instruction, stressing humility and warning against selfishness and conceit. But how do we know what this "humility" is like? We find our answer at the very heart of the gospel —in the staggering humility of Christ, who was in the form of God himself, and yet set that aside that he might take the form of a servant. An assertion of what Christ has done (the heart of Christian faith) is also an assertion of what we must do (the heart of Christian ethics). God has acted in this way toward us, *therefore,* we are to act this way toward our fellow men. The two cannot be separated.

The same fact comes out clearly in the experience of Paul on the road to Damascus (see Chapter 8). Here he finds himself confronted by God. And he asks two questions:

1. Who are you, Lord?
2. What shall I do, Lord? (Acts 22: 8, 10)

First, he must know who this God is who confronts him. And when he does know, then he must do something about it. Since God is that kind of God, Paul seems to be saying, *therefore,* I must find out and do whatever he commands me to do.

These examples make clear that in the New Testament ethics are "therefore" ethics. They represent what we must do because of what God has done. They represent our action in response to God's action. It is all summed up in the statement, "If God so loved us [by sending his Son], we also ought to love one another" (I John 4: 11).

The "Creeds and Deeds" Variation

Popular slogans these days go like this:

> "It's deeds we need, not creeds."

> "It's not what you believe,
> it's what you do, that counts."

But, popular or not, such slogans contain a fundamental fallacy. They fail to take account of the fact that *what you believe influences what you do.* What you believe not only counts; it makes all the difference in the world.

If you believe, for example (as the Nazis did), that the Jews are the scum of the earth, so contaminating to the "pure Nordic race" that they should be wiped out, then you will of course put them in concentration camps and gas chambers and destroy as many of them as you can. The Nazi creed leads to the Nazi deed.

If you believe, however (as Christians do), that God "hath made of one blood all nations of men for to dwell on all the face of the earth" (Acts 17: 26), then you will realize that the Jews are God's children, and you will have to oppose as vigorously as you can their continued slaughter. The Christian creed must lead to the Christian deed.

Note to the Careful Reader: Be careful here. We are on the verge of slipping into a falsification of Biblical faith. We are almost assuming that to know the good is to do it, or (to put it another way) that we sin only because we don't know any better. The Bible doesn't say that if we know that all men are children of God, we will inevitably treat them as such. However, we know that we *should* treat them as such, and the Bible makes us aware, often uncomfortably aware, of this and other demands. But just because we cannot assume that to know the good is to do it is no reason to relinquish the struggle to know the good and *try* to do it. That is our constant obligation as Christians.

Here are a few examples of Biblical convictions that carry ethical implications, creeds (if you will), that demand deeds. Perhaps you can think of others.

It is the Biblical faith that *God is the Creator*. He has a purpose for this world or he would not have created it. Since he has placed us here, it is clear that he wants us to help to carry out his purpose right here where we are. Our job is not to escape from God's world but to *live within it* in such a way that we further his purposes. To believe in creation is to believe in the necessity for ethical action in conformity with the will of God.

It is the Biblical faith that *the Word was made flesh,* that God sent his own Son into the world to live the life of men, not as a superman or a "pretend" man, but as a real man. This means, clearly, that the world, the flesh, and the body are of concern to God, since they represent the arena in which God chose to reveal himself. We cannot indulge in the idle luxury of being concerned merely with "spiritual things" when God so obviously has been concerned with "material things." This is why we can speak of Christianity as the most "materialistic" of all the religions. We are not to reject the body, physical life, the good things around us, but to affirm them and use them joyfully. To put it most concisely from the point of view of Biblical faith, matter matters.

It is the Biblical faith that *God sent his Son to save men.* He apparently thought that we were worth all the anguish and torment of a shameful death upon the cross. He chose to come to us in Christ and win us back to him, even if that was the price that had to be paid. It surely follows that if men are worth that much to God, they must be of worth to us. Anything that is a degradation of the humanity which Christ comes to redeem is a denial of God and of his love. This means that ...

a slum,

a discriminatory clause in a real estate contract,

a sign "For Whites Only,"

... are contrary to God's purpose and are offenses not only against man but against the God who came to save men.

In each case, you see, the belief carries implications in the field of action. And so we have another variation on the theme, "Religion and ethics go together."

With which variation, the defense rests.

An Examination of the Social or Corporate Dimension of Biblical Ethics, Together with a Repudiation of the Way of Legalism or "Pharisaism," to Which Is Annexed a Treatment of the New Testament Faith in "Christian Liberty"

(Why Can't I Live by a Set of Rules?)

A couple of hundred years ago, chapter titles always went like that. They had the great advantage of giving the reader a handy outline of what was coming. But if the title seems too cumbersome for you, you can ignore it and read the next paragraph instead.

This chapter discusses three facts about Biblical ethics:
1. They are corporate ethics rather than individualistic ethics.
2. They denounce "legalism," or living by a set of rules.
3. They emphasize the freedom which belongs to true ethical conduct.

Some Highly Unusual Notions

When the enemies of the early Christians looked for a way to describe them, the phrase they hit upon was, "These men who have turned the world upside down" (Acts 17: 6).

It was an accurate description.

If you were an unsuspecting pagan and one of these Christians got to work on you, before long your world *would* be turned upside down. The things you had held dear, like the pagan gods, would be knocked off their pedestals. Instead of "looking out for Number One," you would be trying to love not only your friends but your enemies as well. Instead of worshiping Caesar, you would be worshiping Jesus—and maybe getting strung up on a cross for doing so.

Community Ethics

This didn't happen just because of certain isolated Christians. The idea of Christians doing things was something that was carried out by groups of Christians working together. When we talk about Christian ethics in the New Testament period, we have to remember that they were *community ethics.* Christians lived and worshiped and acted—together. And the things they did were as down-to-earth as tomorrow's groceries.

All who believed were together and had all things in common; and they sold their possessions and goods and distributed them to all, as any had need. . . . No one said that any of the things which he possessed was his own, but they had everything in common. . . . There was not a needy person among them, for as many as were possessors of lands or houses sold them, and brought the proceeds of what was sold and laid it at the apostles' feet; and distribution was made to each as any had need (Acts 2: 44, 45; 4: 34, 35).

That's how seriously the early Christians took their community ethics. If your neighbor was in need, you didn't just pray for him; you dug into your own pocket and helped him with your own money—only you didn't call it your "own" any more, because you had given it to the community so that anyone in need could be helped. You had to love the people whom Christ had loved. You could not be lolling around in luxury if your "brothers in Christ" were starving.

Today, people look at this early experiment in Christian

living and whisper, with a shudder, "Communism." Actually, this was very different from modern Communism, as any good student of the latter subject can tell you. The striking thing about it is that it shows how far the early Christians were ready to go in translating their beliefs into practice. They didn't just talk about "being concerned with the other chap"; they actually helped him out.

Note to the Careful Reader: But the experiment failed. And just as the reasons for its being tried are significant, so are the reasons for its failure. (1) With a small, intimate group of people there can be a real sharing of the material goods of life. However, when the group gets large, as the Christian community rapidly did, the spontaneous sharing has to be "organized," and the spontaneity inevitably disappears. This does not mean that sharing should stop, but that it must be done differently. (2) Furthermore, the Christians were not stained-glass-window saints. They remained men of the world, tempted to turn any good thing to their own advantage, as happened in the case of Ananias and Sapphira, who tried to "beat the system" and feather their financial nests against a rainy day. (3) Finally, the attempt gradually broke down as the "eschatological expectation" (see Chapter 16) broke down. The early Christians expected the almost immediate return of Christ. When he did not return, they had to revise their manner of living so that their resources would not be used up.

God and the Whole Community

Using that unique experiment as a springboard, let us jump farther into the past, and see how the point was expressed in the Old Testament. We saw (in Chapter 15) that one of the most important Biblical ideas is the notion of the covenant. God enters into special relationship with a whole people. He agrees to be their God, and they agree to be his people.

But what happens, you remember, is that the chosen people invariably break their part of the covenant and worship other gods. And the outcome of this fact is plain for all to see: *a broken covenant means a broken community*. When the covenant relationship between God and man is destroyed, the relationship between man and man is likewise destroyed. Life gets "out of joint," and disaster follows.

In the sayings of all the prophets—Amos, Hosea, Micah, Isaiah, Jeremiah, and the rest—the theme is repeated again and again. Israel has broken its covenant relationship with God. "The Lord has a controversy with the inhabitants of the land," announces Hosea. "There is no faithfulness or kindness, and no knowledge of God in the land" (Hos. 4: 1). And what happens where there is "no knowledge of God in the land"? Hosea is uncomfortably specific. These things happen:

> swearing,
> lying,
> killing,
> stealing,
> and committing adultery;
> they break all bounds and murder follows murder.
>
> (Hos. 4: 2)

Men act this way when the covenant relationship is no longer taken seriously. There is not only "sin in general," but there are "sins in particular."

Why does this happen? Why do people spurn God and thereby destroy their life together? Ezekiel sees, as all the prophets do, that what has upset the applecart is the sin of pride; that is, the feeling that life can be organized apart from God. People repudiate the covenant relationship because they think (falsely) that they can live apart from God, that they can "get by on their own." But this complete repudiation of God brings its own disastrous consequences:

> Because your heart is proud,
>   and you have said, "I am a god,
> I sit in the seat of the gods,
>   in the heart of the seas,"

yet you are but a man, and no god,
> though you consider yourself as wise as a god . . .
> and your heart has become proud in your wealth—
therefore thus says the Lord God:
"Because you consider yourself
> as wise as a god,
therefore, behold, I will bring strangers upon you,
> the most terrible of the nations;
and they shall draw their swords against the beauty of
> your wisdom
> and defile your splendor."

(Ezek. 28: 2, 5-7)

If this is a grim picture, it is also a realistic picture. The whole history of the Old Testament shows that when the covenant relationship with God is repudiated,

> the relationship between man and man *does* go to pieces;
> chaos and disaster *do* follow;
> men *are* set up in conflict with their fellow men;
> the rich *do* despoil the poor;
> the priests *do* become hypocrites;
> religion *does* become a mockery.

Is there no escape? Is this the last word? We have seen that it is not. God did not forsake his people. He chastened them, but he did not forsake them. After the Exile came the restoration. But the time of restoration, when the Children of Israel were restored to their own land, brought its own peculiar difficulties, and we must now take a look at them.

The Development of "Legalism"

When Cyrus, the Persian ruler, began to let the Jews trickle back to their homeland, they developed a way of life which centered upon adherence to a set of rules. (This experience is described in the books of Ezra and Nehemiah.) The feeling was that God had told his people just what to do and not to do, and that everybody should live up to the "do's" and "don'ts" of the code. The priests were to interpret the code and carry out the rituals and ceremonies that were prescribed in it. Thus the code of rules, or the "law," became the measuring stick of achievement. You were "good" if you obeyed the rules, "bad" if you disregarded them.

Legalism and Self-righteousness

Notice what happens when you try to live by rules. There is always the possibility that you will reason like this:

Step One: "Those who obey the laws are good, and God rewards them. Those who disobey the laws are bad, and God punishes them."

Step Two: "There is a man who is prosperous. He must be obeying the law. . . . There is a man who is in trouble. He must be disobeying the law."

Step Three: "I am doing a pretty good job of obeying the law—if I do say so myself. That means God ought to reward me. Now see here, God . . ."—at which point you start ordering God around like a drill sergeant.

Step Three can go another way too: "I'm doing all right for myself. Made a nice little business deal yesterday. That must mean God is extremely pleased with me, and is blessing all my efforts."

Legalism, in other words, leads to self-righteousness, in which I compare how good I am to how bad you are, and how obvious it is that God really likes me a lot better.

The Bible criticizes this point of view sharply. The Book of Job (see Chapter 11) is a specific challenge to it. One of the psalmists points out a truth deeper than legalism: "If thou, O Lord, shouldst mark iniquities, Lord, who could stand?" (Ps. 130: 3). And another one pleads with God, "Wash me thoroughly from my iniquity, and cleanse me from my sin! For I know my transgressions, and my sin is ever before me. Against thee, thee only, have I sinned" (Ps. 51: 2-4).

Laws About Laws

Legalism is like a malignant disease; the more you try to cure it, the worse it gets. Hundreds of laws become confusing, so you try to arrange them in order of importance. And to do this you have to introduce a few more laws:

1. Laws to tell you which laws are most important.
2. Laws to tell you which law to break if you are in a spot where you can't help breaking one law or the other.

By the end of the Old Testament period there were 613 different rules or laws, in addition to explanations and oral traditions about them. And in time the oral traditions came to be as much "laws" as the original laws themselves. Here is how it worked:

The Law: "In the Sabbath [you] shall not do any work" (Ex. 20: 10).

Question: Very well, but what is meant by "work"? Just what things are forbidden on the Sabbath?

Answer: There are 39 different kinds of work prohibited on the Sabbath [and the list of the 39 kinds would be given].

Question: Yes, but aren't some of these things *almost* work but not *actually* work? How can we tell the difference?

Answer: On those questionable details, you must get a special ruling, so that you don't break the law. For example, it is all right for a woman to tie a knot in her sash on the Sabbath; that is not work. But if the same woman should tie the knot in order to carry water jugs from her waist, that would be work, and it would be wrong.

What happens?

It is very clear what happens. You become so worried about breaking one of the rules, or one of the rules about one of the rules, or one of the rulings about one of the rules about one of the rules—that all your time is taken up with a meticulous observance of these details. And the notion of a living personal relationship with God (which is what the law was originally all about) is lost and forgotten. So is the idea of loving your neighbor—who would dare to do a spontaneous act of kindness for his neighbor when such an act might violate one of the demands of the law?

The New Testament Protest

The sharp protest against legalism in the Old Testament is picked up and intensified in the New Testament.

Jesus, for example, is quite unwilling to let life be reduced to a set of rules. Good Jew though he was, he put concern for people above concern for the law. He was willing to break the law about not working on the Sabbath when people's needs were involved. To the surprised horror of the people about him, he healed a sick person on the Sabbath. If the Sabbath laws stood in the way of ministering to human need, then so much the worse for the Sabbath laws. As Jesus put it, "The sabbath was made for man, not man for the sabbath" (Mark 2: 27). It was more important to have regard for your neighbor than to have regard for a law. In a way that utterly shocked his contemporaries, he said on a number of occasions, "It has been said to you of old [and then recited some portion of the law], but *I* say unto you [and then gave a new statement of his own]." This suggests that when Jesus made the apparently contradictory statement, that he had come not to destroy the law but to fulfill it (see Matt. 5: 17), he meant that he came to rescue the law from the kind of ridiculous absurdity to which the Pharisees had brought it, and "fulfill" what had been the original intent of the law—to bring God and man into living relationship. He did this by stressing, out of all the rules and regulations and requirements, the command to love God and to love one's neighbor. (See Chapter 20.)

The thing that makes this discussion so important for us today is that legalism is always the temptation of "religious" people. You probably know individuals who take Jesus' teachings, and try to make a *new* set of rules out of them. Or they develop a new code of rules to fit a particular situation, and then say: "If you obey these rules, you are a Christian. Otherwise not." There are lots of these rules:

1. A Christian doesn't go to the movies
   (at least, not on Sunday).
2. A Christian doesn't smoke.
3. A Christian doesn't drink.
4. A Christian doesn't dance.
5. A Christian spends —— minutes in prayer every day.
6. A Christian always goes to church on Sunday.

This is a new form of legalism. It is living life by a set of rules
(mostly negative, it often turns out). You are "good" if you
obey the rules, "bad" if you break them.

The Case Against Legalism

Why is this so foreign to the spirit of the New Testament?
Why is it so strongly attacked there? Let us summarize the
objections:

Objection One: Legalism forgets that religion is an active
relationship with God in love. It reduces religion to "keeping-
the-rules-so-you-won't-get-caught." It makes outward behavior
more important than inner attitude and motivation. It takes
the spontaneity out of Christian living.

Objection Two: Legalism misunderstands the nature of
God's love. It makes God's love something you have to earn
by keeping the rules, whereas the whole claim of the New
Testament is that God's love cannot be earned; it is a free gift,
offered to people who are *not* worthy of it.

Objection Three: Legalism shifts the center of religious
concern from God to man. Your number one concern becomes
saving your own skin, doing all you can to gain your salvation.
It assumes that you can save yourself, whereas the New Testament proclaims that salvation is God's gift to you, and that you
are to be concerned about God and his children, rather than
being so wrapped up in yourself.

Objection Four: Legalism makes the individual proud. You
are likely to start thinking: Say, I'm really doing pretty well.
Broke only four rules today, out of 613, and that's batting well

in any league. Not bad, old boy; you're really coming along. The minute a person begins to talk this way he is done for. For this is the danger that always threatens the lives of "religious" people—the danger of smugness, or self-satisfaction (particularly when you compare yourself with *certain* people you could mention). Jesus' denunciations of the "good" people of his day should be required reading for anyone who thinks he is a cut above his buddies because he goes to church regularly, or reads his curriculum book, or gives a few dimes to the Red Cross. (Take a long, hard look at Matt., ch. 23, as a speech addressed to you.)

Objection Five: One of Paul's main complaints is that legalism has no power. It may tell you what is demanded of you, but it doesn't give you the power to fulfill the demands. All that legalism could do for Paul was to intensify his misery. Paul, in fact, went even farther, in a statement that scandalized his contemporaries: "If it had not been for the law," he says, "I should not have known sin. I should not have known what it is to covet if the law had not said, 'You shall not covet' " (Rom. 7: 7). It may be (as most thoughtful Jewish thinkers would argue) that Paul is being unduly harsh as he looks back on his preconversion state. But it is still true that there is something enticing about forbidden activity. "Do anything you want in the kitchen," Mother says to Junior, "but don't put beans up your nose." Immediately Junior, who never thought of putting beans up his nose, can think of nothing more exciting, and spends the afternoon trying to carry out the forbidden experiment.

The one real value of the law, Paul went on, was that it was self-defeating. The more you tried it (as he knew from personal experience), the more you realized that it didn't work. But it could be a "tutor" or a "schoolmaster" unto Christ. By this he meant that if you finally realized that the law was a blind alley, you were more likely to turn to the new liberty for living, which had been procured by Christ. This Paul called standing fast in the freedom for which "Christ has set us free" (Gal. 5: 1). It was his answer to the futility of living by rules.

"The Liberty of the Christian Man"

Particularly toward the end of his letter to the Galatians, Paul talks about this liberty or freedom. The Christian is free *from* the law. He is no longer in bondage to hundreds of minute requirements, which can do nothing to save him. He has come to see that these things do not make him "righteous" in the sight of God. His belief in Christ frees him from bondage to the law.

But this freedom is not simply negative. It is "*for* freedom that Christ has set us free" (Gal. 5: 1). Freedom for what? Not simply freedom to do "anything under the sun." Not simply "an opportunity for the flesh," as Paul puts it (v. 13), by which he means a chance merely to be concerned for the self. On the contrary, this freedom means that we can "through love be servants of one another" (v. 13). We are now *free to love,* as we never were before. This is Christian freedom—not to be wrapped up in oneself, but to live a life of outgoing concern for others. To "bear one another's burdens," is to "fulfil the law of Christ" (ch. 6: 2).

SUSPICIOUS READER (*afraid of a trap*): I thought there would be a catch to it. Free to serve. . . . H'mm. A plain contradiction in terms.

But this is not a contradiction. This is one of those living paradoxes of faith in which the New Testament abounds. The author of First Peter makes the same surprising kind of statement: "Live as free men," he writes, and then, in the very same breath, half a line later, he adds, "live as servants of God" (I Peter 2: 16). A man who is "free" can be defined as a man who serves God.

The important point at the moment is that neither Paul nor anyone else can spell out precisely *how,* in every given circumstance, you live out this Christian freedom. You are now free to love your neighbor, but you cannot be given minute instructions on precisely *how* to love your neighbor, since love is not adherence to a series of rules, but a spontaneous concern for the neighbor. What love demands on one occasion may not be what love demands on another occasion. In this sense there are no "rules" connected with Christian ethics. Saint Augustine summarized Christian living from this point of view in a statement that is true and dangerous at the same time. "Love," he said, "and do as you please." Augustine meant that if you truly *did* love, then what you "pleased" to do would be what love demanded in the situation. As a protest against religious legalism, Augustine's point is important, and summarizes Paul's position.

But there is a problem here, as Paul himself is aware. When he began talking this way, the Corinthians, for example, rather gleefully said: "Fine! Dandy! We'll go right along with that. If there are no rules, 'anything goes.' We can do what we please." Paul dealt with this challenge in characteristic fashion, by discussing a specific local problem (I Cor. 10: 23-31). And although the problem itself is a dead issue now, the point that emerges from the discussion is a tremendously live one.

Suppose (Paul says to his readers) you go to a banquet at the home of a pagan friend, and discover that the meat you are to eat has been offered to a pagan idol, say Serapis. Now this doesn't make any difference to you. You know that Serapis doesn't exist, and you can eat the meat with a clear conscience. However, perhaps to some other fellow Christian your action becomes a temptation to sin. He feels that it is wrong to eat meat that has been offered to idols, and that as a matter of principle he shouldn't do it. And yet . . . he sees you do it, and since it is so much easier not to stick out like a sore thumb socially, he imitates you and eats the meat, even though he feels that it is wrong for him to do so. Your action has led him into wrongdoing. So,

> If some one says to you, "This [meat] has been offered in sacrifice," then out of consideration for the man who in-

formed you, and for conscience' sake—I mean his conscience, not yours—do not eat it (I Cor. 10: 28, 29).

Thus the ethic without rules or regulations still provides a real basis for knowing what to do. As Paul puts it, "Let no one seek his own good, but the good of his neighbor" (I Cor. 10: 24). The Christian man is free to seek the good of his neighbor. And "the good of his neighbor" is something he will find, not by turning to page 79 of a book entitled *613 Ways to Love Your Neighbor,* but rather by entering into a living and loving relationship with that neighbor. The heart of the New Testament ethic, then, is a kind of spontaneous love that cannot be reduced to rules but attempts to seek the good of the neighbor.

This still may seem too vague and general, too lacking in specific guidance. We must therefore put more content into this notion of active, outgoing love, by taking a look at some of Jesus' teachings.

The Not-so-simple Teachings of Jesus, with a Footnote on Paul

(What Does It Mean to Love My Neighbor?)

Where have we gotten so far?

We have seen that the "liberty of the Christian man" is at the heart of the New Testament answer to the problem of ethics, and that goodness cannot be "legislated" by compressing it into a set of rules. There is a "spontaneity" that characterizes Christian living at its best.

At the same time we have also seen that this is a dangerous kind of liberty. To be told to "love, and do as you please," may prove to be quite inadequate counsel, particularly if we do not know more specifically what it means to love. Fortunately, the New Testament does not fail us at this point. Over and over again we find down-to-earth examples of what it means to love:

> But if someone who is rich sees his brother in need and closes his heart against him, how can he have any love for God in his heart? (I John 3: 17, Goodspeed trans.) .

The writer is saying bluntly that sometimes you demonstrate your love by digging into your pocketbook.

In this chapter we shall look at ways in which Jesus' teachings cast light on Christian behavior without becoming a new set of laws.

Back to the "Simple Teachings of Jesus"?

But first, let us beware of a very enticing snare which goes:

> Let's forget all this theology business. Let's get back to the simple teachings of Jesus. They give us all the direction we need, and we can forget about sin and salvation and all that.

This may sound fine on the surface, but on a number of counts it is open to serious question.

1. Jesus' significance does not lie primarily in his teachings. Actually they can be paralleled in Jewish rabbinic writings or in Oriental religious teachings long before Jesus' time. To be sure, no one person said all the things Jesus said, or had such a consistently high ethic, but for Christian faith the real significance of Jesus lies, not so much in what he says, but in who he is.

2. When we begin to examine them, we discover that these "simple teachings" are not so "simple" after all. There is nothing very "simple" about the statement, "You, therefore, must be perfect, as your heavenly Father is perfect" (Matt. 5: 48). The "simple truths" of the Beatitudes turn out to be rather complex: "Blessed are the *pure in heart*. . . . Blessed are those who are *persecuted*. . . ." It is not a simple matter to be pure in heart or to endure persecution.

3. Many of the "simple teachings," rather than offering us encouragement, offend us. Rather than making us comfortable, they disturb us. Jesus often casts grave doubts upon our whole manner of living. Think for one minute of some of the things he says.

To the religious leaders of his day: "The tax collectors and the harlots go into the kingdom of God before you" (Matt. 21: 31).

To those closest to him: "Unless you turn and become like children, you will never enter the kingdom of heaven" (Matt.
18: 3).

To the "good" people who think they are "very religious": "You
also outwardly appear righteous to men, but within you are
full of hypocrisy and iniquity" (Matt. 23: 28).

*To the people who think that evil is just the result of social con-
ditioning:* "Out of the heart come evil thoughts, murder,
adultery, fornication, theft, false witness, slander" (Matt. 15:
19).

These are not cheery comments; they are jarring denunciations—a series of "lefts" to the spiritual jaw.

4. Finally, to speak of Jesus' teachings as though they could
be separated from "theology" or "belief in God" is a betrayal
of the very teachings themselves. For Jesus' ethics are through-
and-through *religious* ethics. If you do not believe in the God
of whom Jesus speaks, there is little point to taking his teachings seriously. He tells you to love your enemies, for example,
not because this will "work," or convert your enemies, but because it is God's will that you do so. You are to forgive, not
because this is expedient or clever, but because God forgives
you, and you are to mirror the divine compassion in your own
life. So it goes. When the disciples report that they have subdued demons (and think they are pretty splendid as a result),
Jesus rebukes them: "Do not rejoice in this, that the spirits
are subject to you; but rejoice that your names are written in
heaven" (Luke 10: 20). In other words, it is more important
to do God's will than to be proud of what you have "accomplished."

These comments make it clear that we cannot talk about
Jesus' teachings except in terms of his total mission on earth.

Seeing Jesus' Teachings in Context

Just what is this "total mission" of Jesus? If we remember
the discussion of Jesus' life (Chapters 7-10) it will be clear
that he did not come just to leave us a few pearls of ethical

wisdom. He came to restore the broken relationship between God and man, to announce and to incarnate the fact that God loves sinful men and desires their fellowship, and that the Kingdom of God is now a present reality. Just as the miracles are "signs" of the Kingdom of God, so are the teachings a description of what life in the Kingdom of God is like. They show how one is to live within the Kingdom. For this reason, the teachings cannot be separated from Jesus' *total* mission, and we mutilate his message when we attempt this separation.

The Rigor in Jesus' Teaching

It seems clear that Jesus' teachings represent the unqualified demands of the Kingdom of God. They do not (as we say) "take human nature into account." That is, Jesus does not soften the rigor of his teachings so that they will be easier to follow. The teaching about perfection makes this uncomfortably clear:

Jesus does not say, "Be as good as you can under the circumstances."

He does not say, "Resist as many temptations as you can."

He does not say, "Do your best and let it go at that."

He does not say, "Be perfect according to human standards of perfection."

His demand is the most exacting one possible: "Be perfect, as your heavenly Father is perfect" (Matt. 5: 48).

It is an out-and-out demand, with no concessions made or promised.

It's the same way with specific teachings. Jesus does not say, "Love your enemies as long as it is practicable to do so." No, he says, "Love your enemies"—and offers no concessions. In fact, it is not just enough to love them, you must also pray for them. And Jesus does not agree with Peter that it would be pretty bighearted to forgive a person seven times. On the contrary, Jesus says we must forgive "seventy times seven." But with Jesus this is a special kind of arithmetic, the arithmetic of compassion. For

$$70 \times 7 \neq 490, \text{ but}$$
$$70 \times 7 = \text{Infinity}$$

We must, in other words, forgive limitless times.

The Central Demand

What is the central demand in Jesus' teachings? Surely it is that we are to have absolute trust in God. No "conditions" are attached, no concessions are offered. "You shall love the Lord your God with *all* your heart, and with *all* your soul, and with *all* your strength, and with *all* your mind" (Luke 10: 27). Total commitment to God is the obligation of the Christian. To have this commitment is to be a citizen of the Kingdom of God, and to enter the Kingdom is more important than anything else. There must be a single-mindedness about this pursuit of the Kingdom and this love of God that nothing else can stifle. If your eye causes you to sin, it is better to pluck it out than to be cast into hell. If wealth threatens to keep you out of the Kingdom, you must "sell all that you have, and give to the poor," for, as Jesus points out, "You cannot serve God and money." You must love and serve one or the other. Which one? "You shall love the Lord your God. . . ."

He makes the same point negatively when he says, "Do not be anxious about your life" (Matt. 6: 25). To be anxious is to have less than complete trust in God. Anxiety and complete trust in God are mutually exclusive. Jesus tells of a rich man who was so anxious about the future that he tore his barns down and built bigger ones so that he would have security against possible famine. But he was a fool. He was concerned only with his property. He thought that property was enough, and that with it he could provide ultimate security for himself. But he did not take account of the stern fact, "This night your soul is required of you" (Luke 12: 20).

The emphasis upon complete trust in God is closely related to another emphasis. The second commandment, *which is like the first,* goes, "You shall love . . . your neighbor as yourself" (Luke 10: 27). I do not love God, in other words, just by going off to think deep thoughts. I love God by loving Joe Doakes, or Susie Smith, or whoever my neighbor is.

But who *is* my neighbor? When somebody asked Jesus the question, he replied with a disquieting story about a Samaritan (Luke 10: 25-37). The story is familiar enough, although we do not usually make it disquieting enough. For the point of the story is that a neighbor helps anybody who is in need. The one who "proved neighbor to the man who fell among the robbers" was a Samaritan, which meant, very simply, a mortal enemy of the Jewish people to whom the story was being told. (It is as though an American should illustrate what it means to be a good neighbor by using someone like a Communist as his example.) The person who was helped was "a certain man," not further identified. No inquiries were made,

> about the color of his skin,
> his social background,
> his schooling,
> his loyalty,
> the size of his income.

The only necessary information was that he was in need. The love about which Jesus talks is "universalistic," knowing no bounds. It is all-inclusive.

And that is a rather tall order.

The Greeks Had a Word for It

What do you think of when you hear the word "love"?

> Apple blossoms in April?
> A boy and a girl strolling down an orchard lane?
> A beautiful sky overhead?
> Music (mostly violins) coming out of the sky?
> The whole thing done in 3-D supercolossal Technicolor?

As we use it, the word "love" usually means romantic love, love of one who is "lovable," love which (we fervently hope) will be returned.

There is nothing wrong with that kind of love, except that it doesn't have anything to do with the subject under discussion. There are three different words for "love" in Greek, and unfortunately we have only one English word to cover them all.

> When the Greek talked about "romantic love," he used the word *eros*.

> When he talked about brotherly love and comradeship, he used the word *philia*.

> But when a Christian talked about love, he used the word *agape* (pronounced, roughly, ah-*gaa*-pay).

Agape, Christian love, is love toward the loveless, love toward those who may reject it and treat it contemptuously, but to whom, nevertheless, it must be offered. This is the kind of love Jesus is talking about. Not nice, sugary, romantic love— but absolute, self-giving love, which offers itself to all, regardless of their worth or attractiveness or anything else. (Paul gives us a kind of hymn to *agape*, in I Cor., ch. 13. Try reading it once again, using the word "*agape*" instead of the word "love," and see if it doesn't suggest some new things.)

The significant thing about Jesus is that he didn't just talk about *agape*; he embodied it himself. If you want to know what *agape* is, don't just look at what Jesus said—look at what he did. His whole life is a dramatization of *agape*. He offered himself totally to those in need; he continued to offer himself totally even when people spat upon him and crucified him. The crucifixion is the very pinnacle of *agape*—selfless love in action. Here we see how much God loves. He offers himself totally to those who are unworthy.

And that is the kind of love we are to make real in our lives; *agape* which knows no limits, which gives unstintingly to anyone in need, which is willing to suffer on behalf of anyone else, without thought of reward.

A rather tall order indeed.

One of the Hard Parts

Agape includes *forgiving*. Very few things are more difficult than forgiving. It is perhaps the hardest thing that the Christian has to do. We must forgive "our debtors," as God forgives us "our debts," the Lord's Prayer reminds us. Why are you to forgive? So that you "may be the children of your Father which is in heaven." It is not promised that forgiveness will "work." Jesus does not say, "If you forgive your enemy, then he will stop being your enemy, and love you." Perhaps the enemy will take your forgiveness as a sign of weakness and pummel you all the more. You have to take that risk. You are to forgive, not because it "works," but because God forgives you; forgiving love toward your fellow men is your response to God's forgiving love toward you. This is exceedingly important. When you say, "What she did was simply unforgivable," you are voicing a sentiment that everyone has felt, but it is not a Christian sentiment. The whole point of forgiveness is that you are to forgive just what seems "unforgivable." Otherwise love is not real. You have erected a barrier between yourself and the other person which prohibits the close relationship that forgiving love makes possible.

Another of the Hard Parts

A particularly exacting element in Jesus' teaching is the emphasis on *motivation*. Love which is simply "on the surface" is not real. Real love must permeate the whole of one's being. Consequently, not only the outer act is important, but also the inner attitude which prompts it. The very root of the problem of ethics is motivation:

> You have heard that it was said to the men of old, "You shall not kill; and whoever kills shall be liable to judgment." But

I say to you that every one who is angry with his brother shall
be liable to judgment (Matt. 5: 21, 22).

Presumably you can plead "not guilty" to the charge of having
murdered anyone. But can you plead "not guilty" to the charge
of having been angry? It is anger which is at the root of murder.
Anger, therefore, is the place to attack the problem. Our motives need constant exploration—and purging.

Making an "Impossible" Ideal Relevant

No one who measures his life by Jesus' teachings can ever
say: "I have done everything I should in living the Christian
life. I have 'arrived.'"

No one, that is, but a deluded fool or an insufferable prig.

Does this mean that Jesus' teachings are so far beyond us that
they are irrelevant? Some people come to this conclusion.
"Jesus was too much of an idealist," they say; "he expects too
much of us. His demands are so impossibly high that we'll always fail. So why bother?" Other people feel that this is giving
up the fight too quickly, and pose the problem in this way:
"How can we make Jesus' absolute demands relevant to our
own situation here and now?"

This is the "sixty-four-dollar question" in Christian ethics.
Here are four starters toward an answer of your own.

1. The absolute demands of *agape* furnish us with *a standard by which to judge our motives*. If this seems academic, remember that an action is not judged simply by its "effect"; its
true value may depend upon the motive that prompted it.

Suppose you are walking across a bridge and see two men jump
into the river, one after the other. It looks as though they have both
done the same thing. Actually, they have done very different things.
The first man jumped into the river to commit suicide.
The second man jumped into the river to save him.
The first man was motivated by the desire to destroy life.
The second man was motivated by the desire to save life.
Thus the motives made the two actions as different as night and
day.

The absolute demands of Jesus give us an absolute standard against which our motives can be judged.

2. The absolute demands of *agape* can show us *the ideal possibility in any given situation. Agape* can furnish a standard by which to judge what we ought to do. Most of our choices are not black and white, wholly good or wholly bad. They are all mixed up and confused together, some shade of gray. In choosing between various courses of action, no one of which is wholly good, we can receive help by asking the question, "Which choice comes closest to the ideal of *agape?*" Thus *agape* is always relevant, even if never fully realized (see further, Chapter 22).

3. The absolute demands of *agape* stand as *a judgment over everything we have done.* No matter how much we "accomplish," the demands of *agape* always remind us that we should have done more. Here is one of the places where *agape* is most relevant. If the Christian ethic were pitched lower, it would lose its relevance the minute it was attained. But it never is attained; the Christian can never rest on his ethical oars, feeling that the finish line has been crossed. He has a perpetually "uneasy conscience."

4. This disturbing fact suggests another way in which the absolute demands of *agape* are relevant. They help us to *see our situation as it actually is.* If the ethical demands are the whole story, we are in a situation of frustration and condemnation, since we do not do all that is demanded of us. (Do you honestly "love your neighbor as yourself"?) If Jesus is simply a great ethical teacher, he leaves us in despair, since we cannot live up to what he asks of us.

But ethical demands are *not* the whole story. If Jesus is also the Savior, the one who meets us in the midst of our inadequacy and wrongdoing, the one who says to us, "My grace is sufficient for you" (II Cor. 12: 9), the one who heals and redeems—then we can face life with confidence and hope, rather than despair, conscious that there is a "peace of God," which,

while it "passes all understanding," is nevertheless a reality.
Those who approach God with humble contrition and penitence, asking God's forgiveness, find that they are not alone,
but that God is with them, and is empowering them to face the
struggle once more.[1]

---

[1] Here is the "footnote on Paul" that the chapter title promised:
While there is nothing distinctively new in the ethics of Paul, we
find in his writings a significant attempt to make the *agape* ethic
relevant in a sinful world. Paul's concern with *agape* is not chiefly
a desire to "live out the teachings of Jesus." It is something much
deeper than that. The *agape* of Jesus, a forgiving and sacrificial
love, has shown Paul that God loves him even though he is unworthy of love. Out of gratitude to God for the gift of his forgiving
love, Paul attempts to live the life of *agape* in response.

And even though he does not see all its implications, he makes
some of its implications clearer to us than they were to him. We
can see this fact at work in his attitude toward slavery.

Slavery was an accepted part of the way of life of the Roman
Empire of which Paul was a citizen. Christians today feel that
slavery is a clear violation of *agape* love, and it often comes as a
surprise to discover that nowhere did Paul explicitly condemn the
institution of slavery. (Neither, for that matter, did Jesus.)

However, before condemning Paul too hastily, notice that he
planted the seeds of an attitude toward slavery which, when it came
to full flower, destroyed slavery utterly. Look at his short note to
the Christian slaveowner Philemon.

Philemon's slave, Onesimus, has run away, but has come into
contact with Paul. Paul persuades Onesimus that it is his duty to
return to Philemon, and sends along a brief "covering note" to
his master. In this note he talks of "my child, Onesimus"
(Philemon 10)—hardly the conventional way of describing a slave.
Philemon is to receive Onesimus, "no longer as a slave but more
than a slave, as a beloved brother" (v. 16). "Receive him," Paul
writes, "as you would receive me" (v. 17). Onesimus is not to be
treated as a piece of property, but as a human being—as a brother,
in fact.

To Christians, slaves were "brothers"; no differentiation was to
be made. In another letter Paul describes the Church as a place
where "there is neither slave nor free . . . for you are all one in

Christ Jesus" (Gal. 3: 28). Outwardly the institution of slavery continues; but for the Christian such distinctions have disappeared.

Now on the face of it this sounds like a splendid way to perpetrate injustice—just say that slaves are not "really" slaves, even though they may still be in chains, forced to do backbreaking work eighteen hours a day. But Paul has already introduced the dynamite that will explode the slave situation.

For you cannot treat a man as a "brother" for very long and still treat him as the scum of the earth who exists only to serve your least whim and fancy. And this is what happened as time went on. Christians found that they could not keep slaves and be Christians at the same time. This Christian "leaven" was one of the reasons why the whole slave trade of the Roman Empire began to crumble.

The lesson for us is to look at the sins of our own society and see if the ethic of *agape* does not force us to use the same kind of dynamite. How about our segregated white and Negro churches? our immigration policies? or the food we waste while people in Asia starve?

Becoming Very Specific

(What Does the Bible Say About Sex and
Marriage and The Problem of Work?)

We have taken a look at some elements in the Biblical approach to ethics. Now we must apply these insights to our own situation. For the rest of this book we shall try to "think Biblically" about four problems:

        1. Sex and marriage.
        2. The problem of work or vocation.
        3. Politics and compromise.
        4. War.

    Note to the Careful Reader: These discussions represent *one* person's attempt to "think Biblically." You are not asked to agree. All you are asked to do is to make concrete *for yourself* what God demands of you in these four areas, and to remember that the demand placed upon you cannot be shoved off on somebody else. Jesus made this very clear:

> PETER (*trying to wriggle out of a demand*): Lord, what about *this* man [the beloved disciple standing next to him]?
> JESUS: What is that to you? Follow me!
>   (John 21: 21, 22)

Sex and Marriage

Some people have the queer idea that Christianity thinks that sex is something no "nice" person talks about or thinks about. Now there are a few statements by Paul that might seem to bear this out, and there has also been an ascetic strain in historic Christianity that has been negative toward sex. But this is not the attitude that emerges when one attempts to "think Biblically" about sex and marriage.

SEX IS GOOD

It seems clear, for example, that in the Biblical view sex is good. Sex is a part of God's creation; it is one of his gifts to mankind. It is not inherently sordid or nasty, any more than sunlight is inherently sordid or nasty. This fact comes out clearly in the Biblical account of creation, where the sexual distinction is part of the goodness of creation:

So God created man in his own image, in the image of God he created him; male and female he created them. . . . And God saw everything that he had made, and behold, it was very good (Gen. 1: 27, 31).

"And behold, it was very good" needs to be set against any attempt to suggest that from a religious point of view there is something not quite "nice" about sex. William Temple has pointed out that it is wrong to joke about sex (that is, tell "dirty" jokes) for the same reason that it is wrong to joke about Holy Communion—not because either subject is nasty, but because both are sacred, and to joke about such things is profanity. So the Christian avoids being "crude" about sex, not because sex is bad, but precisely because sex is good.

People sometimes argue:

>*Major Premise:* "Spiritual" things are good and "physical" things are evil.
>*Minor Premise:* Sex is physical.
>*Conclusion:* Therefore, sex is evil.

But this is not good Biblical thinking. Not only is the major premise wrong, but so are the minor premise and the conclusion! In Biblical thinking, man is a unity (see Chapters 13, 17); the physical and "spiritual" are all wrapped up together and cannot be separated from one another. There is not an "evil" physical part of man; on the contrary, man as a totality worships God or builds bridges or engages in sexual activity. Man's sexual drive is a part of that totality and not something separate. It is a God-given gift, which is "very good."

SEX IS A GOOD THING WHICH CAN BE SPOILED

Unfortunately, this is not the whole story. Sex is a good thing but, like other good things, it can be spoiled. Again, the Creation story drives the point home. The main point of Gen., ch. 3, is that man succumbs to the temptation, "You will be like God." This is the fundamental temptation—the temptation to self-sufficiency, which freezes God out of the picture. The fundamental temptation is *not* the temptation to sexual promiscuity, as people often think. But notice that when that fundamental temptation takes ahold of life, it spoils all aspects of life, the sexual aspect included. Sex becomes a means of self-gratification: "Play this game of sex for what *you* can get out of it. Don't worry about the other person. *Use* that other person for your own satisfactions. Don't be inhibited. Express yourself." Instead of being used creatively, as God intended it, as a means of sharing which enriches the lives of both partners, sex is now being used destructively, being perverted into something it was not intended to be. It has become a means of "using" another person, which is to say that the other person is no longer really a "person" but merely a "thing." This is a denial of the Biblical attitude toward persons as children of God.

This, incidentally, is why an overabundance of "necking" or "playing around" almost invariably leads to trouble, since it is either a case of one person exploiting the other person or of two persons experiencing sex simply on the level of "physical thrill." In either case sex is something other than what God intends it to be. It becomes cheapened because it is being wrongly used, so that, instead of contributing to the enrich-ment of life, it contributes to the degradation of life.

THE OLD TESTAMENT VIEW OF MARRIAGE

It is clear in the Bible that the sexual relationship is reserved for those who are united in marriage. It is a means of enrich-ing the marriage relationship both for the mutual sharing of love that it makes possible and for the creation of a family as an expression of love.

Now it is true that in the Old Testament, polygamy (that is, one man having many wives) is taken for granted. But even in this situation, fidelity in marriage is demanded. It is wrong for a man to have sexual relations with a woman not his wife, and the penalties against this sin (which is called "adultery") are very heavy. Not only is the act expressly for-bidden—"You shall not commit adultery" (Ex. 20: 14; com-pare Deut. 5: 18)—but there are instructions about punishing this crime: "If a man commits adultery with the wife of his neighbor, both the adulterer and the adulteress shall be put to death" (Lev. 20: 10).

There is a high stress upon the importance of the family in the Old Testament. The dangers and difficulties of the polyg-amous relationship are sometimes recognized (as in the sto-ries of David), and there is a warm tribute to the part that can be played by a good wife (not wives) in Prov. 31: 10-31.

THE NEW TESTAMENT VIEW OF MARRIAGE

In the New Testament, monogamy (one man and one woman living with each other and no one else) is taken for granted as the normal relationship between the sexes. It is clear in Jesus' teachings that he thinks of marriage in the highest terms and feels that it has God's blessing. There is no suggestion whatever that he thought that marriage was only "second best" to remaining single. In a very important statement he brings together a number of Old Testament ideas about marriage and makes them his own.

Have you not read that he who made them from the beginning made them male and female, and said, "For this reason a man shall leave his father and mother and be joined to his wife, and the two shall become one"? So they are no longer two but one. What therefore God has joined together, let no man put asunder (Matt. 19: 4-6; cf. Mark 10: 6-9).

We can get a further indication of Jesus' attitude toward marriage as ordained by God by looking briefly at what he says about divorce. This is the one matter about which he gives minutely specific ethical advice. Although the different Gospels do not agree exactly as to what he said, the import of his comments is clear. What is wrong with divorce is that when God has joined two people together, they cannot be put asunder by men. Thus to divorce one person and marry another is to be guilty of adultery (Mark 10: 11, 12; compare Luke 16: 18). Matthew represents Jesus as saying that divorce is wrong, "except on the ground of unchastity" (Matt. 5: 32).

Christians have taken differing attitudes about this statement of Jesus. Some have held that he means "no divorce whatsoever under any circumstances." Others have made use of "the Matthean exception," and have felt that divorce is permissible when one of the partners has been unfaithful. Still others have felt that Jesus did not come to legislate a new legalism on this matter and that sometimes to force two people who are no longer in love to live together may be a worse perversion of God's will than to allow them to separate. It is at least clear that we cannot take a word like "adultery" from Jesus' lips and turn it into a legalistic concept. Jesus has something rather arresting to say about adultery.

You have heard that it was said, "You shall not commit adultery." But I say to you that every one who looks at a woman lustfully has already committed adultery with her in his heart (Matt. 5: 27, 28).

The outward act is wrong, but so is the inner thought! Everyone who is honest with himself must admit that he stands convicted by that statement. Consequently our attitude toward adultery cannot be simply an attitude of self-righteous condemnation of someone who gets "caught." It involves an awareness that all of us stand under condemnation, and that all of us need the forgiveness of God, reaching out to us wherever we are, to touch, heal, and transform us.

It is precisely because he has such a high view of marriage, that Jesus looks with such disfavor on divorce.

A BACHELOR SPEAKS HIS MIND

Paul's attitude is more complex. In a number of places he seems to have a scornful attitude toward marriage, notably in First Corinthians, where all he will grudgingly admit is that you'd better marry if you cannot control yourself sexually, since "it is better to marry than to be aflame with passion" (I Cor. 7: 9). This is a far cry from the attitude of Jesus. Remember, however, before you are too rough on Paul, that when he talks about marriage he does not claim to be writing with divine authority, but is simply giving his own point of view (cf. I Cor. 7: 25). Furthermore, as he was expecting the imminent return of Christ, Paul felt that nothing else was very important by comparison. In general he tells people who are married to stay married, and advises those who are not married not to get involved. Better to prepare for Christ's return.

However, in the letter to the Ephesians, Paul (or one of his followers) has a wonderful description of Christian marriage as "under God," and never just a contract of civil law. And while feminine readers will be upset by the suggestion that the man should be head of the household, the main burden of the section (ch. 5: 21-33) is most instructive. The author sees the marriage relationship as analogous to the relationship of Christ

and the Church. Take this for example: "Be subject to one another out of reverence for Christ" (Eph. 5: 21). Not just because you "respect one another's personalities," but out of
reverence for Christ, because Christ can be honored as you
honor one another in the marriage relationship. Or again,
how are husbands to love their wives? They are to love their
wives "as Christ loved the church and gave himself up for her"
(v. 25). The complete selflessness of Christ is to be the husband's model. Even if the man is to be the head of the family,
he cannot be a despot or a tyrant. He is to be selfless, just as the
wife is to be selfless. The whole relationship is to mirror Christ
and his love for the Church. The family can be, in effect, a
sort of "little church," a group of people whose life is not
directed inward upon itself, but outward toward God. Family
life can be "a garden of grace," in which all grow toward the
fuller stature of Christ.

IN THE MEANTIME...

The Bible, then, holds up marriage as a very high good,
which has God's blessing upon it. The decision you have to
make as you approach the possibility of marriage is whether or
not you agree that this is marriage as it ought to be. If you do
not, then you will feel with regard to sex, for example, that
"anything goes, any time, anywhere." Your "reward" will be
that you have spoiled and perverted a potentially great and
noble thing.

If you agree with the Biblical view, on the other hand, you
will do nothing that might lessen for you the ultimate achievement of such a marriage. You will realize that you have been
given a great gift by God and that the choice is yours: you can
use the gift in ways contrary to his intention, in which case it
will be a curse, or you can use the gift as it was intended by him
to be used, in which case it will be a blessing.

The Problem of Work or Vocation

Do you sometimes think, Gee, if only I didn't have to work ... and imagine

sleeping late every morning, or

taking trips to the South Sea Islands, or

watching double-headers every afternoon in summer, and absorbing batting averages every afternoon in winter?

When you do this, you are really changing "vocation" into "vacation." You are thinking of work as an intrusion, a really unwelcome intrusion, upon the pleasant things of life. It's the same way no matter what the "work" is: turning a bolt on an assembly line, sitting behind a desk, selling brushes from door to door, or grinding out algebra assignments for a high school teacher who seems to have been created simply to make life miserable for you.

Our attitude toward work, toward jobs or vocations, has gotten out of kilter. To many people a job has become a nuisance rather than an opportunity. And since work is part and parcel of life, we need to develop a positive attitude toward it. Can the Bible throw any light on this perplexing problem?

God Ordains Work

It is clear in the Old Testament that we are not to sit around idly, being waited on by others. God has placed us here on earth, and he has given us work to do. This applies to the most humble jobs, to the "hewing of wood and the drawing of water" (cf. Deut. 29: 11, Josh. 9: 21, 27), to doing whatever is needed to maintain life and sustain God's created order. "Six days you shall labor, and do all your work," was the way the Fourth Commandment put it. The Eighth Psalm shows how God has entrusted man with the overseeing of his created world:

Yet thou hast made him little less than God,
and dost crown him with glory and honor.

Thou hast given him dominion over the works of thy hands;
   thou hast put all things under his feet,
all sheep and oxen,
   and also the beasts of the field,
the birds of the air, and the fish of the sea,
   whatever passes along the paths of the sea.
                              (Ps. 8: 5-8)

Similarly, in the Creation stories, God ordains work for man to do, and this work is *good*. Work is part of the goodness of creation. Man is to subdue the earth; "and have dominion over the fish of the sea and over the birds of the air and over every living thing that moves upon the earth" (Gen. 1: 28). He is to "till and keep" the Garden of Eden (ch. 2: 15).

Even ordinary, unexciting, daily routine work is to be related to God. When a man does a good job of spring planting, for example, he is not to sit back and congratulate himself. He is to give the glory to God. To pat himself on the back is to deflect attention from God to himself—and this is idolatry. Describing the proper way to plow and sow, Isaiah says of a man who knows how, "He is instructed aright; his God teaches him" (Isa. 28: 26). And after describing the proper way to thresh, he comments, "This also comes from the Lord of hosts; he is wonderful in counsel, and excellent in wisdom" (v. 29). All work is related to God, even such commonplace activities as sowing and reaping.

WE HAVE SPOILED THE MEANING OF WORK

But again, that's not the whole story. Work has gotten spoiled. In the Creation stories, Adam and Eve are placed in the Garden to take care of it. Work is part of God's will for them. This high good is spoiled, however, because of the intrusion of human sin. Just as all of life becomes corrupted and tainted by sin, so also does man's work. Work is not itself a curse, but it comes to be laid under a curse. God says to Adam after he has sinned:

> "Cursed is the ground because of you;
> in toil you shall eat of it all the days of your life; . . .
> In the sweat of your face
> you shall eat bread." (Gen. 3: 17, 19)

Human sin, in other words, really disarranges things. It spoils the true meaning of our work. This does not mean that work is just punishment for sin, for, as we have seen, work is part of God's will for man, but, like everything else, its significance is distorted and lost when men do not do God's will, but follow instead their own wills.

THE NEW TESTAMENT "CALLING"

In the New Testament the notion of a vocation (or being "called" to do something) has an added dimension. The primary sense is the job of helping in the furtherance of the gospel. Your "work" may be as an evangelist. Mine may be as a teacher, or as a prophet. Paul was called to be "a servant of Jesus Christ," and he exercised this vocation by going from place to place preaching, teaching, and writing letters. At the same time he had a means of livelihood, tentmaking, which he pursued to keep himself financially solvent and able to do his other job. But his main work was to bring the "good news" to people. In all of this, he was only making himself available to be used by God. What he accomplished was not to his credit, but to God's greater glory. As he says to the obstreperous Corinthians:

I planted, Apollos watered, but God gave the growth. So neither he who plants nor he who waters is anything, but only God who gives the growth. He who plants and he who waters are equal, and each shall receive his wages according to his labor. For we are fellow workmen for God; you are God's field, God's building (I Cor. 3: 6-9).

The New Testament word for "calling" is, significantly, from the same Greek root as the word "church." The Greek word for church (*ekklesia,* from which we get "ecclesiastical") means literally those who are "called out," or set apart from the rest of the world. Your "calling" is fulfilled within the fellowship of those who are "called out."

Now this does not mean that regular, ordinary jobs are unimportant. Writing to the Thessalonians (who could be just as obstreperous as the Corinthians), Paul faces the problem that a lot of Christians, expecting the immediate return of the Lord, have stopped working. Paul strongly condemns this:

> We hear that some of you are living in idleness, mere busybodies, not doing any work. Now such persons we command and exhort in the Lord Jesus Christ to do their work in quietness and to earn their own living (II Thess. 3: 11, 12).

For those who will not follow this advice there is a short, succinct formula: "If any one will not work, let him not eat" (II Thess. 3: 10).

"Workers" in the New Testament

A number of other passages in Paul's letters deal with advice to the "workers" (really "slaves"). We looked at Paul's attitude toward "slaves" in the last chapter. Here let us see what insight we can draw from Paul's advice to them. Take, for example, these words to the Ephesians:

> Slaves, be obedient to those who are your earthly masters, with fear and trembling, in singleness of heart, as to Christ; not in the way of eye-service, as men-pleasers, but as servants of Christ, doing the will of God from the heart, rendering service with a good will as to the Lord and not to men (Eph. 6: 5-7).

Here is some clear wisdom about the approach to work. The Christian is to do his daily work for God rather than for men. The reward of his work is to be that it is pleasing to God. Whatever your particular work is, it is to be done as unto God, not in such a way that you are merely a "man-pleaser."

Now this is a radical notion. This means doing an honest job on your algebra homework and taking a C— instead of cribbing the answers and getting a B+. This means that the significance of a "nine to five" man is not whether he makes $10,000 a year or not, but whether the work he does is worthwhile in the sight of God.

Pushing the New Testament Teaching

The New Testament does not give us specific answers to twentieth century problems of vocation, neatly laid out on a silver platter. But it does offer some basically sound principles. Let us see how our Protestant forefathers worked these out.

Here is what happened in the early centuries of the Church: The world was looked upon as so evil that, although the *ordinary* Christian might remain within the world and pursue his trade of butcher, baker, or candlestick maker, the really *dedicated* Christian would withdraw from the world and follow a specifically "religious" calling, entering a monastery. If you made a report card for various medieval friends of yours, this would be roughly the way it would come out:

> John Smith, butcher......................C—
> Father Jones, ordinary priest................B
> Abbot Doe, monk.........................A

Now the Protestant Reformers changed all that. They cut across this distinction between "secular" and "sacred" vocations. They felt that this was God's world and that he wanted men to serve him *within* that world, not by withdrawing *from* that world. It was Luther's contention, for example, that the housemaid could serve God in her calling just as effectively as the nun could in hers; that the shoemaker could serve God in his calling just as effectively as the monk could in his. For Calvin, the entire world was to be a monastery, that is, a place where the life of service and praise of God could be lived to the full. From their standpoint, then, our report card would have to be revised so that *potential* grades would read thus:

> John Smith, electrician.......................A
> Pastor Jones of the local church.................A
> Professor Doe, theologian.....................A

Thus Protestants believe that no one calling is intrinsically more sacred or "religious" than any other. It is not God's intention that everyone be a minister or a missionary or a director of religious education; God also "calls" people to carry out their Christian concern in politics, business, schoolteaching, and other professions. Such people can realize God's will in their vocations as they do their jobs with integrity. The first job of the lab technician who is a Christian is not to sing in the church choir; it is to do his experiments thoroughly, honestly, and scientifically. He must not do a shoddy job in the laboratory to get to choir practice on time.

Christ as "Worker"

The term "worker" was, in fact, applied to Jesus himself. While the main understanding of the "work" of Christ refers to his work of salvation for men (his coming to earth, dying on the cross, and being raised again by God in power), there is an interesting reference to him as a worker, or more specifically, a carpenter (see Mark 6: 3). The fact that Jesus worked at a trade is significant. It not only shows us that he identified himself with those who sweated to earn a living; it also reaffirms the *dignity* of work. Work has been sanctified because of the fact that Christ himself worked. It can scarcely be beneath our dignity if it was not beneath his. It can scarcely be degrading if he ennobled it. Anyone who says that real, honest work is just too, too degrading must face the fact that the Son of God did not find it too degrading for him.

Work Is Not the Whole Story

A few minutes ago we saw that the Fourth Commandment stressed the importance of work in God's sight. But another phrase, following hard upon it, goes like this: "But the seventh day is a sabbath to the Lord your God; in it you shall not do any work" (Ex. 20: 10). Work is not the whole story. We are made to work *and* to rest (and also to worship, as the following section will point out). To "rest" means that we stop for a while from shaping the world after our own fashion; that we try to remember that this is, after all, God's world, and that our real job is to try to fulfill his will rather than our own. Furthermore, rest is part of the way in which we are to reflect the divine image within us. We are to rest, as God "rested," according to the bold figure of speech in the Creation story: "And on the seventh day God finished his work which he had done, and he rested on the seventh day from all his work which he had done" (Gen. 2: 2).

Jesus makes a similar point during his visit to Mary and Martha. Martha bustles about, positively bristling with activity, getting more and more flustered. Mary sits and listens to Jesus. Result:

MARTHA (*peeved because she is doing all the work and the kitchen is very warm*): Lord, do you not care that my sister has left me to serve alone? (*Then petulantly*) Tell her to help me.
JESUS: Martha, Martha, you are anxious and troubled about many things; one thing is needful. Mary has chosen the good portion, which shall not be taken away from her (Luke 10: 40-42).

Jesus is not praising laziness, but he is suggesting that we can become so fretful over our work that it ceases to have meaning. Mary was choosing "the good portion," not Martha. For Martha was "distracted with much serving" (Luke 10: 40). It would have been better for her to sit at Jesus' feet than to prepare an unnecessarily elaborate meal.

There is a rhythm of work and rest which needs to be observed. Sleep is the most obvious example of this. Just try going without sleep for three nights in a row and then see how effective a job of work you can do on the fourth morning.

WORK AND WORSHIP

Even more important is the inseparability of work and worship. Worship must be related to work, and work must grow out of worship. In many places in the Christian world, when the Lord's Supper is celebrated, the elements of bread and wine are brought forward by the people at the appropriate time in the service and laid upon the table—symbolic of the way in which man's work (the growing of the grain, the cultivation of the vine) is offered to God for his blessing. When the elements are blessed and distributed, it is an indication that God deigns to accept these symbols and use them as the visible reminders of his presence. Man's work has been received and blessed and transformed. The very word *liturgy*, which we use to describe a specific order of worship, meant originally "work" or "public service." Faithful performance of public service was "liturgy"; any work well done was thus service rendered not only to the public but to God. Paul indicates this tie-up when telling the Corinthians to give to those in need: "The rendering of this service [*liturgy*] not only supplies the wants of the saints but also overflows in many thanksgivings to God" (II Cor. 9:12).

WHERE DO WE GO FROM HERE?

It is clear that we cannot extract from the Bible a detailed blueprint about jobs in twentieth century industrial society. The Bible does not offer information about technological employment. What we are to do is to take the kinds of principles that emerge from this discussion and then relate them to the specific twentieth century situations in which we find ourselves. This is a tough job, but it is part of the obligation of loving God with all our minds.

The Bible and Ballots

(You Mean Religion and Politics Do Mix?)

You've heard statements like:

"Religion and politics don't mix."
"The job of minister is to 'preach the gospel' and not to get
concerned about politics."
"Politics is too 'messy' for the Christian."

These statements are dangerous nonsense.

They are *nonsense* because they ignore the fact that the minute you take "religion" seriously, you've got to be concerned about your fellow men, and in our kind of world concern for fellow men inevitably means concern with the political arena in which men live. Since the "gospel" is concerned not only with individuals, but with individuals in their social relationships, it must be relevant to the way people order their social relationships in politics and government.

They are *dangerous,* because they mean that religion is irrelevant to one of the most important areas of modern life. The decisions made in Congress, for example, affect the destinies of millions of people across the face of the earth. No Christian has the moral privilege of being unconcerned about that fact, or of claiming that politics is so "messy" that the Christian must not soil his hands by getting too close to it. On the contrary, the Christian must demonstrate that politics can be a "realm of grace," a place where, as least in a roughhewn way, men can attempt to do the will of God.

A High Priority Caution—There Is No Social Blueprint in the Bible

An important word of caution is necessary as we begin: The Bible does not give us a blueprint, or a detailed map, or a constitution for a "Christian political order." Whenever you find someone quoting isolated bits of Scripture to "prove" a point with regard to some specific piece of legislation, you are entitled to be suspicious. During the Civil War preachers quoted the Bible to support slavery and to repudiate slavery. In South Africa today, government officials are trying to defend racial segregation on Biblical grounds. What usually happens in such cases is that a person believes something and then goes hunting for "proof texts" in the Bible to back it up. There is no "ready-made" plan for society in the pages of the Bible.

But this does not mean that the Bible is irrelevant. Far from it! For the Bible gives us an indication of the attitudes, the concerns, the motivations, that must inform and direct the kinds of decisions we make on specific issues. One Christian may feel that his concern for minority groups can best be implemented through participation in the Democratic party, while another may feel that the best ends can be achieved by the Republicans, and a third may prefer to remain independent. What none of these people can claim is that the Biblical concern for all men is made effective only through the Democratic party or only through the Republican party or only by maintaining political independence. The Bible does make clear that you must have an attitude of concern for all men, and a particular concern for the downtrodden. Once that is established, then you have to work out for yourself, as honestly and intelligently as you can, how, within the structure of the society you live in, you can best implement that concern.

For example, the fundamental Biblical emphasis that "the earth is the Lord's and the fulness thereof" (Ps. 24: 1) is both a religious and a political statement. The earth is not ours to use in such a way that we exploit our fellow men and make life on earth a hell. How are we to live together in a world that is *God's* world? Similarly, the recurring theme, "You shall love your neighbor as yourself" (Lev. 19: 18; Luke 10: 27), is both religious and political. In what kind of social situation, in what political framework, can I best implement my concern for my neighbor?

"No Other Gods"

Let us frame our discussion of Biblical faith and political responsibility around the first of the Ten Commandments, since, while it seems to be simply "religious," it is actually one of the most "political" statements in the whole Bible.

I am the Lord your God, who brought you out of the land of Egypt, out of the house of bondage. *You shall have no other gods before me* (Ex. 20: 2, 3, italics added).

What does this mean? It means that there is but one God, the living God of Hebrew history. Absolute allegiance must be given to him, and to no one else. *Only to the living God can final and unqualified allegiance be given.* What does this have to do with politics?

Everything.

It means that we can never give our final allegiance to any political system, any economic system, any set of political or social ideals, any nation or group of nations. Our final allegiance belongs to God alone. If we give it to someone else, or something else, that person or thing takes the place of God in our lives. And from the standpoint of Biblical faith, this is idolatry: the worship of an idol or a false god. "My native land" is *not* God, therefore I may not give final allegiance to my native land. The attitude "My country, right or wrong" is an un-Biblical attitude, whether the country is Russia or Germany or India or ... America. The Socialist (or Republican or Democratic or Prohibition) party is not God, therefore I may not be a completely uncritical party member. "My party, right or wrong," is also un-Biblical. The temptation is always to make some man-made object (a country, a political system) into an object of final allegiance. This is idolatry whether in the seventh century B.C. or in the twentieth century A.D. The Christian may worship only the living God.

Now this sounds like dangerous talk! Give allegiance to something higher than the United States? Subversive! Realize that America may be less than a fully "Christian nation"? Seditious! And yet Biblical faith leaves us with no other alternative. Everything, absolutely everything save God himself stands under judgment, and is something less than God.

Light from the Early Church

The early Christians discovered this in no uncertain terms. They were under obligation to worship their government, quite literally. Unless they acknowledged the emperor as divine and declared, "Caesar is Lord," they could be tortured or killed, since anyone who didn't give final allegiance to Caesar gave it to someone else and was obviously a traitor.

But the earliest Christian "creed" of which we have any record read, "Jesus is Lord." Jesus, not Caesar. The Christian was saying, "I will *not* give unconditional allegiance to Caesar; but I *will* give unconditional allegiance to Jesus." To make a statement of faith in those days meant to be involved in politics! Charges were brought against a group of Christians in Thessalonica, for example, that "they are all acting against the decrees of Caesar, saying that there is another king, Jesus" (Acts 17: 7). Obviously, Caesar couldn't have *that* sort of thing going on. Luke adds, "And the people and the city authorities were disturbed when they heard this" (Acts 17: 8). You bet they were! Christianity was risky business in the first century.

The Committee on Un-Roman Activities

To see the full force of this early Christian witness, let us glance at the transcripts of some hearings of the first century Committee on Un-Roman Activities. The Christians are being investigated as a menace to the Roman way of life:

FIRST HEARING

Q: Your name?

A: Simon Bar-Jona, now known as Simon Peter, or Cephas, the Rock.

Q: Married?

A: Yes.

Q: Occupation?

A: Formerly a Galilean tradesman, a fisherman on the Sea of Galilee. Now an apostle of the Lord Jesus Christ.

Q: You are, then, an active member of this band of Christians?

A: I certainly am.

Q: Where were you a year ago today?

A: A year ago today? Probably somewhere in Jerusalem.

Q: No evasions please. . . . Is it true that on the day in question you were appearing before the Jerusalem council?

A: Yes, I appeared before the council on two occasions.

Q: What happened on those two occasions?

A: On the first occasion, another disciple and I were warned not to preach or teach any more about Jesus of Nazareth. (*Reminiscently*) They seemed pretty insistent about it.

Q: Did the two of you promise to obey the orders?

A: Certainly not. We replied, as I remember it, "We cannot but speak of what we have seen and heard."

Q (*to committee members*): Note that, please, gentlemen. The witness admits that he did not take the demands of the council seriously. (*To Peter*) And the second occasion?

A: We were called before the council again, and reminded that we must keep quiet.

Q: And what was your reply?

A: Our reply was, "We must obey God rather than men."

Q: H'mph . . . That's all, Mr. Cephas. Witness dismissed. (*Peter leaves*) There it is, gentlemen, plain as the nose on your face. These Christians won't even obey religious councils, let alone

Caesar. Mr. Cephas' statement, "We must obey God rather than men" is anti-Roman. These Christians are a menace!

SECOND HEARING

Q: Your name, please?
A: Demetrius.
Q: Home?
A: Ephesus.
Q: Occupation?
A: I am a silversmith.
Q: What do you make?
A: Shrines for statues of the beloved goddess, Artemis of the Ephesians.
Q: Are you acquainted with the name of Paul of Tarsus?
A: I am indeed.
Q: Does that mean that you are a Christian?
A: Oh, no, sir! I am not and never have been sympathetic to Christian ideas. Paul of Tarsus is an enemy, not a friend.
Q: Do the other artisans share your antagonism to Paul of Tarsus?
A: Oh, yes, indeed, your honor—I mean, sir. I speak on behalf of eighty-three of my fellow artisans.
Q: Just what has Paul done to you?
A: He preaches a false religion, and he's ruined our business.
Q: Just how has he ruined your business?
A: Well, he tells the people there's only one God, *his* God. Now the fellow's got a gift of gab, so a lot of Ephesians believe him, see. Well, naturally, if they believe in his God, they stop believing in Artemis, and we don't sell any shrines. (*Then, hastily*) I mean, it's an insult to our beloved Artemis, that's what it is, sir.
Q: Did you people do anything to try to stop him?
A: Oh, yes, sir, we put on a demonstration, as you might say. We...

COMMITTEE MEMBER (*interrupting*): We've got all that information in writing; I don't believe it will be necessary to repeat it now. Here it is, sir, confidential document S-2934j, taken from a Christian house of worship. An account by Dr. Lukas of the whole thing, in a manuscript called The Acts of the Apostles, section 19, the last couple of long paragraphs.

Q: Very well. (*Ponders the document, which you had better read yourself, right now*) You are dismissed. (*Demetrius leaves*) Well, gentlemen, here is the same sort of thing all over again. Wherever these Christians go, they stir up trouble. All on account of believing in only one God. It's too dangerous to go on. Oh, I don't mind a man having his own private religion, so long as he obeys the laws of the state, and doesn't stir up any trouble. But this Paul—he has to up and suggest that Artemis isn't real, and bash! the whole economy of a city goes blooey. This Christianity is too revolutionary. We must stamp it out.

THIRD HEARING

COMMITTEE CHAIRMAN: Gentlemen, an extremely dangerous and subversive document has just found its way into my hands, a "letter to the Hebrews." Let me read you a few excerpts. (*Reads*)

These [and here the writer is referring to the people he has just been praising] all died in faith, not having received what was promised, but having seen it and greeted it from afar, and having acknowledged that they were strangers and exiles on the earth. [Note that, gentlemen, "strangers and exiles on the earth," not willing to acknowledge that the Roman Empire is all that a man could want.] For people who speak thus make it clear that they are seeking a homeland. [Seeking a homeland, gentlemen. The Roman Empire is apparently not good enough for them.] If they had been thinking of that land from which they had gone out, they would have had opportunity to return. But as it is [and notice this particularly, gentlemen] as it is, they desire a *better* country, that is, a heavenly one. [And one last sentence, gentlemen. Yes, here it is. Listen to this if you will, please.] Here we have no lasting city, but we seek the city which is to come. [These people think the glorious Roman Empire is second-rate! There is something better, some heavenly country or other. If people begin to think this way, the Empire will go to pieces. People who think this way must be silenced.]

The point should be clear. If you give your final allegiance to God, you cannot give final allegiance to anyone else. This may have difficult consequences. The time may come when, in the name of your faith in God, you have to say no to the president of your boys' club, or to a fraternity house brother, or to a business associate, or to your boss, or even to your Government. German Christians found this out when the Nazis came to power. Russian Christians find it true every day. The same principle applies to American Christians if their Government orders them to do something that is a betrayal of the Commandment, "You shall have no other gods before me." At such times Christians have no choice but to say with Martin Luther: "Here I stand; I can do no other. God help me."

The Necessity of "Involvement"

But there is more to it than just that. For what we have said so far might lead someone to say: "I can't be involved in the messy business of government or politics. It's too sordid. I'll say no all the time." And this would be a tragic distortion of Biblical faith. Consequently, another thing the Bible tells us which is relevant to political responsibility is that *we must be involved in life about us.* We cannot be side-line Christians. The main themes of the Bible all imply this. Look at just a few of them.

The Biblical emphasis on *the importance of history* stresses this. History is where God works; he is concerned about what happens here. He has placed us in history and given us work to do also right here and now. We repudiate our God-given responsibility if we "take a rain check," or refuse to be involved.

The Creation stories stress this. We are placed here to "till the earth." This is an image from an agricultural society of the necessity of work, of keeping life on earth a going proposition. You don't do that as a bystander.

Jesus tells us, in his model prayer, to pray for "our daily bread." People who think Jesus was just concerned about "spiritual things" ought to ponder that fact. If "man does not live by bread alone," as Jesus also said, it is equally clear that he does not live without bread. Daily bread is important. How we get it is important. That all men have enough of it is important.

All these emphases suggest that *how people live together is a religious problem*. If people are hungry, that is a religious problem; if people do not have decent housing, that is a religious problem; if people who have dark skins are not allowed to eat in restaurants with people who have light skins, that is a religious problem—because God loves *all* of his children, and has given us a large share of responsibility in ordering our social life together.

So?

The conclusion should not be hard to draw. The Christian must busy himself with the realm of life in which these issues are debated, and decided. And in the twentieth century this is the realm of politics. This means that the Christian who is trying to "think Biblically" about politics must take the obligations of citizenship seriously. He must work to see that responsible people are nominated for office, campaign to get them elected, vote for them, and put pressures on them once they are in office. He may even feel that it is his Christian vocation to run for office himself.

That Christians must all have this concern does not mean, as we have seen, that Christians are all going to have identical attitudes about specific legislation—solving the housing problem in a slum area, for example. Some will feel that the matter can best be dealt with by private industry. Others will feel that a Federal housing project is the most feasible solution. Christians may have legitimate differences of opinion here. The unpardonable sin is to be unconcerned, and therefore uninvolved.

The Problem of Compromise

"But," someone says, "if I get involved this way, I may have to compromise my principles." And it is true that the "best" or "ideal" course of action is not a possibility very often in the give-and-take of political life. Almost any political choice will involve "compromise." For which of the two following men would you vote as mayor of your town?

☐ *Candidate A:* (He believes that Negroes should be able to swim in the public swimming pool and that there shouldn't be "restricted" housing covenants, so that Jews are forbidden to live in the "nicest" parts of town, but he drinks excessively and isn't much of a churchman.)

☐ *Candidate B:* (He has been a lifelong member of First Church, is a member of the board of trustees, and is a teetotaler, but he believes in racial segregation and thinks that the Jews should be "kept in their place.")

Instructions: Place an "x" in the box opposite the candidate of your choice.

For whom do you vote? Either way you vote, you will be "compromising" some of your belief.

And there is your problem! For there is no Candidate C who combines all the good traits you want. It's either A or B. It's no solution not to vote. That is merely to say by your action that the Christian must remain aloof from concrete political activity, which is in turn a way of saying that Christian faith is irrelevant.

The Christian, therefore, has to realize that God has placed him in the world *here and now,* and that he must be responsible here and now. He cannot sigh and wait for the Kingdom of God when the issues will be black and white. He must choose now between the existing grays. The Bible does not show us people fulfilling God's will by twiddling their thumbs until things are tidied up. It shows us people doing God's will *right where they are,* in the midst of apparently uncreative, unpleasant situations:

in a slave-labor camp in Egypt;

in a rotten city government in Bethel;

under a despotic king named Solomon;

in exile in Babylonia;

under cruel Roman rule.

It was in situations like those that people had to speak and act and legislate and (if they could do none of those things) protest. And we today are called to the same kind of responsibility.

Biblical Faith and Democracy

SUSPICIOUS READER (still worried about subversive tendencies): You've been insisting that no political system can receive our absolute and unqualified allegiance. Maybe the Bible does imply this. But doesn't this mean that there is no real difference between political systems—between, say, democracy and Communism?

Not at all. There are profound differences. The Christian has to make a choice between such political systems. He has to ask himself, "Which political system has the greater possibilities for approximating the will of God in human life?" And when he has answered the question, he must then pitch in and try to make the political system he chooses a better one.

Why must the Christian reject a totalitarian system such as Communism? Precisely because the totalitarian system repudiates the fundamental principle of Biblical thinking, "You shall have no other gods before me." The totalitarian state says: "*I* am your god. You must worship me and me only shall you serve. If anything comes along and demands higher loyalty, be it morality, religion, human decency, or anything at all, you must repudiate it and reject it thoroughly, because I demand your total allegiance." To such a claim, no Biblically minded person can submit. For this is an utter repudiation of the living God.

In what way, then, is democracy closer to "Biblical thinking"? The answer is in terms of the Biblical view of man, with its recognition of both our possibilities and limitations. Reinhold Niebuhr distills a lot of wisdom into two lines when he says:

Man's capacity for justice makes democracy possible; but man's inclination to injustice makes democracy necessary.

The wisdom lies in the fact that belief in democracy is based *both* on man's potentiality and on his corruption of his potentialities. While it is realized that we can create just forms of government, it is also realized that we can destroy the instruments of justice which we create, or, even worse, twist them to our own purposes. Particularly as men gain power this temptation grows upon them. No man or group of men is "good" enough to have unlimited power over other men. And to see that no individual or group of individuals gets unlimited power, a democratic society provides for periodic elections, so that *all* of the people have a "say" rather than just a few. If "man's inclination to injustice" seems to be gaining the upper hand, members of a democratic society can protest against such totalitarian impulses by means of the ballot.

Another example of this kind of provision is contained in the American Constitution, which provides that no one branch of government shall have unlimited power, but that there shall be "checks" and "balances" by other branches of government. The founding fathers realized that democracy was not only "possible" (because of man's capacity for justice), but also "necessary" (because of man's inclination to injustice). Democracy thus makes it possible to guard against idolatry.

SUSPICIOUS READER: Where's the catch?

The catch is right here. It is always possible to become idolatrous about some particular version of democracy, such as the British version, or the American version, or the French version. No existing system ever embodies all the qualities that it should, and the Christian will always have to be on guard to protest and root out those elements in the political life of his own country which perpetuate economic injustice, or exalt one race above another, or give extravagant powers to small groups. The struggle is never over.

That is one reason why it is so exciting.

The Bible and Bullets

(What Does the Christian Do About War?)

> "Got your draft notice yet?"
> "No, but it's due any day now."
> "Going into service right away?"
> "Natch. What else is there to do?"

This kind of situation confronts almost every boy in America today. When he is eighteen, he will face a period of military service. He will be given intensive training in the most up-to-date methods of killing his fellow men; he may even be sent into battle to put his training into practice. Everybody in his society (and that means all of us) is morally involved in the fact that he must do this.

There is a problem here for the Christian, since war—particularly modern atomic war—seems to be a complete violation of the Christian ethic of love. It is hard to reconcile the command to love our enemies with the command to drop atomic bombs on them or kill them with flame throwers. What does the Christian do in this situation?

A Caution

Text-juggling here is no help. Particularly during wartime, militarists produce verses showing God's support of blood-thirsty Israelite wars, while nonmilitarists isolate sayings like "Love your enemies." Anyone can find what he wants in the

Bible by stressing the things that agree with his position and ignoring the things that do not. It is particularly easy to lift statements out of context in playing this fruitless game. When Jesus said, "I bring not peace but a sword," for example, he was not talking about the problem of participation in war.

On the contrary, we must try to discover the *total* Biblical view on this question, and then work out an answer to the question, What shall I do?

Light from the Old Testament

Much of the Old Testament seems to give a frank approval of war, and very brutal war at that. Some of the Old Testament material is even based on a document known as the "Book of the Wars of Yahweh" (see Num. 21: 14). Israel's military victories are often interpreted as the victories of God (see the stories of the conquest of Canaan in Judges). Nahum is a paean of exultation to God for having overthrown the enemy. Fragments of early laws justify revenge, such as "an eye for an eye and a tooth for a tooth," though this is offered as a check on even more indiscriminate revenge, and is thus a symbol of moral advance! There are disturbing passages in the psalms:

> O daughter of Babylon, you devastator!
>   Happy shall he be who requites you
>   with what you have done to us!
> Happy shall be he who takes your little ones
>   and dashes them against the rock!
>
> (Ps. 137: 8, 9)

These instances are deliberately cited as a sober reminder that we cannot use the Bible as a "static" book in which the same truths are found in all places. These are attitudes that modern Christians and Jews would not want to adopt today. It is important to remember that the Bible, as a record of the dealings of God with his people, gives the whole picture of those people. It is not just a record of the "nice" aspects of the relationship, but of the total relationship as it was—good, bad, and indifferent. It is a tribute to the honesty of the Biblical writers and compilers that such passages were not surreptitiously removed as ethical insight deepened, for we find passages in other parts of the Old Testament of a distinctively different character.

This becomes clear in the thunderings of the prophets. Most of the "pro-war" passages in the Old Testament equate the doing of God's will with the military victories of the Israelites. It is the message of the prophets that no such equation can be made. God stands in judgment over the Israelites just as he does over the Assyrians or the Egyptians. He may, in fact, raise up nations to defeat the Israelites precisely because they have wrongly assumed that his will and theirs are identical (see Chapter 8). While this does not represent the outlawing of war, it is clear gain over the suggestion that a military victory equals God's approval.

The prophets also recognize the limits of what can be accomplished by war, political intrigue, and the indiscriminate use of power. Isaiah, for example, warns the people against too great a reliance upon the instruments of force, and he paints a vision of the universal reign of God, in which war shall be no more, and in which he clearly sees that war is not the highest fulfillment of God's holy will:

> He shall judge between the nations,
>   and shall decide for many peoples;
> and they shall beat their swords into plowshares,
>   and their spears into pruning hooks;
> nation shall not lift up sword against nation,
>   neither shall they learn war any more.
>
> (Isa. 2: 4)

The clear imperative of the Sixth Commandment, "You shall not kill" (Ex. 20: 13), is frequently misunderstood. It needs to be said (even though chaplains sometimes make the point too uncritically in wartime) that this prohibition historically applied to those within the tribe of Israel only, and that the Hebrew word is closer to what we mean by "murder" than to "killing." For people today, however, it is increasingly diffi-cult to see much difference between the inhuman slaughter of war and the act of murder.

The Clear Intent of Jesus' Teaching

We find a less ambiguous, though ethically more exacting, picture in the New Testament. Nothing in Jesus' life or teach-ings can be "twisted" into support of killing and warfare. If, as we have seen, he gives us the absolute ethic of the Kingdom of God, it is at just the point under discussion that the de-mands are most stringent.

> Not only must you not kill your enemy; you must not even hate your enemy; you must love him.
>
> Not only must you refrain from retaliation; you must pray for your enemy with active good will.
>
> Not only must you not be angry if someone slaps you; you must "turn the other cheek" and let him slap that one if he wants to. If somebody takes your coat away, you must not get angry or go to court, you must give him your cloak as well.
>
> The people who will be blessed are the "peacemakers." They are the ones who will be called "sons of God."

The ethical outlook of Jesus is one of active, outgoing love, never counting the cost in terms of self, always giving unstint-ingly to the needs of the other person. He inculcates an atti-tude so far-reaching in its demands upon the self that the self will never make demands upon the enemy.

Paul displays the same concern for the fulfillment of the command to love. In a typical passage he says to let love be genuine, to live in harmony with one another, to bless those who persecute, to repay no one evil for evil, to live peaceably with all (as far as it depends upon you), not to take vengeance, but rather to feed the enemy if he is hungry and to give him drink if he is thirsty (see Rom. 12: 9-21).

What Shall the Christian Do?

What shall the Christian do, in the face of the strict demands of Jesus, and their echo in Paul? Must he not refuse to bear arms, or to do other things that would suggest his approval of war?

Since this is such a crucial problem for Christians today, and since there is not one "party line" on the issue, let us look at a statement of the case for Christian pacifism, and then at a statement of the case for the Christian use of force. We shall then conclude with some safeguards which must be borne in mind by advocates of either position.

A Case for Christian Pacifism

The case for Christian pacifism can be stated in some such terms as these: War is utterly destructive of human life and human values, and it can serve no good end. This is particularly true of modern war, as it will be waged with atomic and hydrogen bombs. War is also the complete antithesis of the spirit of Jesus. It is inconceivable that Jesus would sanction war. He talked about loving our enemies, not killing them. Jesus would never shoot another man, or drop bombs on defenseless women and children. Therefore the Christian must follow his Master in this matter, no matter what the consequences. If the consequences are rejection, punishment, persecution, or imprisonment, the Christian must be willing to pay the price in order to witness to the way of love as opposed to the way of violence. The Christian can only act in the faith that if he does God's will, God will accept and make use of this witness in his own way, no matter how "foolish" the witness may appear to men. Ultimate loyalty must be given to Christ and his way—and if Christ's way comes into conflict with the way of a nation, there is no question whom the Christian must serve. He must serve Christ.

All Christians must respect the main substance of the pacifist position even if they do not personally agree with it. Whatever else such a witness may accomplish, it can always remind others that there is a higher way than violence that calls for men's allegiance—a way that the pacifist believes in so firmly that he is willing to pay any personal price to maintain it.

Note to the Careful Reader: Some pacifists will modify the argument at one point, by insisting that pacifism will "work." If we refuse to bear arms against the enemy, they say, the enemy will not harm us but will be transformed and conquered by our example of love, so that the war will cease right there. Since there is "that of God" in every man, we should appeal to "that of God" in the enemy and so change him.

That there is "that of God" in every man is a part of Christian faith. But there is the other part of the truth (as we saw in Chapter 13), which reminds us that the image of God in man has been distorted, so that man is influenced by self-interest as well as by the power of love.

A Case for the Christian Use of Force

There are other Christians who take a different view of the matter. They believe that there may be times when the Christian must use force. Their position is more difficult to state than the pacifist position, and cannot be done so briefly.

The "nonpacifist" would agree with the pacifist that Jesus' ethic is an ethic of sheer, outgoing love, and that it is impossible to make a paratrooper out of him, or put him on the business end of a bayonet. Thus the Christian nonpacifist would join the pacifist in rejecting the extreme flag-waving nationalism which usually infects a nation in time of war. In many situations he would be a pacifist himself. He would probably agree that it would be illegitimate to use force in defending himself in a one-to-one encounter. "If someone socks me in the eye," he might say, "I am forbidden to return the blow. I must bear it, and any more that may follow it, in suffering love."

However, the nonpacifist claims that the situation is different when more than two people are involved, and that in the light of Christian love itself the situation must be re-thought. If you are walking down the street and see a thug beating up a defenseless man, you may believe firmly that Jesus is right about loving your neighbor, but you still have two very difficult problems to solve:

1. Who is your "neighbor" *in this particular situation?*
2. *How* are you to express your "love"?

You cannot refuse to be involved. If you "walk by on the other side," you give your silent approval to the stronger individual in the conflict, in this case the thug. But if you intervene to stop the fight, you will probably have to use force. The thug may be unimpressed with your arguments. But unless you can effectively stop him, how can you say that you are expressing love toward the victim? On the other hand, if you knock out the thug with a large rock, you may be expressing love toward the victim, but this is scarcely love toward the thug, whose skull you have just fractured.

This illustration shows the difficulty of applying "love" in a fairly simple situation, where good and bad are clear-cut. Our real choices are not usually so clear-cut. Perhaps the thug is not "bad" after all; perhaps he is starving and out of work, with four children and a sick wife at home. Perhaps the victim has the controlling interest in a company that has fired the "thug" for inadequate reasons. Perhaps you are a taxpayer who voted against new street lights at the place where the attack took place, thus making it easier for the "thug" to do his work undetected. Thus you are all involved in guilt. To introduce such factors, the nonpacifist would say, underlines the fact that your ethical choice is not a nice neat choice between doing "good" or doing "evil." Whatever you do will involve you in doing some evil.

The Christian is thus "caught" in situations where "what love would do" is not easy to determine, and cannot be simply accomplished. Take a "real life" example. Suppose you were a Christian in Holland at the time of the Nazi invasion. If you were to "love" the invading Nazis to the extent of refusing to use force against them, you would be failing to love the Dutch people in your own village, since many of them would be brutally shot by the Nazi firing squads. On the contrary, if you were to "love" your Dutch countrymen to the extent of trying to save them from the Nazis, you would have to resist the Nazis by force, probably killing them. In neither case would you be "loving" both the Dutch and the Nazis fully. Furthermore, you would face the same basic dilemma if you were a third party on the outside, like America or Spain. To fail to intervene would be irresponsible to the Dutch and a condoning of the Nazis, while to intervene would necessitate the use of force.

The Christian, then, faces the problem of living the ethic of love in a world where this cannot be fully done. No matter what he does he will fall short of the fullness of what love demands. This is true whether the Christian in question is a pacifist or a nonpacifist.

> The *pacifist,* refusing to resist the Nazis, is thereby morally involved in the evil that Nazism represents, and the murders that will be committed by the Nazi firing squad.

> The *nonpacifist,* in resisting the Nazis, commits himself to the necessity of using force and violence to achieve his end.

The nonpacifist would insist that there are times when the latter choice is the one that the Christian must conscientiously adopt. He will have to condone, and even participate in, the use of force, with all the horror that it involves, because for him the alternative involves an unchristian lack of concern for his fellow men. He will argue that to refuse to resist the aggression of a tyrant (such as a Hitler or a Mussolini) is to condemn the conquered peoples to a life of such monstrous injustice and tyranny that even the evils of modern warfare may be a justified way of avoiding such a situation. (If you have seen pictures of what went on in Nazi concentration camps, you will feel the persuasiveness of this argument.) Thus, the nonpacifist will argue, there are times when, in the name of Christian faith and its demand that we act responsibly in the immediate situation, Christians will resort to force.

*   *   *   *

Now to some people the above line of argument will be totally unconvincing. It will appear to them that the nonpacifist simply hasn't the "guts" to take the ethic of love seriously, and that he is inventing all sorts of rationalizations in order to do what everybody else is doing. It needs to be stressed, therefore, that people who take this stand do so out of a tortured awareness of the difficulty of living the Christian life in the twentieth century, and that it is only because an honest facing of the facts impels them in that direction that they go in that direction. There can be conscientious participation in war, just as there can be conscientious objection.

Some Safeguards for All Concerned

Neither the pacifist nor the nonpacifist can say, "My position is wholly good." In either case the Christian is involved in guilt and wrongdoing. This does not mean, however, that the Christian is morally helpless. There are certain things *any* Christian can do in time of war or in times when war threatens:

1. You can refuse to hate. No matter how tense the cold war or how bitter the hot, you can refuse to give in to the vindictiveness and calculated hatred which characterize nations at such times. You can recognize that *you* are involved in the evil of the situation, and that *your* nation bears part of the responsibility for the situation.

2. You can support positive measures that will help to counteract the threat of war. This might mean supporting legislation to send food, clothes, and machines to downtrodden areas.

It might mean sending them yourself (at least the first two).
It might mean support of attempts to rebuild areas that have
been devastated by bombs. It might mean backing all attempts
to get "enemy" nations together around a conference table.
There is almost no limit to the kinds of things it might mean.

3. You can counteract some of the things you may have to do
because you live in a society at war or threatened by war. For
example, although your nation may be "against" another nation, you can continue to be active in the Christian Church,
which embraces men of *all* nations, including the "enemy"
nation, and thus help to keep alive a bridge of good will which
stands above national interests.

4. You can avoid indiscriminate approval or disapproval of
all that is done by your nation, either before, during, or after
a war. (The temptation of the pacifist is to condemn all that
his nation does in time of war; the temptation of the nonpacifist to approve everything.) The Christian must remember
that he is subject to a higher authority than the State; he must
be willing to say the unpopular thing when an important matter or conviction is at stake.

The Ever-present Element in Christian Ethics

It is thus clear that there is no "easy answer" to the problem of the Christian and war. It should be clear also that this
is true of *all* the ethical decisions that the Christian makes. The
issue of war simply underlines the constant ethical problem of
the Christian. He lives in a non-Christian world which does
not accept the Christian ethic, and yet he must seek to live by
the Christian ethic. Some kinds of compromise are always involved. It is part of Christian wisdom to recognize this fact.

This is the note on which any discussion of Biblical ethics
must close. As Christians, attempting to "think Biblically"
about life, we must realize that even our very best falls short,
that no matter how much we do we have not attained, and that
on every level of life ethics are not enough, but need to be

surrounded and encompassed by the renewing love and forgiveness of God, who can pick up and use even our faulty attempts at the doing of his will, and make from them something that we ourselves have been unable to make. For His is the Kingdom and the power and the glory, forever.

Mystery and Meaning

(Now What?)

As we come to the end of this book, it is apparent that
> not all the questions have been answered,
> not all the doubts dispelled,
> not all the difficulties resolved,
> not all the mystery cleared away.

The Christian has the obligation to understand his faith as
fully as possible—to push his questions no matter how perplexing, to face difficulties no matter how shattering, and to do his
best, with God's help, to surmount the problems. As he goes
through life the Christian can expect to receive greater il-
lumination, firmer assurance, deeper knowledge, and sounder
understanding. But it is wrong to assume that finally all the
mystery will disappear and one will have "all the answers"—
whether as a result of "reading one more book," or going to
another conference, or having some particularly clarifying
vision. As long as he lives, the Christian will be forced to say
with Paul, "Now we see through a glass, *darkly*" (I Cor. 13:
12).

No one who is trying to know and love and serve God can
ever claim that he has fully realized his goal. In fact, the greater
his depth of understanding, the greater will be his apprehen-
sion of the sense of *mystery* underlying the relationship between God and man. He will see that he has come up against

something for which he does not have the full answer, and for which he will never have the full answer. Mystery will always remain, mystery that will never be rationally grasped or explained. The Christian, until the end of his life, must confess, "Lord, I believe; help thou mine unbelief" (Mark 9: 24).

What can we say, in the light of this situation?

Mystery as a Gateway to Meaning

We can recognize, for one thing, that mystery need not mean sheer incomprehension. Mystery may, in fact, be the gateway to a deeper understanding of life than would be possible without the element of mystery.

For example:

Here is your best friend in high school. Up until a couple of months ago he has been very attentive in class and has never been known to get behind in his assignments. (As a matter of fact, you have sometimes wished he would, just to show that he is human.) Now, with final exams almost upon him, he doodles in class, and sits for hours with a book in front of him and never turns a page. His greatest interest has always been mathematics, and after school you find him furtively writing poetry! Ask him a question and he doesn't hear you. Ask him what the matter is, and he looks at you glassily, and walks out of the room. Later that evening he returns starry-eyed and goes to bed without a word to anyone. You can't understand what's come over him. He's a mystery to you.

And then somebody says: "Didn't you know? He's in love."

And now you can understand him—at least, you can understand him better than you did before.

Now "being in love" is a mystery, something you can never fully explain or understand. And yet, *by means of that mystery* you can now understand your friend better than you could before. The mystery of "being in love" has helped to clarify your comprehension, rather than clouding it. Mystery can be a gateway to meaning, in other words. It need not lead you up a blind alley.

The mystery of *creation* is not something you can rationally explain, but by means of that mystery you can understand that God's world has purpose and direction, and that you have a job to do here.

The mystery of *resurrection* is not something you can rationally explain, but by means of that mystery you can understand that a victory has been won over sin and death, and that you are the inheritor of that victory.

The mystery of *forgiveness* is not something you can rationally explain, but by means of that mystery you can understand that God loves you for yourself, and that he calls upon you to love others in the same way.

And so on. In the case of all the affirmations of Biblical faith, we are confronted by an element of mystery, of something that cannot be reduced to a neat formula—and yet each of those areas of mystery can be the means to a fuller understanding of the meaning of life.

Meaning in the Midst of Mystery

The other thing to remember is that although Biblical faith confronts us with mystery, it also helps us to see meaning in the midst of mystery. We are not confronted simply with mystery. We are also confronted with enough meaning directly given so that we can live confidently in the face of the remaining mystery. We see through a glass darkly, *but we do see*—not everything, but enough. We see enough so that we can walk in confidence.

We see enough light shed on the mystery of *God* to be willing to commit our lives to him.

We see enough light shed on the mystery of *evil* to be willing to trust God for the rest.

We see enough light shed on the mystery of *sin and salvation* to be sure that God has resources for meeting our deepest need.

Particularly, we see enough light shed on the mystery of *Jesus Christ* to know that he is the "clue" to the meaning of life, not only showing us God as he is, but also showing us ourselves as we are meant to be. In this fundamental assurance, we are able to hold fast to him, reaffirming with the writer of the letter to the Hebrews:

We do not yet see everything . . . but we see Jesus (Heb. 2: 8, 9).

And he is enough.

Index of Questions

Note to the Careful Reader: Let it be absolutely clear that this is not a book of "answers to questions." You can't turn to the pages listed below and find nice, tidy answers just waiting to be learned. What you can find are at least a few resources of Biblical faith from which you can develop your own answers.

Questions about Jesus Christ

Questions about evil

Questions about ourselves

Questions about how we act (ethics)

Index of Scriptural References